Koenig/Schreiber/Dennis
**European Competition
Law in a Nutshell:
A Concise Guide**

European Law in a Nutshell 1

Koenig/Schreiber/Dennis

European Competition Law in a Nutshell

A Concise Guide

THE LEGAL PUBLISHER

lexxion

BERLIN

A catalogue record for this book is available from the German National Library, detailed bibliographical data can be found on the internet at http://dnb.d-nb.de.

ISBN-Print: 978-3-869 65-158-3
ISBN-E-Book: 978-3-869 65-159-0

© 2011 Lexxion Publisher · Berlin
www.lexxion.eu

Cover: Tozman Satz & Grafik, Berlin
Typeset: typossatz GmbH, Berlin

PREFACE

The impact of European Competition Law in the globalised world is universal, as has been experienced, inter alia, by Microsoft or Intel Corp. The Commission's and European Courts' jurisdiction extends not only to undertakings incorporated in EU Member States, but also to undertakings of any nationality whose business affects the internal market in the EU.

Surprisingly for its wide impact, the legal foundations for European Competition Law are modest; only nine Articles in the Treaty of the Functioning of the European Union deal with this field of law, however, further powers and legal details of the application of these Articles are shaped largely by case law. This book is intended to provide guidance in navigating both the huge body of jurisprudence comprised of cases heard before the European Courts as well as decisions issued by the Commission. It aims to present in a clear and concise manner a full range of European Competition Law topics: Cartels, Antitrust, Merger Control, Staid Aid and Public Procurement.

This book examines the theoretical bases of European Competition Law and discusses the application of those concepts in cases which have been investigated by the Commission and heard before the European Courts. Our aim is to offer practitioners as well as legal students a useful overview of the field of European Competition law (in particular without getting bogged down in excessive detail) which will improve the reader's knowledge of both the theory and practice of this area of law.

The authors comprise a tenured Professor of law who is specialised in European Law and is the academic director of MERNI (Master of European Regulation of Network Industries) at Bonn University, a German lawyer and a Solicitor of the Supreme Court of England and Wales. This text benefits from a collaboration between lawyers with both civil and common law backgrounds whose areas of expertise are varied yet complementary. With experience ranging from advising multi-national corporations and governments to pleading before the General Court and Court of Justice, the authors are well placed to analyse European Competition Law and policy.

For her essential support we would like to thank *Mara Hellstern* who not only proofread the text but also enriched it with new ideas. The book was also supported by *Beate Förtsch, Volker Bache, Christopher Hasenkamp, Benjamin Schmitz* and *Philipp Kühn*. Finally, we would like to thank the team of Lexxion for their assistance.

Bonn/Cologne/London, May 2011

Christian Koenig
Kristina Schreiber
Sandra Dennis

TABLE OF CONTENTS

Chapter One

WHY COMPETITION REGULATION
IN THE EUROPEAN UNION?

One of the fundamental aims of the European Union is the creation of an internal market: Article 26(1) of the Treaty on the Functioning of the European Union ("TFEU") sets out that "the Union shall adopt measures with the aim of establishing or ensuring the functioning of the internal market." Complementary to the free movement of goods, persons, services and capital in "an area without internal frontiers" (Article 26(2) TFEU), effective competition between undertakings is a main driver – and not a goal in itself – in the pursuit of a comprehensive internal market as set out in Article 3(3) of the Treaty on European Union ("TEU"):

> *"The Union shall establish an internal market. It shall work for the sustainable development of Europe based on balanced economic growth and price stability, a highly competitive social market economy, aiming at full employment and social progress, and a high level of protection and improvement of the quality of the environment. It shall promote scientific and technological advance."*

Behind the notion of the "internal market" lies the idea that market participants should be afforded the greatest possible degree of economic freedom of action. Therefore the concept of the internal market is based on more than the legal definition of competition, i.e. it does not exist only on the basis of spatial or temporal criteria defining a relevant market. Rather, European law establishes an internal market in which market participants can engage in supply and demand in countless geographic and industry markets within the European Union without being hindered by barriers to such competition. Free from governmental as well as private restrictions, and led by the aim of economic success, participants in the internal market actually help to create the market itself. The regulations on trade contained in Articles 101–109 TFEU serve to further develop and protect this free economic space.

The implementation of the European internal market is undertaken pursuant to Article 3(3) TEU which requires the Union to work for "the sustainable development of Europe" including the development of "a highly competitive social market economy". In order to achieve this goal, a system to protect against distortions of competition is needed;[1] the basic primary law provisions are set out in Articles 101–109 TFEU.

---

1 "Protocol on the internal market and competition" (Protocol No 27 to the Treaty on the Functioning of the European Union), [2007] OJ C306/156. With the introduction of the Treaty of Lisbon the stated object of creating a system that protects competition in the internal market against distortions was moved from its previously prominent place of Article 3 (g) TEC to the "Protocol on the internal market and competition". This move, however, will not lead to a drastic change in the application of competition law, due to Article 51 TEU incorporating all Protocols to that Treaty into the Treaty itself.

Other Union aims – including in particular social progress and a high level of protection and improvement of the quality of the environment[2] – are of equal importance and therefore influence the interpretation of competition law. The Union, either by virtue of primary (made by Member States) or secondary (made by, inter alia, the European Parliament, Council or Commission) lawmaking, is given exclusive competence over the "establishing of the competition rules necessary for the functioning of the internal market" (Article 3(1)(b) TFEU).

Because competitive distortions interrupt the free movement of goods, persons, services and capital in the Union, the TFEU imposes a positive obligation on Member States as well as the Union itself to support the principle of "an open market economy with free competition" (Articles 119(1) and 120 TFEU).

I. THE STRUCTURE OF GENERAL COMPETITION PROVISIONS

The establishment and preservation of the internal market can be challenged in two significant ways: firstly by anti-competitive behaviours by market participants (i.e. undertakings) on either the supply or demand side. For this reason undertakings are prohibited under Article 101 TFEU from seeking to affect competition through coordinated behaviour patterns (see Chapter 3). Undertakings with a particularly strong market position are prohibited under Article 102 TFEU from abusing that *"dominant"* position to distort competition (see Chapter 4). The elements of these offences are satisfied by an undertaking's current or past behaviour, whilst in contrast, merger control – intended to protect the structure of the market – looks forward: such rules prohibit the merger of undertakings when that merger would be likely to damage competition considerably (see Chapter 7). Secondly, distortions of competition can be caused by interventions by Member States and their agents in the market. These so-called *State-directed competition provisions* are contained in Articles 107–109 TFEU and the control of State aids is discussed in Chapter 8. Finally, Member States' purchase of goods or services in the marketplace must also comply with European competition law; analysis of public procurement in the Union takes place in Chapter 9.

II. THE SCOPE OF ARTICLES 101–109 TFEU

Common to all of the instruments of EU competition law is the stated aim of protecting competition from adverse effects. However, in order to protect against such adverse effects, the nature of "competition" itself as a concept under European law must first be ascertained.

---

2   See Article 3 TEU.

1. "Competition" in the Context of European Competition Law

One approach to the meaning of the term "competition" is to consider the functions and purposes of competition in light of the aims enshrined in primary European Union law (Articles 3(3) TEU and 3(1)(b) TFEU). The goal of undistorted competition is incorporated in jurisprudence and Commission practice through the "*functioning*" or "*workable competition*" concept.[3] However, the Court of Justice of the European Union traditionally has been reluctant to define a specific concept of competition. The rules of competition that govern the existence and preservation of effective competition in the internal market support the primary law concept of "an open market economy with free competition" by limiting State over-regulation and encouraging an economically efficient allocation of resources (and thereby also protecting consumers).

The application of the rules of competition depends very much on the nature of each case, as the wording of Articles 101–109 TFEU is broad, and can be interpreted in a number of ways. The facts of an individual case must be analysed in detail to ascertain whether the behaviour in question has negative effects on competition. Such a tailored analysis seeks to prevent abuses of competition, whilst protecting the right of the parties involved to act freely.

Within the scope of the rules of competition, the effects of an infringement of those rules are to be considered on the one hand in terms of the measurable impact on third parties – first and foremost on final consumers – and on the other hand, on the relevant undertakings, i.e. horizontal (e.g. other producers) and/or vertical (e.g. wholesalers) competitors and the undertakings under supervision themselves. In this way, the rules of competition are applied pursuant to an effects-based approach as compared to a form-based approach (a "*more economic approach*").[4]

a) Consumer Protection

The European rules of competition place particular importance on the idea of consumer protection.[5] Therefore in considering whether certain behaviour infringes competition rules, such behaviour is assessed not only in technical terms, but also on the basis of whether it produces negative effects on final consumers.[6] Such negative effects can include, for example, artificially high prices, the availability to consumers of products which are quantitatively inadequate or qualitatively insufficient, or economically undesirable production which precludes the optimum allocation of resources, resulting, in the

---

3 Case 26/76, *Metro*, [1977] ECR 1875, para. 20.

4 Monti, The New Shape of European Competition Policy (2003), p. 3. See also Schmidtchen, Effizienz als Leitbild der Wettbewerbspolitik: Für einen "more economic approach", in Oberender (ed.), Effizienz und Wettbewerb (2005), and Röller, Using economic analysis to strengthen competition policy enforcement in Europe, in van Bergeijk/Kloosterhuis (eds), Modelling European Mergers: Theory, Competition Policy and Case Studies (2005).

5 See Commission, Guidance on the Commission's enforcement priorities in applying Article 82 of the EC Treaty to abusive exclusionary conduct by dominant undertakings, [2009] OJ C 45/7, para. 5.

6 Cf. Case T-168/01, *GlaxoSmithKline*, [2006] ECR II-2969, summary point 10, paras. 118 et seq. (upheld in Joined Cases C-501/06 P, C-513/06 P, C-515/06 P, C-519/06 P, *GlaxoSmithKline*, [2009] ECR I-9291); Joined Cases T-213/01 and T-214/01, *Österreichische Postsparkasse AG*, [2006] ECR II-1601, para. 115; Case T-88/92, *Luxury cosmetic products*, [1996] ECR II-1961, para. 112.

long term, in disadvantages for consumers. Not only the short-term effects of the relevant behaviour are considered, but also the long-term effects as well. Together with the fundamental freedoms granted under the TFEU, the rules of competition relating to market liberalisation and market integration serve to establish and protect a domestic market in which the basic values and aims of the Union, in particular those laid down in Articles 2 and 3 TFEU, are realised. In this context the rules of competition serve not only to protect the interests of final consumers or market competitors, but also to protect the structure of the internal market itself as well as competition within it.[7]

b) Freedom of Action

Another key aspect of European competition law is the "independence postulate" – the idea that every undertaking's business policy should be determined independently.[8] Competition law under the TFEU is based on the principle that every competing undertaking is entitled to determine its behaviour independently, and that any restriction of that freedom of action – for example, as a result of agreements or concerted practices between companies – constitutes an infringement of this right. However, in infrastructure markets with high sunk costs, e.g. expensive broadband telecommunications infrastructure costs, which cannot really be recovered in the event of a market exit, European and national competition authorities do tend to accept that infrastructure sharing between competing undertakings reduces investment risks and they therefore permit – under strict proportionality conditions – a well balanced compromise between such practices and the "independence postulate".

c) Efficiency through Competition

Finally, the concept of competition in Union law is also given weight through the advantages – admittedly existing solely in theory – of "perfect" competition. The advantages of such competition lie, in simple terms, in low prices, with demand matching the supply of qualitatively and quantitatively optimal products, sufficient choice and the most efficient means of production.[9] In contrast to monopolistic markets, competition leads (according to the models of the Chicago School of economic thought) to the best possible allocative efficiency. This optimum is achieved in an economy if no individual can be made better off, without at the same time another person being made worse off, i.e. no change in the existing situation is conceivable which benefits one person yet damages no one else (the "Pareto efficiency"). If such a state were to be reached, an optimal balance would be

---

7   Case C-8/08, *T-Mobile Netherlands BV*, [2009] ECR I-4529, para. 38. As to the debate regarding the extent of legal protection offered by Article 102 TFEU see Whish, Competition Law (6th edn. 2008), pp. 191 et seq. The Commission has pointed out recently that the protection of competitors is of minor interest to it; see Commission, Guidance on the Commission's enforcement priorities in applying Article 82 of the EC Treaty to abusive exclusionary conduct by dominant undertakings, [2009] OJ C 45/7, para. 6, available at <http://ec.europa.eu/competition/antitrust/art82/index.html> (last accessed on 18 April 2011).

8   Joined Cases 40/73 to 48/73, 50/73, 54/73 to 56/73, 111/73, 113/73 and 114/73, *Suiker Unie*, [1975] ECR 1663, para. 173, 174; Case 172/80, *Züchner*, [1981] ECR 2021, para. 13; Case C-7/95, *Deere*, [1998] ECR I-3111, para. 86; Case C-238/05, *Asnef-Equifax*, [2006] ECR I-11125, para. 52; Case C-8/08, *T-Mobile Netherlands BV*, [2009] ECR I-4529, para. 32.

9   Whish, Competition Law (6th edn. 2008), p. 4.

created in which every individual produces and experiences the best possible efficiency. Additionally, inherent in the best possible productive efficiency is that the necessary factors of production such as employee labour and raw materials are used by market participants without avoidable losses. In such a state progressive innovation and dynamic efficiency meet, resulting in the creation and further development of new products.[10]

2. The Investigation of Restraints of Trade

In the last few years the Commission has undertaken a comprehensive modernisation of secondary competition law, with the aim of following a *"more economic approach"* whereby the application of competition rules focuses more strongly on economic welfare efficiency. Previously, European competition law was characterised by a more formalistic approach, which focused on identifying the kinds of behaviour which usually result in negative effects on competition, with very little analysis of the negative effects in an individual case. Today, the question of the economic effects of the relevant behaviour is paramount:[11] whether an infringement of competition law exists is determined first and foremost on the basis of the economic effects of the relevant behaviour, rather than on the existence of a technical or structural violation of competition provisions.

This adjustment to competition policy focuses on a stronger inclusion of economic standards of assessment in competition control, including a paramount analysis of the real effects of a behaviour, supplemented by empirical data, and resulting in a quantitative appraisal of the effects of this behaviour on the welfare aims pursued by the Union. Such an approach relates back to a policy of competition supervision in the Union which aims for an optimal use of limited oversight resources, to focus on the activities which have the greatest impact on competition in the Union. The use of models which have been economically tried and tested makes it easier for the priorities set out in Union policy to be achieved, and increases the transparency of competition-related decisions.

It is intended that the protection and support of competition will be strengthened in future by the specific consideration of competition aspects when assessing the impacts of prospective Union legislation.[12] In 2005 the Commission issued a discussion paper on the application of Article 102 TFEU to exclusionary abuses[13] which set out the principles of the more economic approach to competition policy and discussed their use in assessing infringements of competition rules. The principles discussed in that paper also found their way into the Commission's discussion of priorities in the enforcement of cases of abuse of a dominant position.[14]

The more economic approach does not limit the analysis of potentially anti-competitive behaviour to a consideration of the effects of the behaviour on end-consumers. In-

---

10 This view is controversial; cf. Whish, Competition Law (6th edn. 2008), pp. 5 et seq.

11 Cf. Whish, Competition Law (6th edn. 2008), p. 2.

12 Commission, Better Regulation for Growth and Jobs in the European Union, COM(2005) 97 final, p. 5.

13 DG Competition discussion paper on the application of Article 82 of the Treaty to exclusionary abuses, available on the Internet at<http://ec.europa.eu/comm/competition/antitrust/art82/discpaper2005. pdf> (last accessed on 18 April 2011) .

14 Commission, Guidance on the Commission's enforcement priorities in applying Article 82 of the EC Treaty to abusive exclusionary conduct by dominant undertakings, [2009] OJ C 45/7.

stead, the economic effects of the behaviour in question are to be examined at every stage of the market activity. This concept was addressed in the case of *Glaxo-SmithKline*[15] in which the General Court indicated that a bare restriction of trade would not be sufficient to constitute a restriction of competition under Article 101(1) TFEU. Rather, the definitive test would depend on whether the arrangement in question had a negative effect on end-consumers.[16] The Court of Justice then explicitly overruled this argument – stating that not only the impact on end-consumers should be considered, but rather that the effects of the anti-competitive behaviour at all stages of market activity (*inter alia* the effects on horizontal and vertical competitors) were relevant, and in the case of *Glaxo-SmithKline* in particular, the effects at wholesale level.[17] When describing its more economic approach in newer regulations and guidelines, the Commission often refers to the effects a behaviour has on consumers. However, the Commission defines the concept of "consumers" broadly: "all direct or indirect users of the products covered by the agreement, including producers that use the products as an input, wholesalers, retailers and final consumers",[18] thus not limiting consumers to final consumers. Additionally, the Commission, differentiates between "consumers" generally, and "final consumers" as a specific class of consumers.

a) Example: Retail Price Setting

The Commission's more economic approach becomes a point of discussion particularly in the context of retail price setting as a result of the paradigm shift in US jurisprudence:[19] the setting of mandatory resale prices by manufacturers for their products is, on its face, an offence in contravention of Article 101 TFEU (a *'per se* offence'). However, such price setting can also result in positive developments – for example, by promoting service-oriented offers,[20] making it easier for new entrants to participate in the market and sup-

---

15   See Chapter 3 for a detailed discussion.

16   Case T-168/01, *GlaxoSmithKline,* [2006] ECR II-2969, summary point 10 (upheld in Joined Cases C-501/06 P, C-513/06 P, C-515/06 P, C-519/06 P, *GlaxoSmithKline,* [2009] ECR I-9291).

17   Joined Cases C-501/06 P, C-513/06 P, C-515/06 P and C-519/06 P, *GlaxoSmithKline,* [2009] ECR I-9291, para. 64.

18   Commission, Guidelines on the application of Article 81(3) of the Treaty, [2004] OJ C101/97, para. 84; see also i.e. Commission, Guidance on the Commission's enforcement priorities in applying Article 82 of the EC Treaty to abusive exclusionary conduct by dominant undertakings, [2009] OJ C 45/7, para. 19, n. 2; Commission, Guidelines on the applicability of Article 101 of the Treaty on the Functioning of the European Union to horizontal co-operation agreements (Draft of a Communication from the Commission), SEC(2010) 528/2, para. 47, available on the Internet at <http://ec.europa.eu/competition/consultations/2010_horizontals/guidelines_en.pdf> (last accessed on 18 April 2011).

19   In its decision of 28 June 2007 (No 06-480), the US Supreme Court rejected the previous prohibition on vertical price setting, favouring the so-called "rule of reason" which implements an analysis of the possible anticompetitive effects of a given vertical price setting on a case-by-case basis.

20   Fixed minimum prices can promote the offer of services (e.g. product presentations or high-quality customer service by trained staff) in advance of the purchase decision. In the absence of fixed minimum prices, customers might take advantage of those services offered by service-oriented merchants, but nevertheless buy the sought product from another, price-orientated merchant afterwards who does not offer such services; cf. Schwaderer, WuW 2008, p. 653 (655, 666).

porting innovation.[21] As a result of the changes in the US approach, there was also a discussion in the EU[22] as to whether the existing absolute prohibition should be lifted and replaced with a case-by-case analysis based on the more economic approach of the economic effects of the behaviour – i.e. a "rule of reason". However, ultimately the Commission decided in its new vertical block exemption regulation against the abolition of the *per se* prohibition.[23]

b) Example: Predatory Pricing

The offer of goods for a price below the variable costs of such goods' production and distribution (known as predatory pricing) can be abusive under Article 102 TFEU if a market-dominating company uses such goods to edge out its competitors over the medium to long term. An abuse is constituted in these cases when a company is prohibited from taking part in market competition even though it is as efficient as the market-dominating company, but, for example, cannot withstand the pressures of competition due to a lack of financial power.[24]

On the basis of the more economic approach the Commission now considers that such behaviour is not abusive under Article 102 TFEU if it leads to efficiency advantages which, in the long run, prevent damage to consumers. This can be considered to be the case if, *inter alia*, the behaviour is essential for the achievement of efficiency, any negative effects are offset by positive ones and competition is not restricted.[25]

c) Effects of a Case-by-Case Analysis

The stronger weighting of economic arguments raises two issues for the application of competition law: on the one hand, dynamic and ongoing academic discussions are indicative of the unending nature of the development of economic knowledge. The analysis of competition law with the help of economic models and data remains therefore not only inevitably selective and to be carried out on a case-by-case basis, but can also call into question the legitimacy of institutional decisions taken under Union primary law, in particular the principle of limited European competence (Articles 4(1) and 5 TEU). Indeed, this can be assumed from the fact that the Commission will not subject the economic grounds of its competition policy to such a "constitutional" legitimacy test. On the other hand, it is true that a normative acceptance of economic competition theory does not edge out competition law itself, so that the broad conception of the latter is not narrowed by

21 The guarantee of a certain resale price facilitates the merchants' choice to enter into the market or to invest in new products, because the risk becomes calculable.

22 The Commission's draft of Guidelines about vertical restrictions, SEC(2009) 946/3 of 28 July 2009, e.g. para. 219, reflects this discussion.

23 Fixing the retail price is a strictly prohibited restriction (hardcore restriction) according to Article 4(a) of Regulation (EU) No 330/2010, [2010] OJ L 102/1.

24 Case 62/86, *AKZO*, [1991] ECR I-3359, para. 72; Case T-271/03, *Deutsche Telekom AG*, [2008] ECR II-477, para. 194 (upheld in Case C-280/08 P, *Deutsche Telekom AG*).

25 Commission, Guidance on the Commission's enforcement priorities in applying Article 82 of the EC Treaty to abusive exclusionary conduct by dominant undertakings, [2009] OJ C 45/7, para. 30.

certain terms or the preference of a certain competition model. In this context, the Court of Justice's reluctance to define a specific concept of competition appears wise.

A higher conceptualisation of economic matters (e.g. the use of mathematical econometric methods) in the application of competition law can only increase the transparency and efficiency of the decision-making process if the application of such economic criteria is open to scrutiny and consistent with prevailing law. Additionally, focusing on short term effects should not prevent a consideration of the long-term consequences of business behaviour.

3. The "More Economic Approach" and Consumer Protection

It is clear that, as well as the more economic approach, consumer protection has moved to the foreground of the application of EU competition rules. The more economic approach makes the application of competition rules more flexible, with the result that the positive and negative effects of the relevant behaviour (including the effects on consumers) are analysed in individual cases as if such a standard were included in the provisions of Article 101 TFEU. In this way the more economic approach can actually strengthen consumer protection, in contrast to the more formalistic approach used previously, which could have prohibited behaviours which led (in exceptional cases) to positive effects for final consumers.

III. GENERAL VERSUS SECTOR-SPECIFIC COMPETITION REGULATION

The rules of competition set out in Articles 101–109 TFEU apply regardless of the nature of the goods or services which are offered in the relevant market. A conceptual distinction exists between those general rules and the rules which apply to the regulation of a specific sector (and take note of the particular features of those markets) – i.e. telecommunications, the postal service, energy supply networks, railway networks, etc. The provisions of Articles 101–109 TFEU as well as the regulations relating to specific sectors aim to guarantee a system of genuine competition. Sector-specific regulation can also be concerned with other issues such as security of supply, operational safety or environmental protection. Whilst general competition rules apply equally to all economic actors, sector-specific rules apply only to certain actors, e.g. to those holding a natural (and/or historical) infrastructure monopoly such as an electricity or gas transmission/ distribution grid or railway network. Additionally, a key difference between general and sector-specific competition regulation is the competence of national regulatory authorities in *ex ante* intervention in the market in certain sectors (to govern for example network access and usage as well as price regulation). *Ex ante* regulatory instruments prescribe from the start official methods and standards to which market behaviour must adhere. In contrast, *ex post* regulatory instruments leave the determination of methods and means to the market and only afterward are such approaches analysed by national authorities.

Articles 101–109 TFEU prohibit with direct effect[26] infringements of competition rules and authorise the Commission (e.g. pursuant to Article 7 of Council Regulation (EC) No 1/2003) to order any necessary structural or behaviour-oriented remedial actions. Measures based on Articles 101–109 TFEU are aimed at addressing individual infringements. As these provisions are not intended to shape market structure going forward, it is not possible for Articles 101–109 TFEU to form the basis of an order by the Commission that an undertaking cease a particular behaviour in future. In contrast, the *ex ante* intervention competence of sector-specific regulation is intended to allow for a comprehensive, future-oriented influence on the sector. The liberalisation of previously monopolistic network industries in the economy could not have taken place without the creation of such a regime: Articles 101–109 TFEU alone would not have been sufficient.

The circumstances in which the rules of general competition law can be applied are often not specific, so it can be necessary for the Commission or a national competition authority to develop and make more concrete those conditions before the limits on what constitutes acceptable behaviour by undertakings become clear. Because of this uncertainty, a kind of behaviour which was not previously identified by competition authorities or the courts as unacceptable will often not be fined, but simply not allowed to continue. In general, the legal consequences of sector-specific regulation are more concrete (with a few exceptions such as certain *ex ante* provisos), so that separate from an individual case decision by a national authority, the effect of the rules is apparent. European merger control can be said to occupy a hybrid position. On the one hand such regulation is applicable to all sectors of the economy; on the other, authorisation requirements and merger approval are subject to threshold tests, which resemble sector-specific *ex ante* regulation.

The use of general, non-sector-specific competition regulation to liberalise traditionally monopolistic or state industries is insufficient to ensure real competitive access to liberalised markets. In particular in the case of grid-based network industries (e.g. telephone services, gas and electricity supply to final consumers, transportation networks, etc.), it is not possible for new competitors in downstream service or supply markets to establish (i.e. duplicate) the necessary networks upstream and to maintain the necessary domestic and off-shore physical infrastructure. For example, construction of competing gas pipelines by new market entrants, especially at the distribution grid level (closer to the final consumer than the long-distance transmission grid) would be near-impossible to finance, as well as, in principle, environmentally negative given the high "sunk costs" involved (i.e. expenses which a company cannot really recoup at market price upon exiting the market) and the external effects on the environment. Hence, any newcomer to the market, or at least the financing of such an undertaking, would be deterred in the absence of a special regime supporting market entry via e.g. access to existing physical networks. As already highlighted, particularly in the cases of the energy and railway sectors, a duplication of networks is not desirable, especially ecologically. Thus, if an ex-monopolist, i.e. the "incumbent", refused a competitor access to and use of a network infrastructure which was built up in times of monopoly, this could constitute an abuse of market power (prohibited under Article 102 TFEU). However, if only *ex post* competition control was available, by the time competitive justice was established a newcomer would have suffered death by insolvency. It is precisely in this sort of situation that Union sector-specific

---

26   See Case 66/86, *Ahmed Saeed Flugreisen*, [1989] ECR 803, para. 32.

directives and regulations in the fields of telecommunications,[27] gas, electricity,[28] postal services and railway network infrastructure have created a harmonised *ex ante* access regime regulated by national regulatory authorities in Member States. Such authorities are authorised by sector-specific competition rules and by special *ex ante* regulatory competence to monitor network access conditions and terms of use and to approve compensation fees for use of the network. Given that sector-specific regulation often interferes with the freedom to own and use one's property, there is a strong need for such kinds of action to be justified and necessary. Such justification is found in the achievement of functioning and effective competition in the internal market – ideally, and insofar as possible, without sector-specific regulation.

27   Koenig/Bartosch/Braun/Romes (eds), EC Competition and Telecommunications Law (2009).

28   Koenig/Kühling/Rasbach, Energierecht (2nd edn. 2008); Jones, EU Energy Law (Vol. II, 2005).

Chapter Two

THE PROHIBITIONS OF RESTRAINT OF TRADE UNDER ARTICLES 101 (CARTELS) AND 102 (ABUSE OF A DOMINANT POSITION) TFEU

Both the prohibition of cartels under Article 101 TFEU and the prohibition of abuse of a dominant position under Article 102 TFEU forbid restraints of trade by undertakings and provide for legal sanctioning following such acts. Before the prohibition of cartels (Chapter 3) and the prohibition against abuse of a dominant position (Chapter 4) are discussed in more detail, we will first consider a number of points which apply to these provisions: what constitutes an "undertaking" in European law, who is liable for infringements of Articles 101 and 102 TFEU and what types of behaviour are caught by those prohibitions.

I. THE ELEMENTS OF AN INFRINGEMENT COMMITTED BY AN UNDERTAKING AND THE LEGAL CONSEQUENCES OF THOSE ACTIONS

The concept of an "undertaking" is a key aspect of the prohibitions contained in Articles 101 and 102 TFEU in two ways. First, "undertakings" include more than the common conception of companies operating on a market, which means that a broader range entities are caught by the Article 101 and 102 TFEU prohibitions than might initially be expected. Equally however, certain kinds of entities are not considered to be undertakings and therefore are not subject to the prohibitions contained in Articles 101 and 102 TFEU.[29]

Second, the concept of an "undertaking" plays a role in the determination of responsibility for an infringement of Article 101 or 102 TFEU. In certain circumstances an entity active in a market may not be the undertaking 'responsible' for an infringement – instead, it could be the undertakings' parent company, for example, who ordered the prohibited activity to take place. In that case, it may be more appropriate for liability for any fines issues by the Commission to accrue to the parent instead of the subsidiary undertaking.[30] Notably, Articles 101 and 102 TFEU are silent on the matter, so over time Commission guidance and European jurisprudence have developed a reasonably consistent approach to the issue.

The wording of Articles 101 and 102 TFEU does not itself specify to whom the Commission's sanction of an offending behaviour must be targeted. Rather, they prohibit specific behaviours, e.g. cartel arrangements.

Article 103 TFEU authorises the creation of appropriate regulations or directives to give effect to the principles set out in Articles 101 and 102; under Article 103(2) TFEU

---

29 See Chapter 2, Section II(1) (*Undertakings*).

30 See Chapter 2, Section III (*Legal Consequences of an Infringement of European Competition Law: Who is the Addressee of a Decision?*).

such measures can include fines and periodic penalty payments. Implicit in the issuing of such secondary law instruments is the question of to whom such measures should be addressed, i.e. who has committed the infringement.

However, as will be explained below, on the one hand the notion of an "undertaking" refers to a *functional, activity-related concept* based on observations of real economic behaviour, i.e. the offering of goods or services on a market (an undertaking as a concept of 'economic behaviourism'). On the other hand, the legal entity, i.e. the unit or the person to whom the Commission's sanction of an offending behaviour must be addressed, is determined by law, foremost by corporate law. Therefore the examination of an infringement follows a two-step-approach: first, the operating undertaking (the unit of 'real economic behaviour') must be identified and second, the legal entity, i.e. the unit to whom any decision and/or sanctions should be addressed, must be identified pursuant to corporate law in the relevant jurisdiction. After this exercise has been completed, the existence of an infringement committed by the undertaking identified (and attributed to the relevant legal entity) must be established under Article 101 (cartels) or 102 (abuse of a dominant position) TFEU – i.e. have the behavioural and factual requirements of those provisions been met?

Undertaking's action	Legal consequences of an infringement
Is the entity engaged in an economic activity of real economic behaviour, offering goods or services on a market (an "operating undertaking")?	Who is legally liable for the economic activity of the undertaking, i.e. the legal entity identified pursuant to corporate law in the relevant jurisdiction?
Existence of an infringement: has an operating undertaking fulfilled the behavioural and factual conditions set out in Article 101 (cartels) or 102 (abuse of a dominant position) TFEU?	To whom does the Commission address its decision imposing any sanctions?

II. ELEMENTS OF AN INFRINGEMENT: AN UNDERTAKING'S ACTIONS

The prohibitions on cartels and abuse of a dominant position require that an undertaking has acted in a certain way, and that the undertaking is financially active in a certain market.[31] It is irrelevant whether the undertaking is public or private (Article 106(1) TFEU). Additionally, to prevent any restrictions of competition, Member States are obliged under Article 4(3) TEU to refrain from taking any action which could jeopardise the attainment of the Union's objectives – i.e. they may not promote any behaviour which would be contrary to the prohibitions of cartels and abuse of a dominant position.

---

31   Established in Case C-41/90, *Höfner and Elser*, [1991] ECR I-1979.

1. Undertakings

The prohibitions contained in Articles 101 and 102 TFEU apply to the behaviour of "undertakings" and "associations of undertakings". Neither the TEU nor the TFEU contains a legal definition of the concept of "undertaking", so it has fallen to the European courts to set out a definition of this term which applies not only to cartels and abuses of a dominant position, but also in cases of State aid and mergers.

> The concept of an undertaking is *functional and activity-related*: an "undertaking" in European competition law is "every entity engaged in an economic activity, regardless of the legal status of the entity and the way in which it is financed".[32]

a) Economic Activity

The concept of "economic activity" itself is also functional and broad.

> *Economic activity* is any activity consisting of the offering of goods or services on a given market.[33] There is no need to dissociate the activity of purchasing goods from the subsequent use to which they are put in order to determine the nature of that purchasing activity. Rather, the nature of the purchasing activity is determined according to whether or not the subsequent use of the purchased goods amounts to an economic activity.[34]

Notwithstanding the broad interpretation of the concept in European law, certain areas remain outside the realm of economic activity – for example, the exercise of state sovereignty,[35] the purchase of goods solely for the purposes of private consumption and collective bargaining for terms of employment.[36]

An intention to make a financial profit is not required, which means that charitable organisations can be "undertakings" within European competition law. Individual persons who carry out professional activities may also be caught – for example, opera singers[37] and Italian customs agents[38] have been deemed undertakings.

The *functional interpretation* of the concept of economic activity means that the facts surrounding each activity are to be analysed individually. In this way it is possible for certain elements of the State to fall within the definition of an undertaking (as they are

---

32   Established in Case C-41/90, *Höfner and Elser*, [1991] ECR I-1979, para. 21.

33   Case C-309/99, *Wouters*, [2002] ECR I-1577, para. 47; Cases T-81/07, T-82/07 and T-83/07, *Jan Rudolf Maas*, [2009] ECR II-2411, para. 178.

34   Case C-35/96, *Commission v Italy*, [1998] ECR I-3851, para. 36; Case C-205/03, *Fenin*, [2006] ECR I-6295, para. 26; Case C-113/07 P, *Selex*, [2009] ECR I-2207, para. 102.

35   See Chapter 2, Section II(1)(a)(bb) (*Exercise of Sovereign Power*) for further detail.

36   Established in Case C-67/96, *Albany*, [1999] ECR I-5751, paras. 60 et seq.; Cases C-115/97 to 117/97, *Brentjens*, [1999] ECR I-6025, paras. 57 et seq.; Case C-219/97, *Drijvende Bokken*, [1999] ECR I-6121, paras. 47 et seq.; Case C-222/98, *van de Woude*, [2000] ECR I-7111, paras. 22 et seq.

37   *RAI/Unitel*, Commission Decision of 26 May 1978, [1978] OJ L 157/39.

38   Case T-513/93, *CNSD*, [2000] ECR II-1807, para. 39.

acting economically in a certain market) whilst the entirety of the State would not be considered an undertaking under European competition law.

It is therefore necessary to consider the activity allegedly constituting a competition infringement in isolation, i.e. separate from other activities carried out. In the context of State activity, this means that the first question to be asked is whether the anti-competitive behaviour is separable from activities falling within the State's public remit; only if the answer to that question is yes, does it become relevant whether the behaviour constitutes "economic activity".[39]

When determining the status of an undertaking under European competition law, that undertaking's status under national law is irrelevant.[40] Having regard to the functional, activity-related concept of "undertaking" based on observations of real economic behaviour, i.e. offering goods or services on a market, the *autonomous concept of European Union law* consolidated in the long standing case law of the European courts is paramount. It is irrelevant whether national law stipulates that an entity is not itself a legal person; the supremacy of European law applies. In particular, it is not necessary for a body carrying on economic activity to have legal personality separate from that of the State in order to be regarded as an undertaking.[41] There is also no minimum degree of organisational independence needed. The key element in ascertaining an undertaking's status is simply economic activity. The question of an undertaking's place within a larger organisation (e.g. the State) only comes into play when determining which entity or entities should be held accountable for infringements of Articles 101–109 TFEU.

Examples:
- A non-profit organisation organised a motorcycle event. In connection with that event, the organisation entered into sponsorship, advertising and insurance contracts designed to exploit the events commercially. The fact that certain public powers were vested in the organiser did not stand in the way of this particular activity (the motorcycle events) being classed as an economic activity. It is necessary to distinguish the participation of the organiser in its decision-making public capacity from its role as organiser of a commercial event. Finally, the fact that the organiser was a non-profit-making association had no bearing on determining whether these events constituted an economic activity – an intention to make profit is not necessary.[42]
- Acting as an agent in a sporting context is also economic activity. Such activity involves the provision of services for profit and does not fall within the scope of the specific nature of sport.[43]
- Lawyers who offer, for a fee, services in the form of legal assistance such as the drafting of opinions, contracts and other documents and the representation of clients in legal proceedings are undertaking economic activity.[44]

---

39 Case T-155/04, *Selex*, [2006] ECR II-4797, para 3.
40 Case C-41/90, *Höfner and Elser*, [1991] ECR I-1979, para. 21.
41 Case C-69/91, *Decoster*, [1993] ECR I-5335, para. 15.
42 Case C-49/07, *MOTOE*, [2008] ECR I-4863, paras. 23, 25–28.
43 Case T-193/02, *Laurent Piau*, [2005] ECR II-209, para. 73.
44 Case C-309/99, *Wouters*, [2002] ECR I-1577, paras. 48 et seq.

- Self-employed artists and inventors engage in economic activity if they commercialise their performances or products.[45]
- The publication of song books is an economic activity if it is carried out by charitable organisations such as cultural or charity associations or the church.[46]

aa) A Link between Offer and Purchase, Supply and Demand?

European courts define "economic activity" as the *offer* (supply) of goods or services on a given market and not the purchase (demand) of such goods and services.[47] Whether the *purchase* of goods or services on a given market also constitutes an economic activity is a more complicated question. The activity of the purchasing should not be separated from the later use of the product: European courts have held that the economic or non-economic character of later use of a product determines the character of the purchasing activity itself.[48] This means that purchasing a product only constitutes "economic activity" if the product is then subsequently used (possibly after i.e. further processing) in exercise of an economic activity in a certain market.[49] Therefore, demand side, purchasing activity on a relevant market (e.g. a housing market) by public authorities for the purpose of the provision of public (non-economic, i.e. not market related) services (e.g. social care for homeless people) is excluded from European competition law.[50]

Through this judicial interpretation of the nature of economic activity the scope of the prohibitions on cartels and abuse of a dominant position set out in Articles 101 and 102 TFEU are restricted considerably.

(1) Example: Eurocontrol

Did Eurocontrol's acquisition of prototypes and intellectual property constitute economic activity?[51]

The European Organisation for the Safety of Air Navigation (Eurocontrol) is an international organisation established by various European States (both EU members and non-members) which aims to strengthen cooperation in air navigation and works to achieve harmonisation and integration to create a uniform system of air traffic management.

---

45   Emmerich, in Immenga/Mestmäcker (eds), Wettbewerbsrecht: EG (4th edn., 2007), Article 81(1), para. 32.

46   Emmerich, in Immenga/Mestmäcker (eds), Wettbewerbsrecht: EG (4th edn., 2007), Article 81(1), para. 32.

47   Case T-155/04, *Selex*, [2006] ECR II-4797, para. 65 (upheld in this respect in Case C-113/07 P, *Selex*, [2009] ECR I-2207, para. 102).

48   Case C-35/96, *Commission v Italy*, [1998] ECR I-3851, para. 36; Case C-205/03, *Fenin*, [2006] ECR I-6295, para. 26; Case C-113/07 P, *Selex*, [2009] ECR I-2207, para. 102; Case T-513/93, *CNSD*, [2000] ECR II-1807, para. 36; Case T-319/99, *FENIN*, [2003] ECR II-357, para. 36; Case T-155/04, *Selex*, [2006] ECR II-4797, para. 65.

49   For further discussion see Koenig/Engelmann, EuZW 2004, p. 682.

50   Cf. Emmerich, in Immenga/Mestmäcker (eds), Wettbewerbsrecht: EG (4th edn., 2007), Article 81(1), para. 22.

51   Case T-155/04, *Selex*, [2006] ECR II-4797; Case C-113/07 P, *Selex*, [2009] ECR II-I-2207.

To further its aim of developing a uniform system of air traffic management in Europe, Eurocontrol was involved in various research and development tasks including coordinating national policies on research and development in the field of air navigation and leading joint study and development actions in the sector. Through these activities Eurocontrol acquired and developed prototypes of air traffic management equipment and systems, with a view to establishing new standards and technical specifications.

Eurocontrol created a regime for intellectual property rights for prototypes developed by undertakings with which it had agreed research contracts, and (free) access to that intellectual property by competing undertakings depended on whether the property had been developed under a research contract with Eurocontrol, or whether the product was pre-existing.[52]

At issue was whether Eurocontrol's activities, specifically the acquisition of prototypes, constituted economic activity for the purposes of European competition law.

The General Court held that the acquisition of prototypes and intellectual property rights by Eurocontrol was not an end in itself and did not allow those rights to be exploited for commercial use.[53] Rather, Eurocontrol made available the rights which it owned to interested undertakings at no cost.[54] Of key importance was the use to which the acquired property was put: as it was intended for the purposes of standardisation, and passed on at no cost, the act of acquiring the property could not be considered economic activity.[55]

The European courts have strictly opposed the linking of upstream and downstream activity when considering economic activity. It is incorrect to infer from the nature of upstream activity (here, the acquisition of prototypes and intellectual property) the nature of the downstream activity (standardisation); rather, the nature of economic activity is the offer of goods and services on a given market.[56] It is only correct to infer from the nature of downstream supply activity the nature of the upstream demand activity.

(2) Example: Social Benefits Systems

> Does a body responsible for administering social benefits act as an undertaking if it buys goods on a competitive market in order to make them available to insured persons?

The Court of Justice has established that bodies which pursue exclusively social objectives, such as the management of statutory health insurance and old-age insurance schemes, do not undertake economic activity and so are not undertakings for the purposes of Articles 101–109 TFEU.

On the one hand the underwriter of a social benefits scheme will be considered an undertaking if the method by which benefits accrue follows a capitalisation principle (i.e.

---

52   Case T-155/04, *Selex*, [2006] ECR II-4797.

53   Case T-155/04, *Selex*, [2006] ECR II-4797, para. 76.

54   Case T-155/04, *Selex*, [2006] ECR II-4797, para. 77.

55   Case T-155/04, *Selex*, [2006] ECR II-4797, para. 65 (upheld in this respect by Case C-113/07 P, *Selex*, [2009] ECR I-2207, para. 102).

56   Case T-155/04, *Selex*, [2006] ECR II-4797, para. 65 (upheld in this respect by Case C-113/07 P, *Selex*, [2009] ECR I-2207, para. 103).

benefits received are linked to contributions) rather than a redistributive methodology.[57] This is the case even if the underwriter pursues social aims without an intention to make profit. On the other hand, as in the case of *AOK Bundesverband*, in a scheme such as the compulsory medical insurance required in Germany where benefits to insured persons are based on the principle of solidarity and members receive identical benefits which do not depend on the level of contributions, the underwriter will not be held to be engaging in economic activity.[58]

> To summarise the extensive case law on this point, social benefits underwriters do not act as undertakings if:[59]
> (1)　the objective pursued is a purely social one implemented using a redistributive (non-profit) methodology;
> (2)　the scheme, by law, delivers benefits on the solidarity principle rather than a principle of capitalisation,[60] i.e. equal benefits for all participants without regard to contributions; and
> (3)　the underwriters do not enter into competition with each other or with private institutions.[61]

bb) Exercise of Sovereign Power

The exercise by a State of its sovereign powers does not constitute "economic activity".[62] What exactly constitutes a use of sovereign power is determined according to European rather than national criteria. The classification of an activity as an exercise of sovereign power is to be done restrictively as an exception and on the basis of the *autonomous notion of European Union law*. Additionally, carrying on from the functional interpretation of what constitutes an undertaking, an analysis of the use of sovereign powers must contain a consideration of whether, and to what extent, the relevant activity can be considered in isolation from other activities. Provided that the economic (supply- and market-related) activities of a public body can be severed from those it engages in as a public authority, the various activities must be considered individually and the treatment of certain activities as powers of a public authority does not mean that all other activities are not economic.[63]

57　Case C-244/94, *Fédération Française des Sociétés d'Assurance*, [1995] ECR I-4013, paras. 14 et seq. The term "capitalisation principle" as used by the Court of Justice describes how services granted by the social insurance carrier in question depend exclusively on the amounts of contributions paid by the beneficiaries and the returns of the social insurance carrier's investments (Case C-244/94, loc. cit., para. 17).

58　Joined Cases C-264/01, C-306/01, C-354/01 and C-355/01, *AOK Bundesverband and others*, [2004] ECR I-2493, paras. 51–54. For detailed discussion see Koenig/Engelmann, EuZW 2004, p. 682.

59　For further details see also Roth, GRUR 2007, p. 645 (649 et seq.).

60　Case C-244/94, *Fédération Française des Sociétés d'Assurance*, [1995] ECR I-4013, paras. 16 et seq.; Case C-67/96, *Albany*, [1999] ECR I-5751, paras. 81 et seq.

61　For a summary of the jurisprudence see Joined Cases C-264/01, C-306/01, C-354/01 and C-355/01, *AOK Bundesverband and others*, [2004] ECR I-2493.

62　Case C-343/95, *Diego Calì & Figli*, [1997] ECR I-1547, paras. 22 et seq.

63　Case T-155/04, *Selex*, [2006] ECR II-4797, para. 54.

Examples:
- An exercise of sovereign power occurs in cases of compulsory competence – when an undertaking has no option but to act. For this reason the Court of Justice found that the collection of fees by Eurocontrol could not be separated from its public authority competence in the field of control and supervision of airspace.[64]
- The Court of Justice confirmed this jurisprudence in the case of *Diego Calì & Figli* as regards supervision of the sea to the combat environmental pollution[65] and in the case of *Banchero* as regards restrictions on the opening and regional distribution of tobacco shops.[66]
- Employment procurement activities are not an exercise of sovereign power even if undertaken by a public body. Employment procurement has not always been, and is not necessarily, carried out by public entities.[67]
- The setting and levying of taxes is not an economic activity, but rather an act by a public authority. This is also the case for a municipal advertising tax which is not a consideration for using specific, normal services, but rather serves broadly to finance local and regional authorities. The possible subsidiary purpose of such a tax to compensate for the use of public space for advertising by private individuals does not alter its fundamental status as a tax and does not render this tax income consideration for a service.[68]

b) Associations of Undertakings

Also caught by the prohibition contained in Article 101 TFEU are associations of undertakings.

> "Associations of undertakings" are groups of financially independent undertakings acting together, regardless of the legal form or legal basis of the association.[69]

For the purposes of Articles 101–109 TFEU the concept of an association of undertakings is also understood as applying to associations which themselves consist of associations of undertakings (for example in the case of farmers' unions or groups of unions as well as specialised associations representing specific farming interests).[70]

---

64 Case C-364/92, *Eurocontrol*, [1994] ECR I-43, paras. 18 et seq.
65 Case C-343/95, *Diego Calì & Figli*, [1997] ECR I-1547, paras. 23 et seq.
66 Case C-387/93, *Banchero*, [1995] ECR I-4663, para. 49.
67 Case C-41/90, *Höfner and Elser*, [1991] ECR I-1979, paras. 22 et seq.
68 Opinion of Advocate General Kokott of 28 October 2004, Case C-134/03, *Viacom Outdoor*, [2005] ECR I-1164, para. 73.
69 Case 45/85, *Verband der Sachversicherer*, [1987] ECR 405, paras. 29 et seq.
70 Joined Cases T-217/03 and T-245/03, *FNCBV*, [2006] ECR II-4987, para. 49.

2. Public Undertakings and Those to Which Member States have Granted Special or Exclusive Rights (Article 106(1) TFEU)

Articles 101 and 102 TFEU are applicable to both public and private undertakings and Article 106 makes clear that public undertakings and undertakings to which Member States have granted special or exclusive rights must observe the limitations set out in Articles 101 and 102 as well.

Public undertakings are those controlled by State entities or institutions as, for example, shareholders. Such control is evident when a public body can, directly or indirectly, exert a dominant influence by virtue of its ownership of or financial participation in an undertaking or the rules that govern that undertaking.[71] An undertaking is the beneficiary of exclusive rights if a monopoly is granted to it by a State measure (e.g. postal services, management of airports, etc.) An undertaking is the beneficiary of *special rights* if it, along with a limited number of other undertakings, is granted particular rights by the State.

Article 106(1) TFEU prohibits Member States from enacting or maintaining in force any measure contrary to the rules contained in the Treaties, singling out in particular Articles 18 and 101–109 TFEU. Additionally, the European courts have confirmed that a Member State infringes Article 106(1) in conjunction with Article 102 TFEU if it enacts any law or similar provision which creates a situation where a public undertaking or an undertaking which is the beneficiary of special or exclusive rights cannot avoid abusing its market-dominant position.

Examples:
– The simple granting of an exclusive or special right as per Article 106(1) TFEU does not constitute an infringement of European competition law, even if doing so leads to the creation of a dominant position or monopoly.[72]
– An infringement of Article 106(1) in conjunction with Article 102 TFEU occurs when a situation is created which necessarily causes abusive behaviour, or at least favours one undertaking above others.[73] This sort of favouring would take place if a national regulation stood in the way of equal competition amongst competitors. In the case of *Connect Austria* the Court of Justice found against national legislation which allocated additional radio frequency to a public undertaking in a dominant position which al-

---

71 Article 2 of Commission Directive 80/723/EEC of 25 June 1980 on the transparency of financial relations between Member States and public undertakings (Transparency Directive), [1980] OJ L 195/35; last amended by Commission Directive 2005/81/EC, [2005] OJ L 312/42. This Directive was repealed by Commission Directive 2006/111/EC, [2006] OJ L 318/17 (last amendment by Council Directive 2009/162/EU of 22 December 2009, [2010] OJ L 10/14).

72 Case C-41/90, *Höfner and Elser*, [1991] ECR I-1979, para. 29; Case C-203/96, *Dusseldorp*, [1998] ECR I-4075, paras. 60 et seq.; Case C-266/96, *Corsica Ferries*, [1998] ECR I-3949, paras. 40 et seq.; Case C-451/03, *Servizi Ausiliari Dottori Commercialisti*, [2006] ECR I-2941, para. 23.

73 Case C-41/90, *Höfner and Elser*, [1991] ECR I-1979, paras. 31 et seq.; Case C-323/93, *Centre d'insémination de la Crespelle*, [1994] ECR I-5077, paras. 18, 20 et seq.; Case C-163/96, *Criminial Proceedings against Raso and others*, [1998] ECR I-533, paras. 29 et seq.; Case C-49/07, *MOTOE*, [2008] ECR I-4863, para. 50.

ready owned a license for certain other frequencies without costs, whilst new market entrants were subject to a fee.[74]

– An infringement of Article 106(1) in conjunction with Article 102 TFEU also occurs when a Member State entrusts the task of administration to an undertaking which is itself a competitor in the market place. In the *MOTOE* case, the undertaking responsible for consenting to applications to organise motorcycle events also held such events itself. This circumstance conferred an advantage on the relevant undertaking as it could de facto determine who would be authorised to hold such events and the conditions in which such events were organised – thereby placing that undertaking at an obvious advantage over its competitors.[75]

III. LEGAL CONSEQUENCES OF AN INFRINGEMENT OF EUROPEAN COMPETITION LAW: WHO IS THE ADDRESSEE OF A DECISION?

Articles 101 and 102 TFEU refer to the behaviour of an undertaking, i.e. the unit active on the market (the operating undertaking). However, the question of to whom a decision by the Commission should be addressed can be more complicated. In a simple sense, the addressee of a Commission decision will be the legal person responsible for the operating undertaking's behaviour in the marketplace. This may well be the operating undertaking itself, if decisions regarding the anti-competitive activity were taken by the operating undertaking of its own volition. In other cases it may be that the operating undertaking's actions were directed by another undertaking – e.g. a shareholder or other form of legal owner of the operating undertaking's assets and rights, or a beneficial owner entitled to make decisions or benefit from the operating undertaking, its rights and its goodwill. In such circumstances responsibility for the infringement of competition law and liability for any resulting fine should accrue to the undertaking directing the operating undertaking's behaviour (to reflect its ultimate responsibility for the anti-competitive activity), rather than to the operating undertaking itself.[76] Additionally, it is important to remember that the concept of an "undertaking" within European competition law does not depend upon national corporate law, so an undertaking in the EU context is not necessarily an individual company with a single legal personality.

The consequence of the European judicial practice of considering the nature of the true legal entity responsible for an undertaking's activities in a market is that several legal or natural persons may be treated as the relevant legal entity.[77] Different legal persons together can form, for example, the relevant "undertaking" for the purposes of Articles 101 and 102 TFEU if they belong to the same corporate group and do not determine their market behaviour autonomously of each other.[78] A decision based on Articles 101 and

---

74 Case C-462/99, *Connect Austria*, [2003] ECR I-5197, para. 95.

75 Case C-49/07, *MOTOE*, [2008] ECR I-4863, para. 51.

76 Cf. to the requirement to address a legal entity Joined Cases T-305/94 to T-307/94, T-313/94 to T-316/94, T-318/94, T-325/94, T-328/94, T-329/94 and T-335/94, *PVC II*, [1999] ECR II-931, para. 978.

77 Cf. Case C-97/08 P, *Akzo Nobel*, [2009] ECR I-8237, para. 55.

78 Case T-203/01, *Michelin*, [2003] ECR II-4071, para. 290; Case T-112/05, *Akzo Nobel*, [2007] ECR II-5049, para. 58.

102 TFEU can also be addressed to a legal entity which was not directly involved in the infringement, if that entity exercised a determining influence on the undertaking which actually acted in the market.

> The following considerations apply when determining the addressee of a decision regarding an infringement of European competition law:
> (1) Articles 101 and 102 TFEU refer to the activities of "undertakings";
> (2) all natural or legal persons who exercise a controlling influence on an operating undertaking can be deemed to be responsible for that undertaking's behaviour;
> (3) each legal entity which has exerted a controlling influence on the operating undertaking is responsible for the infringement;
> (4) a controlling influence is presumed (though capable of rebuttal) in cases of a 100 % holding in an operating undertaking's share capital; and
> (5) the burden of proof to disprove a controlling influence rests on the legal entity presumed to be responsible.

Notably, the concept of the legal entity responsible for an operating undertaking's actions in the marketplace should be distinguished from pure shareholders in an undertaking. Shareholders[79] in an undertaking are the natural or legal persons who hold shares in a legal entity (i.e. a company ("Ltd.") or corporation ("Inc.")), and who may, but – importantly – do not necessarily direct the operations of an undertaking or exert a controlling influence over the undertaking's activities.

In order to identify whether shareholders can be held accountable for an operating undertaking's actions in the marketplace, three elements have to be distinguished:

> *shareholders* = natural or legal persons
> holding shares in an
> *undertaking* = e.g. a company or corporation
> owning and/or exerting a controlling influence over the activities of the undertaking, thereby benefitting directly from the
> *undertaking´s* assets, rights, staff, goodwill and intellectual property (IP).

This basic scheme helps to analyse complex corporate structures and determine the liability of an operating undertaking and/or its parent and/or the corporate group as a whole for an infringement of Article 101 or 102 TFEU.

Example: Akzo Nobel

The Commission imposed a fine on a number of undertakings including Akzo Nobel, BASF and UCB for cartel infringements under Article 101 TFEU.[80] The Commission's decision was addressed to Akzo Nobel and its subsidiaries jointly and severally, even though

---

79 For ease of reference we refer to "shareholders" and "shares" in an undertaking, but it should be noted that other, non-shareholder corporate structures exist as well. In such cases, the form of ownership in an undertaking may differ, but the basic analysis in determining the influence exerted over the actions of the undertaking remains the same.

80 *Choline chloride* (COMP/37.533) Commission Decision of 9 December 2004.

only the subsidiaries were active in the marketplace, and not the parent company itself.[81] Akzo Nobel owned 100 % of the share capital of the subsidiaries.[82]

Akzo Nobel challenged the Commission's finding that it and its subsidiaries constituted a single economic unit committing the infringement, and therefore the parent company was liable for its subsidiaries' actions. Akzo Nobel argued instead that it had exerted no decisive influence over its subsidiaries' commercial decisions – the subsidiaries had committed the anti-competitive infringements independently and so Akzo Nobel should not be held accountable for their behaviour.[83]

The Court of Justice upheld the General Court's decision that Akzo Nobel could be held accountable for the behaviour of its subsidiaries and confirmed that in cases where a parent company owns 100 % of the shares in a subsidiary, there exists a rebuttable presumption that the parent company exercises a decisive influence over its subsidiary.[84] The burden of proof rests on the parent company to defeat this presumption, and it may adduce evidence of the organisational, economic and legal circumstances of the relationship to prove that the subsidiary engaged in the relevant market behaviour of its own volition.[85]

IV. MEMBER STATES

Article 4(3) TEU, which refers to Member States' "sincere cooperation" and obliges them to refrain from any measure which could jeopardise the attainment of the Union's objectives, together with Article 106(1) TFEU, ensures that member States are also bound by Articles 101 and 102 TFEU. If Member States were not also bound by these Articles, the effectiveness of those provisions would be much reduced.[86]

It is not necessary that the infringements of Articles 101 and 102 TFEU are committed by public undertakings or undertakings to which Member States have granted exclusive rights. Member States may not actively support breaches of competition law, promote infringements of competition regulations, or transfer legislative competence to private economic participants such that the Member State is effectively 'authorising' the infringement of Article 101 or 102 TFEU.

A breach of Article 4(3) TEU via support for activity which infringes Articles 101 and 102 TFEU (other than within the scope of Article 106(1) TFEU) occurs only when there has been an underlying competition infringement by an undertaking.[87] Absent such an offence, no breach of Article 4(3) TEU can have occurred.

---

81 *Choline chloride* (COMP/37.533) Commission Decision of 9 December 2004, paras. 167–176.

82 Case C-97/08 P, *Akzo Nobel*, [2009] ECR I-8237, paras. 7 et seq.

83 For details see Case T-112/05, *Akzo Nobel*, [2007] ECR II-5049, paras. 33 et seq., 38.

84 Case C-97/08 P, *Akzo Nobel*, [2009] ECR I-8237, para. 63.

85 Case T-112/05, *Akzo Nobel*, [2007] ECR II-5049, paras. 65, 67; upheld in Case C-97/08 P, *Akzo Nobel*, [2009] ECR I-8237, para. 65.

86 Case 231/83, *Cullet/Leclerc*, [1985] ECR 305, para. 16; Joined Cases C-94/04 and C-202/04, *Cipolla*, [2006] ECR I-11421, para. 46; Case C-198/01, *CIF*, [2003] ECR I-8055, para. 45; Case C-446/05, *Doulamis*, [2008] ECR I-1377, para. 19.

87 Case C-2/91, *Meng*, [1993] ECR I-5751; Case C-185/91, *Reiff*, [1993] ECR I-5801; Case C-245/91, *Ohra*, [1993] ECR I-5851; Case C-153/93, *Delta*, [1994] ECR I-2517.

1. Member States as Addressees of Commission Decisions

European courts frequently have considered Member States' breaches of Articles 101 and 102 TFEU by virtue of Article 4(3) TEU in the context of fee systems for various professions. This area has produced a large number of cases in which Member States had imbued a professional organisation with the ability to set fee structures, thereby limiting the competitive freedom of affected undertakings.

An infringement of Articles 101 and 102 TFEU and subsequent breach of Article 4(3) TEU results only if a Member State has transferred *extensive* legislative competence for fee systems to a private person,[88] e.g. to a professional association whose members engaged in the relevant market[89] and which represents, first and foremost, the interests of its economically-active members.[90] In such cases the Member State effectively delegates responsibility for decisions affecting the economic sphere to private economic operators.[91]

No such delegation occurs if the receiving professional organisation can be characterised as experts independent of the economic operators concerned, if that organisation is required by law to set fees or tariffs taking into account the interests of the public as well as undertakings in other sectors or users of the service in question and if the Member State retains its power to make decisions of last resort.[92]

> Does a Member State infringe Article 101 TFEU in conjunction with Article 4(3) TEU if it transfers the establishment of minimums and maximums for lawyers' fees to a national Bar association and then enacts those provisions by consent?

In Italy the scale of lawyers' fees was established every two years by the national Bar association (CNF) and was then presented to the Minister of Justice. He then had to approve or reject this decision for it to be used by other national bodies. The fee system set out the minimum and maximum amounts of lawyers' fees, which were established concretely in each case by judicial decree according to the difficulty of the case and work undertaken by the solicitor. In exceptional cases the national court might set fees below the minimum or above the maximum.[93]

---

88 Case 13/77, *INNO/ATAB*, [1977] ECR 2115; Case 267/86, *van Eycke*, [1988] ECR 4769, para. 16; Case C-446/05, *Doulamis*, [2008] ECR I-1377, paras. 20–22.

89 In contrast Case 35/99, *Arduino*, [2002] ECR I-1529, paras. 44 et seq.; Joined Cases 94/04 and 202/04, *Cipolla*, [2006] ECR I-11421, paras. 46 et seq., as the professional organisations worked out merely non-binding proposals.

90 Case C-309/99, *Wouters*, [2002] ECR I-1577, paras. 59 et seq.; cf. Case 13/77, *INNO/ATAB*, [1977] ECR 2115; Case 267/86, *van Eycke*, [1988] ECR 4769, para. 16; Case C-446/05, *Doulamis*, [2008] ECR I-1377, paras. 20–22.

91 For a summary of jurisprudence see the Opinion of the Advocate General, Case C-446/05, *Doulamis*, [2008] ECR I-1377, para. 66.

92 Case C-185/91, *Reiff*, [1993] ECR I-5801, para. 24; Case C-153/93, *Delta*, [1994] ECR I-2517, paras. 16–18, 23; Joined Cases C-140/94 to C-142/94, *DIP*, [1995] ECR I-3257, paras. 18–19; Case C-35/96, *Commission v Italy*, [1998] ECR I-3851, para. 44; Case C-35/99, *Arduino*, [2002] ECR I-1529, paras. 36 et seq., 40 et seq.; Joined Cases C-94/04 and C-202/04, *Cipolla*, [2006] ECR I-11421, paras. 48 et seq.

93 Case C-35/99, *Arduino*, [2002] ECR I-1529.

Indicating an infringement of Article 101 TFEU in conjunction with Article 4(3) TEU:	Indicating no infringement of Article 101 TFEU in conjunction with Article 4(3) TEU:
The CNF was comprised solely of lawyers, so these individuals set the rates of charge set for their own professional group.	The fees system had no legal effect without the approval of the Minister of Justice.
The CNF was not bound by legal criteria in its adoption of resolutions and consequently could make decisions according only to the interests of that professional group.	The fees to be applied were determined in each case by judicial decree. The fee system regulated only the basic framework from which the court could deviate in individual cases.

The Court of Justice held that Italy did not infringe Article 4(3) TEU through Article 101 TFEU because the State character of setting the fee structure was preserved by the need for approval at Ministerial level, and consequently the private economic participants in the form of the CNF did not possess final responsibility.[94]

2. Responsibility Accruing to an Undertaking

The legal entity related to the acting undertaking remains responsible for a competition infringement alongside a Member State as long and so far as the Member State leaves that undertaking scope for action or room for manoeuvre. The applicability of Articles 101 and 102 TFEU to an undertaking is not limited by the fact that the relevant anti-competitive behaviour was sanctioned or encouraged by national legislation.[95] What is critical is whether the national legislation "preclude[s] undertakings from engaging in autonomous conduct which prevents, restricts or distorts competition"[96] and whether the restriction of competition is attributable to the autonomous conduct of the relevant undertaking.[97] If these conditions are not met, the undertaking related legal entity cannot be held accountable for the infringement of competition provisions. The European courts have construed these conditions restrictively[98] – it is necessary that the relevant restraint of trade have been caused exclusively by national legislation or other governmental decree.[99]

---

94 Case C-35/99, *Arduino*, [2002] ECR I-1529, paras. 43 et seq.; also Joined Cases C-94/04 and C-202/04, *Cipolla*, [2006] ECR I-11421, in particular paras. 49, 54.

95 Case 231/83, *Cullet/Leclerc*, [1985] ECR 305, para. 17; Case T-148/89, *Trefilunion*, [1995] ECR II-1063, para. 118.

96 Joined Cases C-359/95 P and C-379/95 P, *Ladbroke Racing*, [1997] ECR I-6265, para. 34. See also Joined Cases 40/73 to 48/73, 50/73; 54/73 to 56/73, 111/73, 113/73 and 114/73, *Suiker Unie*, [1975] ECR 1663, paras. 65 et seq., 71 et seq.; Case C-219/95 P, *Ferriere Nord SpA*, [1997] ECR I-4411, para. 25; Case C-198/01, *CIF*, [2003] ECR I-8055, para. 52; Case T-271/03, *Deutsche Telekom AG*, [2008] ECR II-477, para. 85 (confirmed in Case C-280/08 P, *Deutsche Telekom AG*).

97 Joined Cases C-359/95 P and C-379/95 P, *Ladbroke Racing*, [1997] ECR I-6265, para. 33; Case T-513/93, *Consiglio Nazionale degli Spedizionieri Doganali*, [2000] ECR II-1807, para. 58.

98 Case C-198/01, *CIF*, [2003] ECR I-8055, para. 67; Case T-513/93, *Consiglio Nazionale degli Spedizionieri Doganali*, [2000] ECR II-1807, para. 60; Case T-168/01, *GlaxoSmithKline*, [2006] ECR II-2696, para. 70 (confirmed in Cases C-501/06 P, C-513/06 P, C-515/06 P, C-519/06 P, *GlaxoSmithKline and others*, [2009] ECR I-9291).

99 Case T-271/03, *Deutsche Telekom AG*, [2008] ECR II-477, paras. 87, 89 (confirmed in Case C-280/08 P, *Deutsche Telekom AG*).

a) Example: Deutsche Telekom

> Does the fact that a national regulatory authority approved the prices charged by an undertaking in a dominant position absolve that undertaking from responsibility under Article 102 TFEU?[100]

Prior to the full liberalisation of the telecommunications markets, Deutsche Telekom enjoyed a legal monopoly in the retail provision of fixed line telecommunications services.[101] Following liberalisation, Deutsche Telekom faced varying degrees of competition from competitors, but in the view of the Commission, retained a dominant position in the relevant markets in this case.[102]

The Commission alleged that, to varying degrees over a number of years, Deutsche Telekom had infringed Article 102 TFEU by engaging in abusive pricing in the form of a 'margin squeeze'.[103] A price margin squeeze exists when a dominant undertaking applies exclusionary pricing schemes to products offered on both the wholesale and the consumer (retail) markets. In this case, Deutsche Telekom offered access at the wholesale level as well as to end-users directly. Its competitors, in order to offer services to end-users, had to purchase wholesale access from Deutsche Telekom. The margin squeeze existed in that the charges to be paid to Deutsche Telekom for wholesale access were so high that competitors had no choice but to charge their end-users prices higher than those prices Deutsche Telekom charged its own end-users for similar services. Deutsche Telekom countered by arguing that, because the prices for wholesale access as well as the prices for retail access to the network were approved in advance by the German telecommunications regulator, the structure of the market was established through administrative intervention, and responsibility for the structure of the market rested with the regulatory authority, rather than with Deutsche Telekom. Deutsche Telekom also pointed out that it was obliged under German law to request price adjustments from the regulatory authority only in specific circumstances.[104]

The German telecommunications regulator was involved in the setting of Deutsche Telekom's prices at both the wholesale and end-user levels:

- Wholesale access: Deutsche Telekom had to apply for regulatory approval of its wholesale prices. The prices to be charged by Deutsche Telekom had to correspond (objectively) to efficient expenses for the services provided (the relevant criterion under the German Telecommunications Act). Following regulatory approval, Deutsche Telekom was permitted to charge only the approved prices.
- End-user services: in the area of end-users Deutsche Telekom offered narrow band (ISDN) and broadband (ADSL) services, which were subject to different forms of regulation. The narrow band service was established in the price cap regulations via individual infrastructure services being included in a basket and a maximum price

---

100 Case T-271/03, *Deutsche Telekom AG*, [2008] ECR II-477; upheld in Case C-280/08 P, *Deutsche Telekom AG*.

101 Case T-271/03, *Deutsche Telekom AG*, [2008] ECR II-477, para. 1.

102 Case T-271/03, *Deutsche Telekom AG*, [2008] ECR II-477, paras. 2, 36.

103 Case T-271/03, *Deutsche Telekom AG*, [2008] ECR II-477, para. 37.

104 Case T-271/03, *Deutsche Telekom AG*, [2008] ECR II-477, para. 77.

for those services then being set by the regulatory authority. How Deutsche Telekom divided the prices for the individual services it provided was left to its discretion; though it had to obtain authorisation for the individual service prices, the regulatory authority nonetheless approved the maximum basket price. For the period until 2002 Deutsche Telekom offered its narrow band service for prices below the maximum basket price. From 2002 the relevant prices for narrow band connection services were equal to the basket maximum. The broadband services were regulated with one additional remuneration control which meant that Deutsche Telekom did not require regulatory approval to begin with, however in the case of a possible offence against the German Telecommunications Act, additional controls could be implemented by the regulatory authority.

Although Deutsche Telekom's scope for price setting in the relevant period had been restricted by sector-specific regulation, competitors of Deutsche Telekom stated subsequently that on account of considerable price reductions by Deutsche Telekom for end users on pre-payment plans, they could not profitably offer end users' services in competition with those offered by Deutsche Telekom.

The Commission found that this price margin squeeze infringed Article 102 TFEU. Of particular issue in this case whether the price margin squeeze, and therefore the competition law infringement, were imputable to Deutsche Telekom, given the role played by the State in the setting of prices.

Indicating Deutsche Telekom was responsible for an infringement of Article 102 TFEU:	Indicating Deutsche Telekom was not responsible for an infringement of Article 102 TFEU:
A price margin squeeze could have been avoided by lowering pre-payment prices, as well as by increasing the retail prices charged to final customers.	The pre-payment prices were approved by the regulatory authority ex ante, which meant that Deutsche Telekom's ability to act independently was eliminated.[105]
1998 to 2001	
Until the end of 2001, Deutsche Telekom could increase the totality of end users' prices through price restructuring.[106] It lowered its end users' prices for narrow band services in this period below the State-agreed maximum prices and could successfully have applied for permission to increase the price of a specific product.[107]	
The participation of the regulatory authority did not mean that Deutsche Telekom would bear no responsibility regarding its prices. On the one hand, Deutsche Telekom ultimately had an influence on the prices approved as the	Deutsche Telekom argued that as regards end users' prices, it had no scope to act as a result of the maximum price set by the regulatory authority. Since the telecommunications regulatory authority was responsible for the maximum

---

105   Deutsche Telekom's argument, Case T-271/03, *Deutsche Telekom AG*, [2008] ECR II-477, paras. 38, 70.

106   Commission's argument, Case T-271/03, *Deutsche Telekom AG*, [2008] ECR II-477, para. 43.

107   Case T-271/03, *Deutsche Telekom AG*, [2008] ECR II-477, paras. 100, 105, which, it should be noted, has not happened, cf. paras. 126, 130.

Indicating Deutsche Telekom was responsible for an infringement of Article 102 TFEU:	Indicating Deutsche Telekom was not responsible for an infringement of Article 102 TFEU:
licence decision was based on its application.[108] On the other hand even a review of the price licence applications on the basis of Article 102 TFEU by the regulatory agency would not have removed Deutsche Telekom's responsibility: the regulatory authority is not responsible for the compliance with Article 102 TFEU. As it was not the German competition authority, but the telecommunications regulatory authority, it was only concerned with observing Article 4(3) TEU, and not broader competition provisions. Ultimately, the telecommunications regulatory authority did not actually check compliance with Article 102 TFEU.[109]	price, it should also have checked the basket maximum price for price dumping and unfair prices. The regulatory authority would have had to refuse an application for such prices as an abuse of Article 4(3) TEU in conjunction with Article 102 TFEU. The simple possibility of making an application for a price change is not to be equated with an autonomous freedom to set prices. The ex ante regulation serves to shape the market structure by State interventions and replaces the market structure responsibility of a regulated undertaking.[110]
From 2002	
From 2002, Deutsche Telekom could have raised end users' prices for broadband services on the basis of its own (even if legally qualified) judgement.[111] An increase relating to the narrow band connection services was no longer possible as those services were now included in a separate basket. Nonetheless, the two end users' services must be considered together (both narrow band and broad band connection services). On the one hand, Deutsche Telekom's competitors received only combined access to both end users' pre-payment products at the wholesale level.[112] On the other hand, both end users' products were tied closely to each other: broadband services constitute an upgrade from narrow band services and not a separate product.	At most Deutsche Telekom was able to set prices for broadband services independently from 2002. However, this ability was limited extensively: the basis for the change to broadband services was the adjusted price for narrow band services. Additionally, Deutsche Telekom, as regards its price setting for broadband services, had to follow the material requirements of the German Telecommunications Act and therefore was not allowed to raise prices above the costs of the efficient provision of services. Furthermore, the regulatory agency could control subsequently whether these prices met the requirements of the German Telecommunications Act.[113]

The General Court found that, between 1998 and the end of 2001, Deutsche Telekom could have applied for higher end users' prices, but rather than do so, it lowered its end users' prices.[114] Additionally, from 2002 it could have reduced the price margin squeeze

---

108 Case T-271/03, *Deutsche Telekom AG*, [2008] ECR II-477, para. 107.

109 Case T-271/03, *Deutsche Telekom AG*, [2008] ECR II-477, paras. 100, 109–124.

110 Deutsche Telekom's argument, Case T-271/03, *Deutsche Telekom AG*, [2008] ECR II-477, paras. 71, 73–79.

111 Commission's argument, see Case T-271/03, *Deutsche Telekom AG*, [2008] ECR II-477, para. 43, see also para. 145.

112 Case T-271/03, *Deutsche Telekom AG*, [2008] ECR II-477, paras. 147–151.

113 Deutsche Telekom's argument, Case T-271/03, *Deutsche Telekom AG*, [2008] ECR II-477, paras. 72, 80–83, 144.

114 Case T-271/03, *Deutsche Telekom AG*, [2008] ECR II-477, para. 131.

by increasing the prices it charged for broadband services.[115] Ultimately, even though Deutsche Telekom's ability to act was restricted by the national regulatory regime, scope for independent action still existed and Deutsche Telekom behaved abusively.

The General Court held (and the Court of Justice upheld) that, although the national regulatory authority had indeed had an effect on the prices set by Deutsche Telekom, in order for a national legal framework to render Articles 101 and 102 TFEU inapplicable to the anti-competitive activities of an undertaking, the restrictive effects on competition must originate solely in the national law, and not leave open the possibility that competition may be distorted by the autonomous conduct of the undertaking.[116] Consequently, as Deutsche Telekom was found to have had sufficient scope during the period of infringement to raise its retail prices and thereby avoid the margin squeeze,[117] it was considered to be liable for the infringement of Article 102 TFEU.

As regards the actions of the German telecommunications regulatory authority, the General Court noted that that body, like all organs of the State, is bound to respect the provisions of the TFEU; however, as a telecommunications regulatory authority, that body is distinct from a competition authority and may have objectives which differ from those of European competition policy.[118] Thus the possibility exists that the German regulatory authority may well have itself infringed European competition law, but in any case, even if it had considered the implications for competition law of the charges proposed by Deutsche Telekom, the Commission cannot be bound by the decision of a national body in European competition matters.[119]

In other cases the Court of Justice has found a sufficient ability to act economically independently, for example, in the form of a slight price range set out in State regulation,[120] the existence of a guideline for a production quota without a corresponding guideline for retail prices[121] and the State distribution of 85 % of production and the setting of retail prices.[122] The General Court has accepted a sufficient ability to act independently if the enactment of a fee system was made through State means, however, did restrict certain rates of charge or fee thresholds which should be considered by the establishment of the fee system.[123] Even in the case of extensive exclusion of price competition (having been replaced by State regulation) sufficient ability to act competitively can still exist in view of other competitive factors.[124]

---

115 Case T-271/03, *Deutsche Telekom AG,* [2008] ECR II-477, para. 151.

116 Case T-271/03, *Deutsche Telekom AG,* [2008] ECR II-477, paras. 87 and 88.

117 Case T-271/03, *Deutsche Telekom AG,* [2008] ECR II-477, paras. 140 and 151.

118 Case T-271/03, *Deutsche Telekom AG,* [2008] ECR II-477, para. 113.

119 Case T-271/03, *Deutsche Telekom AG,* [2008] ECR II-477, para. 120.

120 Joined Cases 209/78 to 215/78 and 218/78, *Heintz van Ladewyck SARL,* [1980] ECR 3125, para. 133.

121 Case C-219/95 P, *Ferriere Nord SpA,* [1997] ECR I-4411, para. 25.

122 Case C-198/01, *CIF,* [2003] ECR I-8055, paras. 73 et seq.

123 Case T-513/93, *Consiglio Nazionale degli Spedizionieri Doganali,* [2000] ECR II-1807, para. 62.

124 Case C-198/01, *CIF,* [2003] ECR I-8055, paras. 68 et seq.; cf. also Case 26/76, *Metro,* [1977] ECR 1875, para. 21.

To summarise, sufficient scope of independent economic action exists if:

(1) at the State level only general specifications regarding an undertaking's ability to act independently are set out; and

(2) at the State level concrete alternative forms of action are established or permitted; such is the case if:

(a) a limit on an undertaking's ability to act applies only 'in one direction' (certain behavioural alternatives are limited); or

(b) an undertaking is responsible for submitting requests for authorisation and can influence the structure and content of the authorisation; or

(c) an undertaking can make a new application for authorisation in future, so the existing authorisation is of a temporary nature only.[125]

b) Example: Fines

If a national regulatory regime prescribes anti-competitive behaviour by an undertaking, in the interest of legal certainty, penalties generally cannot be imposed on that undertaking.[126] As regards the imposition of penalties for breaches of competition law (but notably not for e.g. the imposition of an injunction) the existence of national law which precludes an undertaking from acting autonomously can constitute a mitigating factor in its infringement of competition rules (in the sense of waiver of penalties) if the undertaking has acted in reliance on the State's statement of non-applicability.[127]

If national regulations merely permit, promote or simplify anti-competitive behaviour, undertakings remain responsible for their own behaviour. They infringe Article 101 or 102 TFEU independently and therefore cannot rely on their trust of the State in the area of national law as regards their conformity with EU law. Penalties can be also imposed on undertakings for offences against competition law in such situations. In any case the extenuating circumstances of reliance on national norms is to be noted in the calculation of penalties.[128]

V. MARKET DEFINITION

The concept of "market definition" describes the process by which a relevant product market is identified on the basis of product, geographic and temporal criteria. The definition of the relevant market serves to demarcate the exact area in which an undertaking supplies a certain product in competition with other undertakings, i.e. competes for customers. The relevant market identifies the framework within which competition law is to be applied. The principle purpose of defining a market is to allow for a consideration of the competitive strengths of the relevant undertakings. The degree to which competing undertakings are actually able to constrain the behaviour of the undertaking in question,

---

125   In detail Schreiber, Das Zusammenspiel der Regulierungsinstrumente in den Netzwirtschaften Telekommunikation, Energie und Eisenbahnen, 2009, pp. 103 et seq.

126   Case C-198/01, *CIF*, [2003] ECR I-8055, para. 53.

127   Case C-198/01, *CIF*, [2003] ECR I-8055, para. 54.

128   Case C-198/01, *CIF*, [2003] ECR I-8055, paras. 56 et seq.

and the degree of real competition on the market (i.e. that an undertaking cannot behave independently of its competitors or set uncompetitive prices) are key factors in analysing the competitive situation.[129]

Notably, this concept within the realm of competition law differs from the colloquial concept of, for example, the market or area in which a company sells its products, or more generally, a particular industry or sector.[130]

Only once the relevant market has been identified can it be determined whether there has been a "prevention, restriction or distortion" of competition as per Article 101 TFEU.[131] Market definition is also a key aspect of investigating whether an undertaking possesses a market-dominating position for the purposes of Article 102 TFEU, as such determination can only be made once the size of the whole market is known. This is a key question in considering the application of Article 102 TFEU: whether an undertaking is guilty of an infraction depends on its market strength. A determination of market strength, in turn, depends on how the relevant market is defined – a wide market definition may result in a low market share, whereas a narrow market definition can lead to a high market share.

1. The Principles of Market Definition – Criteria and Methods

The Commission set out its views on the manner in which the relevant market should be determined in its 1997 notice on the definition of the relevant market for the purposes of Community competition law.[132] The Commission and European courts continue to adhere to the principles described in that notice.

Market definition always considers the extent to which an undertaking is affected by competition in a market. Fundamentally, an undertaking's or group of undertakings' ability to distort competition depends on whether it or they can act independently of their competitors.

Undertakings are subject to three main types of competitive constraints: demand substitutability, supply substitutability and, in exceptional cases, potential competition.[133]

Thus determination of market definition depends on an economic and empirical review of market data. However, such review is only possible after a preliminary consideration of the potential relevant market in order to narrow parameters and make a final determination. Therefore in practice, market definition proceeds in two steps – first a preliminary analysis and then a more detailed and concrete determination.[134]

---

129 Commission, Notice on the definition of the relevant market for the purposes of Community competition law, [1997] OJ C372/5, para. 2 (the "Commission Notice on the definition of the relevant market").

130 Commission Notice on the definition of the relevant market, para. 3.

131 For the purposes of Article 101 TFEU it is not necessary to determine the specific market in question if the distortion of competition can be ascertained without exact market definition, Case T-38/02, *Groupe Danone*, [2005] ECR II-4407, para. 99; *Bananas* (Case COMP/39188) Commission Decision, para. 140.

132 Commission Notice on the definition of the relevant market, [1997] OJ C372/5-13.

133 Commission Notice on the definition of the relevant market, para. 13.

134 Cf. Commission Notice on the definition of the relevant market, paras. 25–35.

a) The Role of the Consumers of a Product

The concept of "demand side substitutability" considers the behaviour of consumers who buy a product, whether for, for example, end-consumption, resale or as a component part for further production. If these consumers will swap to another supplier if the existing one increases the prices of or decreases the quality of its product, then that supplier is not able to act independently of the market – such a supplier must adhere to the demands of its consumers and cannot raise prices without losing consumers. The relevant market encompasses all actual alternative products or suppliers to which a consumer can easily swap.[135] Demand substitution is the most important factor in determining the relevant market, as it constitutes the most immediate and effective disciplinary force on the suppliers of a particular product, as customers are easily able to swap to other producers or suppliers.[136]

Different methods and approaches to the concept of demand substitution have developed over time. This evolution offers a clue to the importance in each case of the specific facts of that case, as well as how resilient those facts are. The initial analysis undertaken in determining a relevant market considers the characteristics and intended use of a product.[137] At the next stage, the "SSNIP test" and various quantitative tests are undertaken.

aa) SSNIP Test

The "SSNIP test" ("Small but Significant Non-Transitory Increase in Price") is a thought experiment asking a hypothetical question: if the price of a product was raised permanently by 5 to 10 %, would consumers of this product change to another product?[138]

If the answer to this question is yes, and the resulting loss of sales cannot justify the increase in price, then both products belong to the same market.[139] If a price increase would drive consumers to other products, then these products are substitutable, and therefore in the same market. The SSNIP test is repeated with other products, until a set of products is identified where a permanent price increase would be profitable, as there are no further substitutes available.

Market data used for the SSNIP test can be historic[140] or can be gathered contemporaneously through questionnaires put to customers asking how they would act in the event of a permanent price increase.[141]

---

135 Cf. Commission Notice on the definition of the relevant market, para. 13.

136 Commission Notice on the definition of the relevant market, para. 13.

137 Commission Notice on the definition of the relevant market, para. 36.

138 Commission Notice on the definition of the relevant market, para. 15.

139 Commission Notice on the definition of the relevant market, para. 17.

140 Commission Notice on the definition of the relevant market, para. 38.

141 The legal basis for such questionnaires is Article 19 of Council Regulation (EC) No 1/2003 of 16 December 2002 on the implementation of the rules on competition laid down in Articles 81 and 82 of the Treaty, [2003] OJ L1/1; for further information see Chapter 6 (*The Commission's Competence*).

However, this method is only really effective where the price of a product is of determining significance – it loses its effectiveness, for example, in the medical market where price may not be the determining factor in consumption.[142]

Additionally, the SSNIP test is also inappropriate in determining market definition in cases of demand side power (in contrast to supply side power). In such cases, the starting point is then the supplier, and the price test serves to identify any alternative distribution channels or outlets for the supplier's products.[143]

The general starting point of the SSNIP test is the current market price, however care must be taken if this price is already artificially high, due for example, to existing market abuse. If monopoly prices already exist, then consumers may be more ready to change to alternative products which satisfy their needs less well. In that case, a high degree of substitutability may exist, even if not indicated by responses to a hypothetical price change.[144] In such instances the hypothetical price in a competitive environment must be determined, taking account of the fact that the prevailing market price might already have been substantially increased.[145]

bb) Quantitative Tests – Price Cross-Elasticities

Other tests can also be used to determine market demarcation.[146] The most prevalent of these is price cross-elasticity. The SSNIP test relies on changes in demand resulting from a change in price. On the other hand, an investigation of price cross-elasticity considers the causality of price changes: if the price of a similar product is increased or decreased, does the price of the product being investigated also change?[147] As with the SSNIP test, the effects of a change in one product's price on the price of other products are examined – only the perspective is different. In the SSNIP test, the effect of price changes on demand is measured; with price cross-elasticity, the question is rather the extent to which price changes for one product cause price changes for another on the supply side (without considering whether such changes alter demand).

b) The Role of Other (Potential) Suppliers of a Product

Another approach to market definition considers supply rather than demand side substitution. This test is useful when a change in selling price would make it worthwhile for a supplier to alter its production, as would be the case when the price of a product was increased permanently, and it would be lucrative for a supplier (and without great cost or risk) to swap production to that product.[148]

---

142 Cf. Morse, Product Market Definition in the Pharmaceutical Industry, Antitrust Law Journal No 2 (2003), Vol. 71, 633 (638).

143 Cf. Commission Notice on the definition of the relevant market, para. 17.

144 This issue is the subject of the "Cellophane Fallacy" discussion – cf. Whish, Competition Law (6th edn. 2008), pp. 30 et seq.

145 Cf. Commission Notice on the definition of the relevant market, para. 19.

146 Cf. Commission Notice on the definition of the relevant market, para. 39.

147 Cf. Case T-271/03, *Deutsche Telekom AG*, [2008] ECR II-477, paras. 83, 149 (confirmed by Case C-280/08 P, *Deutsche Telekom AG*); Commission Notice on the definition of the relevant market, para. 39, n. 5.

148 Cf. Commission Notice on the definition of the relevant market, para. 20.

One example of this circumstance would be the paper industry. For the consumer, normal writing paper is not generally interchangeable with high-quality paper used for reproductions of art. However, on the manufacturing side, it is relatively straightforward to swap to production of a different type of paper, as this can be done simply by changing the settings on production machinery.[149]

Analysis of the supply side therefore can be useful in certain circumstances for making the relevant market more precise.

> Different products are included in the relevant market when:
> (1) the competitive production conditions for a group of products are technically comparable;
> (2) those products are themselves technically comparable;
> (3) consumers consider those products all to be part of a similar range;[150] and
> (4) the manufacturing (supply) side has strong incentives to swap from the production of product A to the production of B due to relatively low swap costs.

c) The Potential Competition

Potential competition, in particular the question of whether a third party in the market could generate competitive pressure, is not usually taken into account when defining markets as undertakings only tend to alter their behaviour in such cases if the barriers to entry to the market are particularly low.[151] However, the issue of market entry barriers can only be carried out at a subsequent stage, once the position of the undertakings involved on the relevant market has already been ascertained.[152]

2. Product, Geographic and Temporal Market Demarcation

A distinction should be drawn between product, geographic and temporal market demarcations. The *product market* encompasses products of the same or similar kind, while the *geographic market* focuses on the geographic range of a product – how close a supplier needs to be to a consumer. In some cases the two must be relatively close to each other; in others, a distance of hundreds of kilometres is acceptable. Finally, the *temporal market* describes products for which timing is important, for example items which are only available or in demand seasonally.[153]

---

149 Cf. Commission Notice on the definition of the relevant market, para. 22.

150 Füller, in Hirsch/Montag/Säcker (eds), Competition Law: European Community Practice and Procedure, 2008, 1-11-014.

151 Cf. Ritter/Braun, European Competition Law: A Practitioner's Guide (3rd edn. 2004), p. 36.

152 Cf. Commission Notice on the definition of the relevant market, para. 24.

153 The temporal dimension of market demarcation has become important for petroleum products. The Commission limited the relevant market at that time to the time period of the oil crisis in 1973/1974; see Case COMP/28841, Commission Decision [1977] OJ L117/1. The Court of Justice did not reject the Commission's market demarcation, Case 77/77, *BP*, [1978] ECR 1513, paras. 18, 29.34.

VI. EXAMPLES: MARKET DEMARCATION IN PRACTICE

The principles described above provide a basis for analysis of the relevant market, but they seldom lead to unequivocal boundaries of a market. For this reason, building upon the basic rules of market demarcation are a number of additional methods and considerations. In addition, the large body of Commission decisions and European jurisprudence has led to the development in practice of differing approaches to different sectors and kinds of cases.

1. Demand Side Substitutability – the Classic: *United Brands*

The 1978 decision in the case of *United Brands*[154] can be considered a classic example in determining the relevant market. Even today, reference is often made to this decision in which the Court of Justice considered the relevant market in high detail. Even though at that time the "more economic approach" was not in use, this judgement remains illustrative today.

Does there exist a relevant market consisting solely of bananas, or is it more appropriate to consider bananas as an "integral part of the fresh fruit market"?[155]

United Brands argued that bananas should be classed in the same market as other fresh fruit available in shops, as bananas and other fruits are sold together, at similar prices and for the same purpose (consumption between meals or as a dessert).[156] The Commission, on the other hand, argued that there is a demand for bananas which is distinct from the demand for other fresh fruits, particularly as bananas possess certain qualities that make them an important part of the diet of certain sections of the public.[157]

In terms of availability, bananas also posses certain special qualities, for example that they ripen year round, so that seasons do not have to be taken into account and consequently their price can be adjusted in the times of year when other fruits are in plentiful supply.[158] Two studies undertaken had indicated that the banana is only affected by falling prices of certain fruits at certain times of the year – the importing of bananas was flexible, and marketing strategies adjustable, so that the conditions of competition were "extremely limited" and the price of bananas adapted to circumstances where supplies of other fruits are plentiful without any serious difficulties.[159] Essentially, the market for bananas was distinct from the market for other fruits, as bananas were not affected by competitive pressures from those other fruits – consumers of bananas were not enticed away from bananas by the availability of other fruits.[160]

---

154 Case 27/76, *United Brands*, [1978] ECR 207, paras. 12–35.
155 Case 27/76, *United Brands*, [1978] ECR 207, para. 12.
156 Case 27/76, *United Brands*, [1978] ECR 207, paras. 13, 18.
157 Case 27/76, *United Brands*, [1978] ECR 207, paras. 19, 21.
158 Case 27/76, *United Brands*, [1978] ECR 207, paras. 23, 33.
159 Case 27/76, *United Brands*, [1978] ECR 207, paras. 23, 33.
160 Case 27/76, *United Brands*, [1978] ECR 207, paras. 34, 35.

The Court of Justice, with its finding of non-substitutability between bananas and other fruits, approved the Commission's finding of a distinct relevant market for bananas. However, from the judgement it remained unclear precisely what degree of substitutability was required for products to comprise the same relevant market. It was clear that not all consumers of a product must depart from that product on the basis of substitutability in order for there to be a separate relevant market; instead, for the purposes of the SSNIP test it is sufficient if a large enough number of consumers swap to other products in the event of price increases that such an increase does not become profitable. For example this means that a price increase is not lucrative if approximately 10 % of customer profits do not increase or even go down as a result of the increase.

2. Comparable Products – Neighbouring Markets

It can be problematic to establish a clear market demarcation between comparable products and neighbouring markets. It must be determined whether a distinct product market exists, or whether several neighbouring markets exist vertically or horizontally.

Vertically neighbouring markets are those in which one product is necessary for the use of another product, e.g. the market for staples which are necessary for the use of office staplers, or the market for spare parts used to repair other, primary products. Horizontally neighbouring markets are those which contain comparable, but not substitutable products – e.g. the markets for passenger car tyres and truck tyres.

a) Clearstream Banking

At issue in the case of *Clearstream Banking* was whether there was one relevant market for clearing services for securities or instead, two markets separate from each other for 'primary' and 'secondary' clearing and settlement services. The Commission was of the view that two markets existed – the primary market being the clearing and settlement of securities by the same entity which holds the securities in safe custody, with the second market being clearing and settlement carried out by intermediaries, i.e. operators other than the entity in which the securities are held in custody.

This case dealt with the question as to whether Clearstream had infringed competition rules by refusing to supply cross-border securities clearing and settlement services to Euroclear Bank, established in Belgium. Clearstream was the sole final custodian of German securities kept in collective safe custody, which was the only significant form of custody frequently used in securities trading. The process of buying and selling securities differs from the purchase and sale of other kinds of assets as there is a need to monitor ownership of securities.

Therefore the securities clearing and settlement process is an essential step for the completion of a securities trade. Clearing is the process by which the contractual obligations of the buyer and the seller are established. Settlement is the transfer of securities from the seller to the buyer and the transfer of funds from the buyer to the seller. Securities need to be physically or electronically deposited with an entity and held by that entity. As Clearstream was the sole authorised final custodian of German securities, every bank offering trading services had to use the services offered by Clearstream to finalise a securities trade.

There were two possible ways to complete a securities trade: Either the bank (as a customer) had access to the services of Clearstream itself (*'primary* clearing and settlement') or a bank (also as a customer) used the services of another bank which itself had direct access to the services of Clearstream (*'secondary* clearing and settlement').[161]

The Commission argued (and the General Court held) that the provision by Clearstream of primary clearing and settlement services to customers who had accepted its general conditions occurs on a market separate from the provision of secondary services, even though the result of these services being carried out was the same (completing a trade). For customers who required primary clearing and settlement services in order to be able efficiently to provide secondary clearing and settlement services, secondary clearing and settlement were not a valid alternative. Secondary clearing and settlement services were in fact more expensive and slower. On the basis that there was no substitutability either on the demand side (costs and speed) or on the supply side (Clearstream was the sole authorised service provider), the two markets must be considered separate.[162]

The Commission therefore concluded that Clearstream had a dominant position on the relevant market (the market being comprised of primary clearing and settlement services), as such transactions of securities issued and kept in collective custody were carried out in Germany only by Clearstream, the sole securities depository bank in Germany.[163]

b) Spare Parts

The case of *Hugin* dealt with whether the refusal of a manufacturer of cash registers to supply spare parts to independent companies not in its sales network constituted an abuse of a dominant position. A key factor was whether the supply of spare parts constituted a specific market or whether it was part of the market for cash registers.[164] Manufacturer Hugin possessed a relatively small part of the market share for cash registers, but it was the only manufacturer of spare parts for machines made by it, and so consequently it possessed a monopoly in that regard.[165]

To determine what the relevant market for spare cash register parts was, it was necessary to consider the category of customers who require such parts. The Commission found that the main consumers of spare parts were companies who specialised in servicing and repair of cash registers.[166] Therefore demand substitutability had to be assessed from the point of view of these undertakings, and for them, Hugin-brand spare parts could not be substituted with spare parts from other brands.[167] Consequently the rele-

---

161   For further details of the complicated circumstances of this case see *Clearstream* (COMP/38096) Commission Decision, paras. 1–38.

162   Case T-301/04, *Clearstream*, [2009] ECR II-3155, paras. 47–73, in particular paras. 65–68.

163   Case T-301/04, *Clearstream*, [2009] ECR II-3155, paras. 62 to 68, 73.

164   Case 22/78, *Hugin*, [1979] ECR 1869, para. 5.

165   Case 22/78, *Hugin*, [1979] ECR 1869, para. 3.

166   Case 22/78, *Hugin*, [1979] ECR 1869, paras. 6, 7.

167   Case 22/78, *Hugin*, [1979] ECR 1869, para. 7.

vant market was the market for Hugin spare parts needed by independent undertakings, rather than the market for cash registers as a whole.[168]

c) Tyres

The case of *Michelin* considered in some detail the differences between types of tyres, as well as potential demand and supply side substitutability.

The Court held that there was no interchangeability between new and spare tyres; these were different markets as the competition structures of each are very different (with car manufacturers playing a strong role in the market for new tyres).[169] Additionally, no interchangeability existed between tyres for cars and vans and tyres for heavy vehicles;[170] as well as not being substitutable on the demand side, on the supply side swapping production between these two types of tyres required substantial time and investment due to the considerable differences in the production technology of each type of tyre.[171] Finally, new tyres and retreads were not interchangeable for market demarcation purposes.[172] In contrast to the *United Brands*[173] decision, it was not enough that some users considered these two types of tyres interchangeable.

As regards security and reliability, a retread tyre has a lower value than a new tyre. The market for remoulded tyres was a secondary market which was dependent on the offer situation and price situation at the new tyre market, because each of the remoulded tyres was produced from an originally new tyre and the number of the possible retread renewals of a tyre was limited.[174]

3. Supply Side Substitutability

a) Tetra Pak

aa) The Relevant Product Market

This case concerned the markets in machinery for the aseptic and non-aseptic packaging of liquid foods in cartons and the corresponding markets for cartons – whether they comprised one product market, or two.[175] Of key importance was that (in the decisive time period) aseptic machinery and cartons were not sufficiently interchangeable with non-aseptic packaging systems using other materials, on the grounds of a lack of substitutable production equipment – undertakings producing non-aseptic materials were not able to

---

168 Case 22/78, *Hugin*, [1979] ECR 1869, para. 8.

169 Case 322/81, *N.V. Nederlandsche Banden-Industrie-Michelin*, [1983] ECR 3461, para. 38.

170 Case 322/81, *N.V. Nederlandsche Banden-Industrie-Michelin*, [1983] ECR 3461, paras. 39, 40.

171 Case 322/81, *N.V. Nederlandsche Banden-Industrie-Michelin*, [1983] ECR 3461, para. 41.

172 Case 322/81, *N.V. Nederlandsche Banden-Industrie-Michelin*, [1983] ECR 3461, para. 48. Two different markets were also ascertained in Case T-203/01, *Michelin*, [2003] ECR II-4071, paras. 25, 44.

173 See VI. 1. of this chapter.

174 Case 322/81, *N.V. Nederlandsche Banden-Industrie-Michelin*, [1983] ECR 3461, para. 51.

175 Cf. Case T-83/91, *Tetra Pak*, [1994] ECR II-755, para. 65.

produce aseptic cartons.[176] Given the lack of supply side substitutability, two different product markets existed.[177]

bb) The Relevant Geographic Market

Tetra Pak denied that the relevant geographical market covered the whole of the Union; it argued that, instead, various Member States constituted separate markets for the products in question because the objective conditions of competition were not the same for all traders throughout the (then) European Community. However, the General Court held that the existence of subsidiaries at national level, as well as the practice of dairies obtaining supplies at a local level, were not sufficient to prove that differing competitive conditions existed in different Member States. The fact that consumers had the opportunity to source machinery or cartons from other Member States (helped by the low transportation costs of those products) meant that the whole of the Union should be considered the relevant geographic market.[178]

b) Possibility of Adaptation and Transportation Costs

aa) The Relevant Product Market

The product in question in the case of *Kish Glass* was a type of float glass for which demand side substitutability did not exist, as swimming glass of different strengths is not interchangeable for final consumers. The question then became one of supply side substitutability, and the General Court upheld the Commission's decision that, although there was only one main supplier of cut glass in imperial measures, other undertakings currently producing under metric measures could alter their production relatively quickly and without excessive expense.[179] Thus the relevant product market was the market for glass of all strengths, not just those in imperial measures.[180]

bb) The Relevant Geographic Market

The relevant geographic market in *Kish Glass* was determined primarily on the basis of transportation costs, and whether they demarcated a geographic market.[181] At issue was whether transportation costs were such that the relevant geographic market should be limited to Ireland or Ireland and the United Kingdom, or extended to cover the whole of the (then) Community or at least the northern part of it. The court upheld the Commission's decision that transportation costs were not sufficient to indicate a separate market from the (then) Community as a whole, nor were there technical or regulatory barriers

---

176 Case T-83/91, *Tetra Pak*, [1994] ECR II-755, para. 69.

177 Case T-83/91, *Tetra Pak*, [1994] ECR II-755, paras. 71–73.

178 Case T-83/91, *Tetra Pak*, [1994] ECR II-755, paras. 94 and 98.

179 Case T-65/96, *Kish Glass*, [2000] ECR II-1885, para. 65.

180 Case T-65/96, *Kish Glass*, [2000] ECR II-1885, para. 69.

181 Case T-65/96, *Kish Glass*, [2000] ECR II-1885, paras. 81 et seq.

to the Irish market. Thus the relevant geographic market was the (then) European Community or the northern part of it.[182]

4. Regulated Industries

When examining the supply side substitutability of a product, the specific qualities or characteristics of a particular sector of the economy should be considered. In particular as regards regulated industries, this may include a demarcation of the market according to certain legal requirements imposed upon market participants.

a) Telecommunications Sector: Deutsche Telekom AG

The case of *Deutsche Telekom*[183] considered whether Deutsche Telekom had infringed Article 102 TFEU by operating abusive pricing in the form of a 'margin squeeze' by charging its competitors prices for wholesale access that were higher than the prices it charged for retail access to the network. Of particular importance in determining the relevant market was to distinguish between the market in access to the network infrastructure owned and operated by Deutsche Telekom and the market in services provided to final users over networks, such as telephone call services.[184]

The Commission distinguished two separate markets in relation to access to the local network: the wholesale market (the upstream market in local network access offered by infrastructure owners to their competitors) and the retail market (the downstream market in access services offered by telecommunications operators to their own end users).[185] The Commission acknowledged that on the supply side a number of conceivable alternatives to the local networks did exist – i.e. fibre-optic networks, wireless local loops, satellites and upgraded cable TV networks. However, none of those alternatives could be considered as equivalent to the local network in Germany, as they were not sufficiently developed in order to be substitutable.[186] Thus the relevant markets were the market in local network access for competitor at the wholesale level, and the market in access to narrowband and broadband connections at the retail level.[187]

---

182   Case T-65/96, *Kish Glass,* [2000] ECR II-1885, para. 82.

183   Case T-271/03, *Deutsche Telekom AG*, [2008] ECR II-477 (confirmed in Case C-280/08 P, *Deutsche Telekom AG); Deutsche Telekom AG* (Case COMP/37.451, 37.578, 37.579) Commission Decision 2003/707/EC, [2003] OJ L263/9, in particular pp. 18–22.

184   *Deutsche Telekom AG* (Case COMP/37.451, 37.578, 37.579) Commission Decision 2003/707/EC, [2003] OJ L263/9, in particular pp. 18–22, para. 59; cf. also Commission guidelines on market analysis and the assessment of significant market power under the Community regulatory framework for electronic communications networks and services, [2002] OJ C165/6, para. 65.

185   *Deutsche Telekom AG* (Case COMP/37.451, 37.578, 37.579) Commission Decision 2003/707/EC, [2003] OJ L263/9, para. 61.

186   *Deutsche Telekom AG* (Case COMP/37.451, 37.578, 37.579) Commission Decision 2003/707/EC, [2003] OJ L263/9, para. 83.

187   *Deutsche Telekom AG* (Case COMP/37.451, 37.578, 37.579) Commission Decision 2003/707/EC, [2003] OJ L263/9, para. 91.

b) Pharmaceutical Sector: Astra Zeneca

At issue in the case of *Astra Zeneca* was whether national markets for medicines within the (then) European Community were distinct enough to comprise separate relevant geographic markets, or if the Community as a whole should be considered the relevant geographic market.

Of particular importance was that different price, reimbursement or allowance plan regulations existed in each Member State, as well as different brands and packaging strategies, marketing strategies and prescription regulations. Harmonisation at the European level was limited to regulations concerning safety and quality control, and it was held that this standardisation was not extensive enough to render the relevant geographic market the whole of the (then) Community, rather than individual Member States.[188]

5. Tied Services

In the case of *British Airways*[189] the General Court considered whether a separate market existed for travel agent services, or whether those services were part of the same market as other airline travel services.

At the time, travel agents acted as sales representatives of airlines which then entered into a direct contract with customers and paid a commission to the agents, as well as in some cases offering rebates to the travel agents (known as tying). The travel agents were independent intermediaries who performed an independent service activity and who competed with each other for sales.[190] It was also the case that a mutual dependence existed between the travel agents and the airlines, which were not capable of selling air transport services effectively.[191]

In the relevant period, approximately 85 % of flights sold in the United Kingdom were sold through travel agents, therefore such services could be considered irreplaceable for airlines.[192] As the travel agents engaged in an economic activity for which no appropriate substitute existed,[193] such services were held to form a market distinct from the airline market.[194]

---

188   *AstraZeneca* (Case COMP/37.507) Commission Decision, p. 113, para. 503.

189   Case T-219/99, *British Airways,* [2003] ECR II-5917 (confirmed in Case C-95/04 P, *British Airways,* [2007] ECR I-2331).

190   Case T-219/99, *British Airways,* [2003] ECR II-5917, paras. 92 et seq (confirmed in Case C-95/04 P, *British Airways,* [2007] ECR I-2331).

191   Case T-219/99, *British Airways,* [2003] ECR II-5917, para. 95 (confirmed in Case C-95/04 P, *British Airways,* [2007] ECR I-2331).

192   Case T-219/99, *British Airways,* [2003] ECR II-5917, para. 99 (confirmed in Case C-95/04 P, *British Airways,* [2007] ECR I-2331).

193   Case T-219/99, *British Airways,* [2003] ECR II-5917, para. 100 (confirmed in Case C-95/04 P, *British Airways,* [2007] ECR I-2331).

194   Case T-219/99, *British Airways,* [2003] ECR II-5917, para. 100 (confirmed in Case C-95/04 P, *British Airways,* [2007] ECR I-2331).

6. Relevance of Distribution Channels

The relevant market can also be demarcated according to a product's distribution channels.

a) Beer Supply Agreements

The case of *Roberts* illustrated that the manner in which a product is distributed can affect its relevant market. Here, the General Court confirmed that the retail market for beer is distinct from the market where beer is supplied to pubs and private clubs. Even though the product is essentially the same, the method of distribution was key in determining market demarcation.

From the point of view of the final consumer, the pub and club sector differed from the retail sector as sales in such establishments are associated with the provision of services, and the consumption of beer does not depend essentially on economic considerations.[195] The two sectors differed from the point of view of breweries as well – distribution to pubs and clubs was characterised by specific systems for the sector, the need for special equipment to dispense draught beer and the prices charged were generally higher than in the retail sector.[196]

b) Bronner – Access to Essential Facilities

At issue in *Bronner* was whether a refusal by a press undertaking which held a large share of the daily newspaper market and which operated the only nationwide newspaper home delivery scheme to allow the publisher of a rival, smaller newspaper to have access to that scheme constituted an abuse of a dominant position under European competition law.

The General Court considered "whether home-delivery schemes constitute a separate market, or whether other methods of distributing daily newspapers, such as sale in shops or at kiosks or delivery by post, are sufficiently interchangeable with them to have to be taken into account also".[197]

Although the establishment of a home delivery service was not a commercially viable option for the smaller newspaper, it could nonetheless distribute its product through other means, e.g. by post or through sale in shops or kiosks.[198] Additionally, there were no technical, legal or economic obstacles which would make it impossible, or even unreasonably difficult, for any publisher of daily newspaper to establish (alone or with others) its own home delivery scheme.[199] Thus the General Court held that in this case, the refusal of the dominant firm to supply services to its competitor did not constitute an abuse of its dominant position.

---

195 Case T-25/99, *Roberts*, [2001] ECR II-1881, para. 30.

196 Case T-25/99, *Roberts*, [2001] ECR II-1881, paras. 30–31.

197 Case C-7/97, *Bronner*, [1998] ECR I-7791, para. 34.

198 Case C-7/97, *Bronner*, [1998] ECR I-7791, para. 43.

199 Case C-7/97, *Bronner*, [1998] ECR I-7791, paras. 43 et seq.

7. One Product – Two Markets

Wanadoo Interactive SA was a subsidiary of the French Telecom group and provided ADSL services in France. A key issue in the *France Télécom* case was whether there existed one market for residential internet access in France, or two separate markets for high- and low-speed access.

Wanadoo argued that there was only one market for internet access, in the form of a continuum from low-speed to high-speed, and pointed out the emergence of medium-speed ADSL services in support of this perspective.[200] In contrast, the Commission was of the opinion that differences in usage, technical specifications and performance, price and the nature of subscribers for the services meant that two separate markets should be distinguished.[201]

The Commission also found substitutability between high- and low-speed ADSL services, but notably, the substitutability was highly asymmetrical: customers very rarely would migrate from high-speed access to low-speed access, but far more frequently would move from low- to high-speed access.[202] Additionally, a survey conducted by the Commission found that 80 % of high-speed subscribers would not alter their subscription in response to a price increase of 5-10 %, indicating a lack of demand side substitutability.[203] Consequently the General Court upheld the Commission's determination that there was insufficient substitutability between high- and low-speed ADSL services to constitute one market instead of two separate markets, and that the sole relevant market was that of high-speed (only) internet access to residential customers.[204]

This finding implied that a product consisting of "high speed internet access" was part of two separate markets depending on the point of view of the analysis (which abusive behaviour was being investigated). From the perspective of behaviour in connection with a product consisting of "low speed internet access", both high speed and low speed access are part of the relevant product market. In contrast, looking at behaviour relating to high-speed access only, low-speed access is not part of this relevant product market.

---

200 Case T-340/03, *France Télécom,* [2007] ECR II-107, para. 73 (confirmed in Case C-202/07 P, *France Télécom,* [2009] ECR I-2369).

201 Case T-340/03, *France Télécom,* [2007] ECR II-107, para. 77 (confirmed in Case C-202/07 P, *France Télécom,* [2009] ECR I-2369).

202 Cf. *Wanadoo Interactive* (Case COMP/38.233) Commission Decision, paras. 193–202.

203 Case T-340/03, *France Télécom,* [2007] ECR II-107, para. 90 (confirmed in Case C-202/07 P, *France Télécom,* [2009] ECR I-2369).

204 Case T-340/03, *France Télécom,* [2007] ECR II-107, para. 91 (confirmed in Case C-202/07 P, *France Télécom,* [2009] ECR I-2369).

Chapter Three

THE PROHIBITION ON CARTELS
UNDER ARTICLE 101 TFEU

Article 101(1) TFEU sets out a prohibition on cartels, which includes anti-competitive agreements as well as decisions and coordinated behaviour patterns by undertakings or amongst groups of undertakings.

Article 101 TFEU
"1. The following shall be prohibited as incompatible with the internal market: all agreements between undertakings, decisions by associations of undertakings and concerted practices which may affect trade between Member States and which have as their object or effect the prevention, restriction or distortion of competition within the internal market, and in particular those which:
   (a) directly or indirectly fix purchase or selling prices or any other trading conditions;
   (b) limit or control production, markets, technical development, or investment;
   (c) share markets or sources of supply;
   (d) apply dissimilar conditions to equivalent transactions with other trading parties, thereby placing them at a competitive disadvantage;
   (e) make the conclusion of contracts subject to acceptance by the other parties of supplementary obligations which, by their nature or according to commercial usage, have no connection with the subject of such contracts.
2. Any agreements or decisions prohibited pursuant to this Article shall be automatically void.
3. The provisions of paragraph 1 may, however, be declared inapplicable in the case of:
   – any agreement or category of agreements between undertakings,
   – any decision or category of decisions by associations of undertakings,
   – any concerted practice or category of concerted practices,
   which contributes to improving the production or distribution of goods or to promoting technical or economic progress, while allowing consumers a fair share of the resulting benefit, and which does not:
   (a) impose on the undertakings concerned restrictions which are not indispensable to the attainment of these objectives;
   (b) afford such undertakings the possibility of eliminating competition in respect of a substantial part of the products in question."

Instead of competing with each other on arms' length terms, members of a cartel act according to agreed behaviour patterns and thus restrict the development of better products and the evolution of lower prices. The existence of a cartel is indicated (in a simple sense) by the actions of multiple undertakings to coordinate their behaviour on a relevant market by agreeing to restrict or exclude competition. The patterns of behaviour prohibited by Article 101 TFEU seek to reduce the entrepreneurial risks of competition, thereby weakening consumers' negotiating power as well as discouraging innovation as a strategy and driver to overcome entrepreneurial risks.

I. THE STRUCTURE OF THE PROHIBITION

The substance of the prohibition on cartels is contained in Article 101(1) TFEU, with Article 101(3) providing for certain exceptions to the basic prohibition. Since it is possible that coordinated behaviour amongst undertakings can also lead to positive, desirable effects, in exceptional circumstances behaviours which restrict competition can be permitted. Desirable effects are achieved, for example, if the coordinated behaviour is necessary for an undertaking to join the market and otherwise does not prevent, restrict or distort competition to an appreciable degree.[205] Another example of a positive effect of what seems on the surface to be anti-competitive behaviour might be industry-wide cooperation for technical advancements or standardisation.[206]

In conjunction with Council Regulation (EC) No 1/2003 on the implementation of the rules on competition laid down in [then] Articles 81 and 82 of the Treaty,[207] Article 101 TFEU can be seen as a *prohibition subject to specific legal exemptions and associated controls*. The exemption to the basic prohibition on cartels does not require a decision by the Commission, but rather exists in law *per se* if the conditions of Article 101(3) TFEU are satisfied.[208]

If the conditions of Article 101(1) TFEU are satisfied, without any of the exceptions contained in Article 101(3) applying, Article 101(2) specifies the legal consequence of such infringement: *"[a]ny agreements or decisions prohibited pursuant to [Article 101] shall be automatically void"*. Such practices are also void *per se*, with no further action by the Commission or national competition authorities required. The undertakings involved bear the risk of their agreements or decisions being rendered unenforceable, which consequently affects the economic attractiveness of committing such an infringement of Article 101 TFEU in the first place. Additionally, the Commission can impose on each undertaking involved in the infringement a fine at the rate of up to 10 % of the undertaking's last annual turnover[209] if the infringement of Article 101 TFEU was intentional or negligent.[210]

---

205 Case 56/65, *L.T.M./M.B.U.*, [1966] ECR 282, 304; Case T-328/03, *O2 (Germany)*, [2006] ECR II-1231, para. 68.

206 See for example Commission Regulation (EC) No 772/2004 of 27 April 2004 on the application of Article 81(3) of the Treaty to categories of technology transfer agreements, [2004] OJ L 123/11.

207 [2003] OJ L 1/1.

208 Article 1(2) of Council Regulation (EC) No 1/2003 of 16 December 2002 on the implementation of the rules on competition laid down in Articles 81 and 82 of the Treaty, [2003] OJ L 1/1.

209 Article 23(2) of Council Regulation (EC) No 1/2003.

210 See Chapter 6 (*The Commission's Competence*) for an in-depth description of the Commission's powers.

II. CONCERTED PRACTICES

Behaviours which involve decisions and coordinated behaviour patterns which are likely to affect trade between Member States fall within the scope of Article 101 TFEU.

1. Agreements between Undertakings

An "agreement" is created if two or more undertakings express their intention to behave in a certain manner in the marketplace.

The decisive indicator of an agreement is the existence of a "concurrence of wills between at least two parties", the form of which is unimportant, provided that the agreement is a faithful expression of the parties' intentions.[211] Thus an agreement can come about expressly or impliedly, orally or in writing. The behaviour patterns envisaged by Article 101(1) TFEU can arise through an isolated or individual action, exist in a series of actions or be demonstrated by sequential behaviour.[212] Finally, concerted practices can also be indicated by the behaviour of associations of undertakings.

a) Intention, rather than Actual Behaviour, is Paramount

It is unimportant whether the relevant parties actually behave in the way indicated by the concurrence of wills. Instead, it is sufficient for an undertaking to be present at a meeting in which several other undertakings agree to behave in a coordinated manner in the market, regardless of whether the first undertaking later actually behaves in accordance with the agreement. The only way for such an undertaking not to be caught by the Article 101(1) TFEU prohibition would be for it to disassociate itself explicitly from the contents of the meeting.[213]

Examples:
– In the case of *Sarrió SA*, the General Court agreed that cardboard manufacturers and cardboard suppliers who met regularly to share information, agree common price increases and allocate market share, and who subsequently carried out a series of concurrent and uniform price rises, infringed the prohibition on cartels. The General Court found that even undertakings which did not abide by the outcome of meetings characterised by an anti-competitive purpose were still participants in the anti-competitive behaviour, as they had not publicly distanced themselves from what was agreed in those meetings.[214] By not objecting to the anti-competitive agreement such undertakings gave their competitors the impression that they would take account of the results

---

211   Case T-41/96, *Bayer AG,* [2000] ECR II-3383, para. 69.
212   Case C-49/92 P, *Anic Partecipazioni SpA,* [1999] ECR I-4125, para. 81.
213   Recently *Carglass* (Case COMP/39.125), Commission Decision, p. 129, para. 476.
214   Case T-334/94, *Sarrió SA,* [1998] ECR II-1439, para. 118.

of the meeting and abide by the agreed decisions.[215] In this manner such undertakings also made a relevant contribution to the behaviour prohibited by Article 101(1) TFEU.[216]

- It is not necessary to be an active participant in prohibited meetings of undertakings; passive participation is sufficient. In the case of *Tréfileurope Sales* it was noted that an undertaking had participated, partly passively, in meetings between producers of steel mesh products. At those meetings the participants exchanged information about the state of the market and its prospects and concluded agreements on prices of certain products – clearly anti-competitive behaviour.[217] The Court confirmed in *Aalborg Portland* that "it is sufficient for the Commission to show that the undertaking concerned participated in meetings at which anti-competitive agreements were concluded, without manifestly opposing them [and] it is for that undertaking to put forward evidence to establish that its participation in those meetings was without any anti-competitive intention by demonstrating that it had indicated to its competitor that it was participating in those meetings in a spirit that was different from theirs".[218]

b) Horizontal and Vertical Coordination

Originally, the concept of agreement in Article 101(1) TFEU was envisaged to apply only to the classical scenario of *horizontal* cooperation between competing manufacturers, as for example in the case of agreements regarding the retail price of a certain product.

> *Horizontal agreements* are agreements between competitors, i.e. undertakings trading in competition with each other in a market, for example at a certain value added step in the product or distribution chain.

Examples:
- Coordinated behaviour between several producers of beef[219] was in principle the same type of anti-competitive behaviour as a contract between breweries which forbade any sales of beer to a bar owner who was already bound to one of the participating breweries.[220] In such cases the undertakings involved are all active at the same point in the production chain, i.e. 'horizontally'.
- The Commission was of the view that hardcore restrictions cannot be justified – in particular horizontal agreements which have as their object (a) the fixing of prices when selling products to third parties; (b) the limitation of output or sales; or (c) the

---

215 Case T-7/89, *Hercules Chemicals*, [1991] ECR II-1711, para. 232; Case T-141/89, *Tréfileurope Sales*, [1995] ECR II-791, para. 85; Joined Cases T-25/95 and others, *Cimenteries CBR*, [2000] ECR II-491, para. 1389 (confirmed in Joined Cases C-204/00 P and others, *Aalborg Portland A/S*, [2004] ECR I-123, para. 82).

216 Cf. Joined Cases C-189/02 P and others, *Dansk Rørindustri A/S*, [2005] ECR I-5425, para. 143.

217 Case T-141/89, *Tréfileurope Sales*, [1995] ECR II-791, paras. 80 and 85.

218 Joined Cases C-204/00 P and others, *Aalborg Portland A/S*, [2004] ECR I-123, para. 81.

219 Case C-209/07, *Competition Authority/Beef Industry Development Society and Barry Brothers (Carrigmore) Meats*, [2008] ECR I-8637.

220 Joined Cases T-49/02 and T-51/02, *Brasserie nationale SA, Brasserie Jules Simon et Cie SCS and Brasserie Battin SNC*, [2005] ECR II-3033, paras. 83, 85.

allocation of markets or customers.[221] In the area of cooperation for the purposes of product innovation, the undertakings involved must remain free to pursue research and development in other areas or after conclusion of the cooperation, as well as to protect and assert their rights in their intellectual property.[222]

However, since the decision of the Court of Justice in the case of *Consten & Grundig* it is clear that vertical agreements between a manufacturer and its distribution partners can also fall foul of the prohibition in Article 101(1) TFEU.[223]

> *Vertical agreements* are agreements between undertakings which operate at different levels of the production or distribution chain, in particular adding value at different stages.[224]

Examples:
– An agreement between a beer supplier and a publican (rather than amongst beer suppliers) was a vertical agreement which fell within the prohibition contained in Article 101(1) TFEU.[225] The same was true in the case of, rather than beef producers entering into an agreement, organisations which represented the agricultural producers, and organisations which represented slaughterhouse operating authorities agreed on minimum prices for certain categories of cows and the temporary suspension of beef imports in certain Member States.[226]
– Vertical agreements are found above all in *distribution systems*. For example, Nintendo concluded contracts with its distributors which had the effect of limiting parallel trade[227] of Nintendo game console cartridges within the EU. Those contracts obliged distributors to sell Nintendo products only to certain categories of buyers (e.g. final consumers) and required distributors not to export the products or sell the products to exporters.[228] At the same time Nintendo imposed explicit export bans or similar conditions on its customers, retailers and wholesalers through formal distribution agree-

---

221 Article 4 Commission Regulation (EU) No 1218/2010 of 14 December 2010 on the application of Article 101(3) of the Treaty on the Functioning of the European Union to certain categories of specialisation agreements, [2010] OJ L335/4; cf. also Article 5 Commission Regulation (EU) No 1217/2010 of 14 December 2010 on the application of Article 101(3) of the Treaty on the Functioning of the European Union to certain categories of research and development agreements, [2010] OJ L335/36.

222 Article 5(1)(a) and (b) of the R&D Block Exemption Regulation.

223 Joined Cases 56/64 and 58/64, *Consten & Grundig*, [1966] ECR 321.

224 See for example the definition in Article 1(1) of Commission Regulation (EU) No 330/2010 on the application of Article 101(3) of the Treaty on the Functioning of the European Union to categories of vertical agreements and concerted practices, [2010] OJ L102/1 (the "Vertical Agreement Block Exemption Regulation").

225 Case C-234/89, *Delimitis/Henninger Bräu*, [1991] ECR I-935.

226 Joined Cases T-217/03 and T-245/03, *FNCBV and FNSEA*, [2006] ECR II-4987.

227 Parallel trade is particularly relevant where a manufacturer sells its products to distributors in different Member States for different prices. If a distributor acquires the product in a low price country and exports it to a high price country, he raises his profit margin.

228 *PO Video Games, PO Nintendo Distribution and Omega – Nintendo* (Cases COMP/35.587, COMP/35.706 and COMP/36.321), Commission Decision 2003/675/EC of 30 October 2002, [2003] OJ L255/33, paras. 283 et seq.

ments as well as general terms and conditions for sale.[229] Compliance with such agreements and terms and conditions was monitored by Nintendo, and any distributors who did not comply were boycotted or otherwise induced to cooperate (e.g. by making the allocation of additional distribution agreements for other geographic areas dependent on such cooperation).

– Whilst certain vertical agreements benefit from an exemption to the prohibition in Article 101(3) TFEU,[230] the Commission has made clear that hardcore restrictions shall not benefit from that exemption; in particular those which have as their object:

- the restriction of a buyer's ability to set its sale price independently (though a supplier may still set a maximum sale price or suggest a sale price, provided that the effect of such a suggestion is not that it amounts to a fixed or minimum sale price due to pressures or incentives);
- the restriction of the territory into which, or the customers to whom, a buyer may sell the relevant goods or services, unless there exists a specific justification for such restriction;
- the restriction of sales to final consumers by members of a selective distribution system;
- the restriction of cross-supplies between distributors within a selective distribution system, even if those distributors are operating at different levels of trade; or
- a restriction on the ability of a supplier of components to sell such components as spare parts to end users or to repairers or other service providers.[231]

c) Contracts and Gentlemen's Agreements

For the purposes of Article 101(1) TFEU, an "agreement" is defined under European jurisprudence, rather than national law (and does not have to constitute a valid and binding agreement under national law).[232] The concept of an "agreement" presumes no legal liability or even the existence of measures for its enforcement.[233] Therefore such agreements can also include 'gentlemen's agreements'.

> *Gentlemen's agreements* do not involve legally binding contracts; rather, they encompass all correspondence which indicates a concurrence of wills.

There has been some debate, particularly at the edges of what can be considered concerted practices, as to what degree of enforcement capabilities or binding obligations are necessary to constitute an "agreement". On the one hand, Article 101(2) TFEU states explicitly that any agreements or decisions prohibited pursuant to Article 101 shall be automatically void; of course, in order for an agreement to be rendered void, it would

---

229 *PO Video Games, PO Nintendo Distribution and Omega – Nintendo* (Cases COMP/35.587, COMP/35.706 and COMP/36.321), Commission Decision 2003/675/EC of 30 October 2002, [2003] OJ L255/33, paras. 285 et seq.

230 Article 2 of the Vertical Agreement Block Exemption Regulation.

231 Article 4(a)–(e) of the Vertical Agreement Block Exemption Regulation.

232 Case C-277/87, *Sandoz,* [1990] ECR I-45, para. 2.

233 Recently *Carglass* (Case COMP/39.125), Commission Decision, para. 474.

have to have been legally binding in the first place. Nonetheless, it does not follow that an agreement or decision *must* be legally binding *in order* to be caught by Article 101 TFEU.

The question then exists as to whether an agreement must be binding in any form at all – e.g. if not legally, then perhaps factually or morally binding. European jurisprudence is not entirely clear on this point. In a number of cases[234] the General Court has held that it is not necessary for undertakings to consider themselves to be bound either in law, in fact or morally in order for an "agreement" to have been reached; it is sufficient for them to have expressed their joint intention to conduct themselves on the market in a specific way. This reflects the fact that there is no clear distinction between the circumstances leading to an "agreement" and the circumstances that constitute "concerted practices" – a variety of behaviours and intentions can exist within the range of what is prohibited under Article 101(1) TFEU.[235]

The Commission's approach occupies something of a middle ground: in order to constitute an agreement it is sufficient that the undertakings involved follow a 'common plan'. Such a plan is evidenced by the parties involved agreeing to act (or refrain from acting) in a way that limits, or is likely to limit, their individual business behaviour in a market.[236] The effect of this approach can be seen clearly as regards the burden of proof: the burden of proof in establishing the existence of an agreement lies with the Commission (or a national competition authority) in that they must show the existence of a 'common plan' amongst the relevant undertakings. Asking for a 'common plan' rather than a factually binding agreement is, in practice, more manageable.

Finally, unilateral actions do not fall within the scope of Article 101(1) TFEU; for an "agreement" to exist two or more parties are required.[237] Offences relating to unilateral actions are caught by Article 102 TFEU, provided the undertaking concerned is in a dominant position.

aa) Example: Unilateral Behaviour or Agreement between Parties?

In the case of *Bayer* the Court of Justice considered, on appeal from the General Court, whether an anti-competitive agreement existed between certain Bayer subsidiaries and wholesalers in a number of Member States, or if Bayer had acted unilaterally.[238]

The price of a certain medicine (called Adalat) was fixed in most Member States by national health authorities. The price set in the UK was significantly higher than the price set in France or Spain, with the result that wholesale purchasers of Adalat in France and Spain found it profitable to purchase more of the product than was needed in those countries and export the excess to the UK (known as parallel trade). Naturally, this activity reduced the sales of (and profit made by) Bayer's UK subsidiary. Bayer began to decrease the amount of Adalat sold to wholesalers in France and Spain whom it suspected

---

234 Case T-347/94, *Mayr-Melnhof Kartongesellschaft*, [1998] ECR II-1751, para. 65; Case T-9/99, *HFB Holding and others*, [2002] ECR II-1487, para. 200; Case T-53/03, *BPB plc*, [2008] ECR II-1333, para. 82.

235 Cf. for example *E.ON/GDF* (Case COMP/39.401), Commission Decision of 8 July 2009, [2009] OJ C 248/5, para. 171; *Power Transformers* (Case COMP/39.129), Commission Decision, para. 113.

236 *E.ON/GDF* (Case COMP/39.401), Commission Decision of 8 July 2009, [2009] OJ C 248/5, para. 166.

237 Case T-41/96, *Bayer AG*, [2000] ECR II-3383, paras. 69, 71 et seq.; Case T-325/01, *DaimlerChrysler*, [2005] ECR II-3319, paras. 83 et seq.

238 Joined Cases C-2/01 P and C-3/01 P, *Bundesverband der Arzneimittel-Importeure*, [2004] ECR I-23.

of engaging in parallel trade. When those wholesalers became aware of this strategy, they attempted different means of obtaining additional supplies, even though they were aware that Bayer wished national supplies not to be exported.

Whilst it was clear that Bayer was seeking to restrict parallel trade, it was less clear whether an "agreement" existed between Bayer and the French and Spanish wholesalers. Absent such an agreement, the alleged competition infringements would not fall within the parameters of Article 101 TFEU. The Court of Justice upheld the General Court's finding that an agreement under Article 101(1) TFEU required a concurrence of wills between at least two parties: a unilateral policy which can be implemented without the cooperation of another party is not an agreement for European competition purposes. In this case, there was clearly no concurrence of wills between Bayer and the wholesalers, as the wholesalers had attempted to circumvent the restrictions Bayer imposed on them. The fact that the wholesalers continued purchasing from Bayer after they became aware of Bayer's attempts to halt parallel trade was irrelevant.

Notably, the Courts emphasised that whilst European law (under what are now Articles 34–36 TFEU) prevents Member States from enacting measures restricting inter-state trade, no such restrictions on private undertakings exist, unless an undertaking is in a dominant position, in which case Article 102 (rather than Article 101) applies.

bb) Examples: Cartel Agreements and Common Plans

- A cartel agreement exists if legally and financially independent undertakings enter into a contract regarding certain behaviours, i.e. the restriction or distortion of competition. Such was the case in *GlaxoSmithKline*, where (in contrast to the *Bayer* case discussed above) a pharmaceutical undertaking entered into agreements with its wholesalers which provided for a "dual-pricing" system, depending on where certain medicines would be sold. A lower price was set for medicines which would be sold to Spanish hospitals and chemists, and a higher price was set for medicines that would be exported to other Member States. The Court of Justice held that such agreements constituted an attempt to restrict parallel trade, and consequently fell within the realm of Article 101(1) TFEU.[239]
- The Commission also regularly addresses *common plans* amongst competitors in a market. The *Carglass* case concerned an "overall plan" to regulate the market adopted by several manufacturers of auto glass who participated in numerous meetings, exchanged telephone calls and faxes, allocated customer contracts through coordination of prices and supplies and exchanged commercially sensitive information.[240] Handwritten notes by an employee of one of the undertakings involved also made explicit reference to an agreement between the competitors.[241]
- A "common plan" also existed between E.ON and GDF, who entered into an anti-competitive agreement and coordinated their behaviour patterns in the natural gas sector. In 1975, Ruhrgas (a German gas supplier which was later purchased by E.ON) and GDF

---

239   Joined Cases C-501/06, C-513/06 P, C-515/06 P and C-519/06 P, *GlaxoSmithKline*, [2009] ECR I-9291, paras. 58–61, 63, 66 et seq.

240   *Carglass* (Case COMP/39.125), Commission Decision, in particular para. 487.

241   *Carglass* (Case COMP/39.125), Commission Decision, para. 493.

(a French natural gas supplier) agreed to build a pipeline which would bring gas from Russia to Germany and France. At the same time, they agreed not to sell gas in each other's territory – a market-sharing agreement (however not illegal when it was agreed in 1975). From 2000 the European gas markets were opened to competition. The Commission alleged that E.ON and GDF had been engaging in anti-competitive behaviour for a number of years, continuing that behaviour even after they became aware that the 1975 agreement was illegal. The companies involved had claimed in 2004 that they had long regarded the 1975 agreement as "null and void", but the Commission maintained that the parties remained in contact with each other even after 2000 (when the gas market liberalisation directive 98/30/EC was to have been adopted in national law) and continued their market sharing activities until 2005; they also discussed the newly liberalised market and monitored each other's actions.[242]

2. Decisions by Associations of Undertakings

The prohibition contained in Article 101(1) TFEU also applies to decisions by associations of undertakings. The most common associations of undertakings are trade associations, though many other bodies with statutory, regulatory or disciplinary duties can be caught as well.

Decisions by associations of undertakings can occur in different ways, for example through a vote of the members of a trade association, or in the form of a decision taken by an executive or governing body of the trade association. It is not necessary that the measure is legally binding; it is sufficient that member undertakings are bound by it.[243]

Examples:
– A "decision by an association of undertakings" for the purposes of Article 101(1) TFEU includes, for example, a decision by the Dutch law society regarding partnerships between members of the Bar and people in other professions, even if the law society is a public-law body.[244] In making such a decision, the law society was not exercising sovereign competence,[245] but rather was acting as a regulatory body for a profession whose members were engaged in economic activity.[246] Additionally, the law society made its decisions without regard for the general population's interest, which would be characteristic of an exercise of sovereign powers.[247]

---

242 *E.ON/GDF* (Case COMP/39.401), Commission Decision of 8 July 2009, [2009] OJ C248/5, paras. 1, 3 et seq.

243 Cf. already above Chapter 2 II.1.c).

244 Case C-309/99, *Wouters,* [2002] ECR I-1577, paras. 64, 71, 115.

245 Case C-309/99, *Wouters,* [2002] ECR I-1577, para. 57.

246 Therefore Dutch lawyers are regarded as undertakings within the context of Article 101 (1) TFEU; cf. Case C-309/99, *Wouters,* [2002] ECR I-1577, paras. 49 and 58.

247 Case C-309/99, *Wouters,* [2002] ECR I-1577, para. 62.

- FIFA is considered an association of undertakings, as its members are themselves associations of undertakings – national groupings of football clubs for whom the practice of football is an economic activity.[248]

3. Concerted Practices

The catch-all definition of concerted practices for the purposes of Article 101 TFEU encompasses a form of coordination between undertakings where they knowingly substitute cooperation with each other for the risks of competition.[249] No formal agreement need have been concluded.

In spite of the already wide conception of concerted practices, European courts as well as the Commission tend to take a broad view of what constitutes an "agreement" or "decision" in this context, as it can often be difficult to find proof of concerted practices.[250] The Court of Justice has commented that the definitions of such terms as "agreement", "decisions of undertakings" and "concerted practice" are intended to catch forms of collusion having the same nature, and which are "distinguishable from each other only by their intensity and the forms in which they manifest themselves".[251]

In practice, case law has developed categories to help identify what constitutes "concerted practices". Typical cases of concerted practices involve the exchange of information between competitors and the coordination of market presence.

a) Typical Market Behaviour

The concept of concerted practices should be distinguished from the reality of market-based reactions by undertakings to the behaviour of their competitors. Reacting to the actions of competitors is considered normal market conduct, and therefore does not fall within the realm of concerted practices even if the competitors' behaviour shows a parallel pattern. *Actual parallel behaviour*, i.e. the individual decision by an undertaking to alter its prices to match its competitors', therefore is not caught by Article 101 TFEU. On the other hand, Article 101 TFEU may still apply if the parallel conduct is such that it leads to conditions of competition which do not correspond to the normal conditions of the market,[252] i.e. higher prices or a decreased availability of products.

The boundary to the realm of concerted practices is crossed when *market behaviour is coordinated* by an undertaking on the basis of special information, e.g. the announcement of a price increase. From the perspective of the intent behind an undertaking's action, engaging in concerted practices takes place when an undertaking anticipates that other undertakings will adapt to the changes in the market (e.g. the price increase). It can

---

248 Case T-193/02, *Laurent Piau,* [2005] ECR II-209, para. 72.

249 For further information about the Commission's view of concerted practices see *Professional videotape* (Case COMP/38.432), Commission Decision of 20 November 2007, para 104.

250 For further information regarding burden of proof and the Commission's obligation to adduce evidence see Chapter 6.

251 Case C-8/08, *T-Mobile Netherlands,* [2009] ECR I-4529, para. 23.

252 Case 48/69, *ICI,* [1972] ECR 619, paras. 64, 67.

be recalled that the independence postulate does not remove from undertakings the right for them to adapt themselves intelligently to the existing or anticipated conduct of their competitors. Nevertheless, such freedom to act does not extend to permitting direct or indirect "contact" between undertakings, the object or effect of which is to influence the conduct on the market of an actual or potential competitor, or to disclose to such a competitor the course of conduct which an undertaking has decided to adopt or is completing adopting on the market.[253] On that basis, the exchange of market information can fall within the prohibition contained in Article 101(1) TFEU if it removes a degree of uncertainty as to the operation of the market and such exchange is liable to have an adverse influence on competition between market participants.[254]

Examples: Actual or Coordinated Parallel Behaviour?
– In *Acerinox*, an undertaking operating in the stainless steel sector claimed that the alignment of certain of its prices was a result of parallel conduct in an oligopolistic market, rather than a concerted practice with its competitors. However, Acerinox had nonetheless attended a meeting with its industry competitors at which the application of a uniform surcharge was discussed. The General Court ruled (and it was upheld by the Court of Justice) that although parallel conduct alone is not definitive proof of concerted practices unless such practices constitute the only plausible explanation for such conduct,[255] Acerinox's previous behaviour was sufficient evidence of participation in a cartel under Article 101(1) TFEU (notwithstanding Acerinox's claim that it had distanced itself from the original meeting with its competitors).[256]
– The case of *Ahlström* addressed whether a quarterly announcement of prices by European wood pulp producers to their consumers constituted coordinated parallel behaviour.[257] The Court of Justice found no proof of concerted practices, as on the facts of the case concertation was not the only plausible explanation of the parallel conduct.[258] It was held that the system of price announcements could be regarded as a "reasonable response to the fact that the pulp market constituted a long-term market and to the need felt by both buyers and sellers to limit commercial risk. Further, the similarity in the dates of price announcements may be regarded as a direct result of the high degree of market transparency, which does not have to be described as artificial".[259] Finally, the price communications did not have the effect of lessening each undertaking's un-

---

253   Cf. Joined Cases 40 to 48/73, 50/73, 54 to 56/73, 111/73, 113/73 and 114/73, *Suiker Unie*, [1975] ECR 1663, para. 174; Case C-77/95, *Züchner*, [1996] ECR I-5689, para. 14; Case C-7/95 P, *Deere*, [1998] ECR I-3111, para. 87; Case C-8/08, *T-Mobile Netherlands*, [2009] ECR I-4529, para. 33.

254   Cf. Case C-7/95 P, *Deere*, [1998] ECR I-3111, para. 90; Case C-194/99 P, *Thyssen Stahl AG*, [2003] ECR I-10821, para. 81; Case C-8/08, *T-Mobile Netherlands*, [2009] ECR I-4529, para. 35.

255   Joined Cases C-89/85, C-104/85, C-114/85, C-116/85, C-117/85 and C-125/85 to C-129/85, *Ahlström*, [1993] ECR I-1307, para. 71; Case T-48/98, *Acerinox*, [2001] ECR II-3859, para. 43.

256   Case T-48/98, *Acerinox*, [2001] ECR II-3859, para. 45.

257   "Quarterly announcements" constituted a well-established trading practice on the European pulp market, whereby at the beginning of each quarter producers communicated to their customers and agents the prices they wished to obtain that quarter for pulp.

258   Joined Cases C-89/85, C-104/85, C-114/85, C-116/85, C-117/85 and C-125/85 to C-129/85, *Ahlström*, [1993] ECR I-1307, paras. 126 et seq.

259   Joined Cases C-89/85, C-104/85, C-114/85, C-116/85, C-117/85 and C-125/85 to C-129/85, *Ahlström*, [1993] ECR I-1307, para. 126.

certainty as to the future attitude of its competitors – at the time when each undertaking announced its prices, it could not be sure of the future conduct of the others.[260] The entrepreneurial risk of the undertakings acting on the same market (horizontally) was not reduced by such announcements; the only reduction in risk occurred for undertakings acting vertically on different levels of the market (i.e. sellers and buyers). Therefore the undertakings' behaviour at the level of the horizontal market did not infringe Article 101(1) TFEU.

b) Unilateral Actions – Explicit Disapproval

In the same way that the unilateral actions of one party cannot constitute an "agreement" under Article 101(1) TFEU, unilateral action also cannot amount to concerted behaviour.

Nonetheless, communication in one direction only, i.e. from one competitor to another, without the second competitor reciprocating, can still add up to concerted practices. This would be the case if, for example, one competitor informed another of its intentions or future behaviour at the behest of the second competitor (or even if the information was unsolicited) if the second competitor accepts the communication without reservation or objection.[261]

Examples:

– In the case of *Westfalen Gassen Nederland*, the Commission alleged that competitors in the Dutch market for industrial and medical gases had colluded for a number of years to fix prices and agree periods of non-competition.[262] Westfalen argued that it had attended meetings with its competitors, but had refused to participate actively. The General Court held that silence by an undertaking at a meeting of competitors when anti-competitive behaviour was discussed was not "tantamount to an expression of firm and unambiguous disapproval" and that passive participation in an infringement is capable of rendering an undertaking liable.[263] Additionally, Westfalen failed to adduce evidence proving that it had not taken account of the unlawful concerted practices discussed at a meeting with competitors when later determining its own conduct on the market.[264]

– The General Court has also found concerted practices in the (apparently one-sided) communication by a chemicals undertaking to its competitors of information regarding how it intended to behave in the market and its views on pricing.[265] The fact that an undertaking had "eliminated, or at the very least, substantially reduced the uncertainty as to the conduct to be expected from it on the market" (and failed to distance itself

---

260   Joined Cases C-89/85, C-104/85, C-114/85, C-116/85, C-117/85 and C-125/85 to C-129/85, *Ahlström*, [1993] ECR I-1307, paras. 64 et seq.

261   Joined Cases T-25/95 and others, *Cimenteries*, [2000] ECR II-491, para. 1849.

262   Case T-303/02, *Westfalen Gassen Nederland BV*, [2006] ECR II-4567.

263   Case T-303/02, *Westfalen Gassen Nederland BV*, [2006] ECR II-4567, para. 124.

264   Case T-303/02, *Westfalen Gassen Nederland BV*, [2006] ECR II-4567, para. 133.

265   Case T-279/02, *Degussa*, [2006] ECR II-897, paras. 135, 137.

publicly from what occurred at anti-competitive meetings) was sufficient to amount to concerted practices.[266]

c) "Activation" Necessary?

One topic of debate is whether the scope of what constitutes concerted practices is limited by the need for actual conduct in the market "activating" what was discussed in the concertation.

European jurisprudence has confirmed that mere parallel conduct is not sufficient proof of concerted practices unless concertation is the only plausible explanation for such conduct.[267] Nonetheless, it is questionable whether it is possible to prove concerted practices when no corresponding steps were taken in the market, i.e. no "activation" occurred.

Example:
The Court of Justice dealt with this question in the so-called Polypropylene cases.[268] Several manufacturers of this material had met regularly for years in confidential meetings to discuss their business policies and set targets or minimum prices for their products. The agreements included measures for the enforcement of those prices, concurrent price increases and a splitting of market share. When several Polypropylene manufacturers appealed the Commission's decisions, the Court of Justice had to consider whether, in order for a concerted practice to exist, there must be conduct on the market pursuant to the undertakings' collusive behaviour.[269]

It can be recalled that the independence postulate does not take away an undertaking's right to adapt itself intelligently to the existing or anticipated conduct of its competitors.[270] Nonetheless, the scope of Article 101(1) TFEU is such that any contact between undertakings, the object or effect of which is to create conditions of competition which do not correspond to the normal conditions of the market, is prohibited.[271] Notably, such "contact" does not presume that anti-competitive effects have actually been felt on the market; Article 101(1) TFEU applies to concerted practices which have the prevention, restriction or distortion as their object "or" effect, not their object "and" effect.

Thus case law has established that "although the concept of concerted practice presupposes conduct of the participating undertakings on the market, it does not necessarily imply that that conduct should produce the concrete effect of restricting, preventing or distorting competition".[272]

In the later case of *T-Mobile Netherlands* the Court of Justice confirmed various principles set out in the Polypropylene cases and reiterated that if, following concertation,

---

266　Case T-279/02, *Degussa*, [2006] ECR II-897, para. 133, 135, 137.

267　Joined Cases C-89/85, C-104/85, C-114/85, C-116/85, C-117/85 and C-125/85 to C-129/85, *Ahlström*, [1993] ECR I-1307, para. 71; Case T-48/98, *Acerinox*, [2001] ECR II-3859, para. 43.

268　E.g. Case C-51/92 P, *Hercules Chemicals*, [1999] ECR I-4235; Case C-199/92 P, *Hüls*, [1999] ECR I-4287; Case C-49/92 P, *Commission v Anic Partecipazioni*, [1999] ECR I-4125.

269　Case C-49/92 P, *Commission v Anic Partecipazioni*, [1999] ECR I-4125, para. 119.

270　Case C-199/92 P, *Hüls*, [1999] ECR I-4287, para. 160; Case C-7/95 P, *Deere*, [1998] ECR I-3111, para. 87.

271　Case C-7/95 P, *Deere*, [1998] ECR I-3111, para. 87; Case C-199/92 P, *Hüls*, [1999] ECR I-4287, para. 160.

272　Case C-199/92 P, *Hüls*, [1999] ECR I-4287, para. 165; Case C-49/92 P, *Commission v Anic Partecipazioni*, [1999] ECR I-4125, para. 124.

an undertaking remained active on the market, there existed a rebuttable presumption that concerted practices had affected the undertaking's conduct on the market (with the burden of proof resting on the undertaking to prove its conduct was not affected by the concerted practices).[273]

d) Information Exchange

A typical example of concerted practices can be found in the exchange of information between competitors. Such exchange can lead to a distortion of competition, as uncertainties about the behaviour of competitors are reduced by an artificial market transparency.

Information exchange can take various forms: data can be shared directly between competitors or it can be shared indirectly through a common agency (e.g. a trade association), a third party such as a market research organisation or through the companies' suppliers or retailers.[274]

However, because an exchange of information can also produce positive effects (e.g. an increase in competitive intensity) an exact analysis of the anti-competitive effects of such behaviour, taking particular account of the structure of the relevant market, is necessary. Broadly, an exchange of publicly-available information is permitted, as well as information such as large-scale statistical data. Individual information or statistical data which is capable of being used for anti-competitive purposes (in particular individualised data) is not permitted to be shared.[275]

The Commission has also issued guidelines on the applicability of Article 101 TFEU to horizontal cooperation agreements, setting out in detail the circumstances in which horizontal cooperation agreements may be exempted from competition rules on the basis of Article 101(3).[276]

aa) Example: T-Mobile Netherlands

The case of *T-Mobile Netherlands* centred around one meeting of representatives of Dutch mobile telecommunications operators in June 2001. At that meeting, they discussed, *inter alia*, the reduction of standard dealer remunerations for certain telephone subscriptions, and in the course of their communications, confidential information was revealed.

The Dutch competition authority took the view that this activity constituted a restriction of competition and levelled fines on several undertakings. In a preliminary reference from a Dutch court, the Court of Justice considered in what circumstances the presumption of a causal connection between concerted practice and market conduct existed (and

---

273 Case C-49/92 P, *Commission v Anic Partecipazioni*, [1999] ECR I-4125, paras. 122 et seq.; Case C-8/08, *T-Mobile Netherlands*, [2009] ECR I-4529, para. 51.

274 Commission, Guidelines on the applicability of Article 101 of the Treaty on the Functioning of the European Union to horizontal co-operation agreements, [2011] OJ C11/1, para. 55.

275 Commission, Guidelines on the applicability of Article 101 of the Treaty on the Functioning of the European Union to horizontal co-operation agreements, [2011] OJ C11/1, para. 74.

276 Commission, Guidelines on the applicability of Article 101 of the Treaty on the Functioning of the European Union to horizontal co-operation agreements, [2011] OJ C11/1. See Chapter 3, Section VI(2) (b) (*Horizontal Agreements*).

in particular, whether such a connection existed if the concerted practice was an isolated event rather than a series of concerted practices over a lengthy period).

The Court of Justice referred to two of the Polypropylene cases, *Hüls* and *Anic Partecipazioni,* and noted that in those cases, the Court had found that the presumption of a causal connection between concerted practices and market conduct applied when (a) there was concerted action and (b) the undertaking concerned remained active on the market.[277] In terms of the degree of concerted action, or period of time over which the concerted action needed to have taken place, the Court concluded that in differing factual circumstances (e.g. the subject-matter of the concerted action and the particular market conditions), different degrees of concertation might be appropriate for anti-competitive purposes.[278]

For example, if the undertakings concerned wanted to establish a cartel with a complex system of concerted actions relating to a multiplicity of aspects of market conduct, regular meetings over a long period of time might be necessary. On the other hand, as was the case in the matter before the Court in *T-Mobile Netherlands*, it may be that a one-off meeting between competitors is sufficient for them to implement an individual anti-competitive object.

Thus the Court of Justice concluded that "what matters is not so much the number of meetings held between the participating undertakings as whether the meeting or meetings which took place afforded them the opportunity to take account of the information exchanged with their competitors in order to determine their conduct on the market in question and knowingly substitute practical cooperation between them for the risks of competition".[279] If it can be established that one undertaking acted in concert with another, and then remained active on the market, the rebuttable presumption arises that the concerted practices had an effect on the undertaking's conduct in the market.[280]

bb) Example: Infrastructure Sharing

In the mobile telecommunications markets there is an established practice of infrastructure or network sharing,[281] i.e. the common use of network components by several network providers in an effort to reduce those providers' operating costs. In order for such agreements to be permitted under European competition law, each of the undertakings cooperating together must protect its competitive independence.[282]

Any agreement dealing with infrastructure sharing must be analysed on the facts of the individual case to determine whether it is compatible with Article 101 TFEU.

In the case of T-Mobile Deutschland and O2 Germany, the Commission noted firstly in its decision that the network sharing agreement was mainly technical in nature and did

---

277 Case C-8/08, *T-Mobile Netherlands,* [2009] ECR I-4529, para. 58.

278 Case C-8/08, *T-Mobile Netherlands,* [2009] ECR I-4529, para. 60.

279 Case C-8/08, *T-Mobile Netherlands,* [2009] ECR I-4529, para. 61.

280 Case C-8/08, *T-Mobile Netherlands,* [2009] ECR I-4529, para. 61.

281 For a detailed description of the different models of infrastructure sharing see Koenig/Neumann, CR 2001, pp. 589 et seq.; Lichtenberger/Ruhle/Uhlirz, JRP 2003, pp. 79 et seq.; Ruhle, K&R 2002, pp. 358 et seq.

282 Koenig/Neumann, CR 2001, p. 589 (591); Ruhle, K&R 2002, p. 358 (359).

not have as its object the restriction of competition, then went on to undertake a detailed analysis of the potential effects of the agreement on competition in the German mobile telecommunications market.

The Commission found that there would be almost no adverse effect on competition and that the undertakings' competitive independence would be maintained in a number of ways; for example:

- the proposed agreement did not limit the parties' commercial freedom to share sites with other undertakings (and both parties planned to continue to do so);[283]
- the parties retained independent control over their core networks and service platforms, including the nature and range of services provided and the freedom to increase their network coverage and capacity;[284] and
- the extent of information to be shared between the parties would be limited to technical and location data for network sites – no competition-sensitive information would be shared between the parties beyond the minimum necessary to allow network planning.[285]

On this basis, the Commission found no infringement of Article 101 TFEU.

III. RESTRICTION OF COMPETITION

A fundamental element of the prohibition contained in Article 101(1) TFEU is that the agreement, decision or concerted practice in question must be capable of affecting (i.e. restricting or distorting) trade between Member States. Such a restriction or distortion of trade flows limits the development of competition on markets and therefore is contrary to the aim of the establishment of the internal market as per Article 3 TEU.[286]

A restriction of competition under Article 101(1) TFEU occurs if the relevant behaviour is capable of restricting, limiting or distorting competition. It should be noted that in European law, the question of distortion or restriction of competition between Member States is concerned with whether abusive conduct *could* have such an effect – it is not necessary that the conduct has *in fact* appreciably affected trade between Member States.[287]

Caught by Article 101(1) TFEU are measures which both *actually* affect trade between Member States, as well as those which have as their *object* such an effect. If the purpose of an agreement[288] is to hinder competition, Article 101(2) TFEU (rendering such agree-

---

283 *Network sharing Germany (T-Mobile Deutschland GmbH + Viag Interkom GmbH & Co)* (Case COMP/38.369), Commission Decision, [2004] OJ L75/32, para. 100.

284 *Network sharing Germany (T-Mobile Deutschland GmbH + Viag Interkom GmbH & Co)* (Case COMP/38.369), Commission Decision, [2004] OJ L75/32, para. 102.

285 *Network sharing Germany (T-Mobile Deutschland GmbH + Viag Interkom GmbH & Co)* (Case COMP/38.369), Commission Decision, [2004] OJ L75/32, para. 103.

286 Cf. in particular Protocol (No 27) of the TFEU.

287 Case 322/81, *Michelin*, [1983] ECR 3461, para. 104; Case 56/65, *L.T.M./M.B.U.*, [1966] ECR 282, 303 et seq.; Case C-209/07, *Beef Industry Development Society and Barry Brothers*, [2008] ECR I-8637, para. 15; Case C-8/08, *T-Mobile Netherlands*, [2009] ECR I-4529, para. 29.

288 Unless otherwise specified, the term "agreement" is used to denote "agreements", "decisions" and "concerted practices" under Article 101(1) TFEU.

ment void) will apply to that agreement, even if competition has not actually been affected. Such is also the case in circumstances of concerted practices, following the Court of Justice's decision in *T-Mobile Netherlands.*[289]

Agreements which have the effect of restricting trade, even if that effect was unintended, are also caught by the voiding provision in Article 101(2) TFEU. Such an effect occurs if the coordinated behaviour either limits the competitive freedom of the undertakings involved (the independence postulate) or affects competition in the market, for example, increasing costs to consumers or damaging market structure.

1. Enabling Entry into the Market and Stimulation of the Market – a Rule of Reason Test?

Certain agreements are not considered restrictions of competition – for example, those which seek to create more competition in a market[290] or require coordinated behaviour to allow for new market entrants.[291] It can be argued that, if certain kinds of agreements are not deemed to be restrictions of competition on the basis that they have 'positive' effects on the market, this implies that the European courts are applying a 'rule of reason' in their judgements. In cases where the relevant behaviour is deemed not to restrict competition, that behaviour is not caught by Article 101(1) TFEU and therefore the exemption contained in Article 101(3) is equally inapplicable. The *rule of reason* is a test applied in the United States to behaviours that are *prima facie* restrictions of competition. A consideration of the competitive advantages and disadvantages of the measure in question is carried out, and if the positive effects outweigh the negative effects (even if those negative effects include a degree of restriction of competition), the measure is permitted to proceed.

Although there have been signs that the logic of a rule of reason is creeping into certain cases before the European courts[292] (in one case the Court of Justice made explicit reference to the question of a rule of reason having a place in the context of Article 101(1) TFEU, but refused to apply it[293]), the European courts have rejected the suggestion that a rule of reason exists in European law.[294] It is safe to say that the rule of reason is not generally applied in European competition law today.

Example: Roaming Agreements
In the case of *O2 (Germany) v Commission* the General Court expressly rejected the application of a rule of reason to Article 101(1) TFEU.

---

289 Case C-8/08, *T-Mobile Netherlands,* [2009] ECR I-4529.

290 Case 258/78, *Nungesser,* [1982] ECR 2015, paras. 56 et seq.; Case C-306/96, *Javico,* [1998] ECR I-1983, paras. 19 et seq.

291 Case 56/65, *L.T.M./M.B.U.,* [1966] ECR 282, para. 304; Case T-328/03, *O2 (Germany),* [2006] ECR II-1231, para. 68.

292 Cf. for example Case 26/76, *Metro,* [1977] ECR 1875, paras. 20–22; Case C-250/92, *DLG,* [1994] ECR I-5641, paras. 28–45.

293 Case C-235/92 P, *Montecatini,* [1999] ECR I-4539, para. 133.

294 Cf. Case T-328/03, *O2 (Germany),* [2006] ECR II-1231, para. 69.

O2 Germany and T-Mobile Deutschland had, *inter alia*, agreed to share national roaming services for their telecommunications customers. At issue in this case was the manner in which an analysis of a restriction or distortion of competition should be undertaken. The Commission asserted that the agreement restricted competition because of the restrictive nature of shared roaming in general.[295] O2 argued that the Commission had failed to carry out a proper analysis of whether the proposed roaming agreement restricted competition – in particular, the Commission had not examined what the conditions of competition would have been in the absence of the agreement. To the Commission, this assertion was tantamount to asking it to apply a rule of reason to Article 101(1) TFEU, in contradiction to established case law.

The General Court held that a method of analysis taking into account the competitive situation that would exist in the absence of an agreement did not amount to carrying out an assessment of the pro- and anti-competitive effects of the agreement at the stage of considering whether Article 101(1) TFEU applied (and thus applying a rule of reason).[296] Rather, the analysis required in light of Article 101(1) TFEU consisted essentially of taking account of the impact of the agreement on existing and potential competition and the competitive situation in the absence of the agreement, those two factors being intrinsically linked.[297]

However, the General Court also held that the Commission failed to examine whether, in the absence of the roaming agreement, O2 might have been entirely or partially absent from the 3G mobile telecommunications market in Germany. In this context, broad and general statements regarding the restrictive nature of roaming agreements are not sufficient. A more detailed examination of the facts of the individual case was necessary, not only for the purpose of granting an exemption but, even prior to that, for the purpose of analysing the effects of the agreement on competition to determine whether Article 101(1) TFEU was even applicable.[298] The General Court was of the view that an agreement is not capable of restricting competition if, without the existence of the relevant agreement, one party would be unable to compete on the relevant market at all.

2. Restrictions on Competition in Detail

Article 101(1) TFEU identifies a list of behaviours which are specifically caught by that Article, including *inter alia* the fixing of purchasing or selling prices (Article 101(1)(a)) and the sharing of markets or sources of supply (Article 101(1)(c)).

Beyond these examples, the European courts use as a starting point in identifying prohibited restrictions on competition the principle that every undertaking's business policy should be determined independently (the independence postulate).

> Behavioural coordination between undertakings appears anti-competitive when that cooperation affects the undertakings' economic behaviour.

---

295   Case T-328/03, *O2 (Germany)*, [2006] ECR II-1231, para. 64.
296   Case T-328/03, *O2 (Germany)*, [2006] ECR II-1231, para. 69.
297   Case T-328/03, *O2 (Germany)*, [2006] ECR II-1231, para. 71.
298   Case T-328/03, *O2 (Germany)*, [2006] ECR II-1231, paras. 74, 79.

In order to identify whether such an infringement has occurred, it is necessary to undertake a market analysis considering, *inter alia*, the nature of the relevant products, the position in the market and intention of the parties involved as well as the legal and economic circumstances surrounding the potential infringement. Thus restricting new entrants' access to a market[299] or preventing of parallel trade[300] can be caught by Article 101 TFEU.

The analysis of a potential infringement is not limited to the activities of the parties directly involved in the infringement; it also includes a consideration of the possible effects on third parties or consumers. Additionally, in particular as regards vertical agreements, the Commission and European courts have confirmed that the effects of an anti-competitive agreement should be considered not only in the context of competition between the parties involved, but also competition between an involved party and a third party.[301]

a) The Meaning of Market Definition under Article 101(1) TFEU

Market definition serves to identify the relevant market as that area in which the undertakings in question operate in competition with each other.[302]

Following substantial jurisprudence, an exact definition of the relevant market is necessary for the purposes of Article 101 TFEU if, without such definition, it is impossible to determine whether the agreement in question is liable to affect trade between Member States and has as its object of effect the prevention, restriction or distortion of competition within the internal market.[303]

Agreements under Article 101(1) TFEU often specify their own range of application, in which case it is easy for the Commission to define the relevant market. In such cases, the relevant market is simply the range of application specified by the agreement.

Examples:
– In the shipping case of *CMA CGM* the General Court recognised that the Commission did not define the relevant market for all the services in question, but noted that the agreement in that case was intended to regulate the terms of sale of transport services of containerised cargo to shipping undertakings in the (then) European Community. The Court held that in these circumstances, the Commission had demonstrated "to the

---

299 *European sugar industry*, Commission Decision, [1973] OJ L140/17.

300 Case 40/70, *Sirena/Eda*, [1971] ECR 69, para. 10. Parallel trade exists when products are acquired in a low price country to be exported to a high price country. Due to such parallel trade, manufacturers in the importing country have to compete with imported and therefore cheaper products. Market foreclosure resulting from agreements between undertakings prohibiting parallel trade often infringes Article 101 TFEU. Cf. Cases C-468/06 to C-478/06, *Sot. Lélos kai Sia*, [2008] ECR I-7139, para. 65; for cases in the pharmaceutical sector see Case T-168/01, *GlaxoSmithKline*, [2006] ECR II-2969; confirmed in Joined Cases C-501/06 P, C-513/06 P, C-515/06 P and C-519/06 P, *GlaxoSmithKline*, [2009] ECR I-9291.

301 Case 32/65, *Italy v Council and Commission*, [1966] ECR 458; *EATE*, Commission Decision, [1985] OJ L219/35, para. 47.

302 For details see Chapter 2.

303 Case T-62/98, *Volkswagen*, [2000] ECR II-2707, para. 230; Case T-213/00, *CMA CGM*, [2003] ECR II-913, para. 206; Joined Cases T-49/02 to T-51/02, *Brasserie nationale SA, Brasserie Jules Simon et Cie SCS and Brasserie Battin SNC*, [2005] ECR II-3033, para. 144.

required legal standard that the agreement in question is capable per se of affecting trade between Member States to an appreciable extent", and therefore a more specific definition of the relevant markets was not required.[304]

- An exact definition of the relevant market was also unnecessary in the case of *Volkswagen*, where a vehicle manufacturer imposed on its authorised Italian dealers the obligation to sell vehicles only to Italian customers. Such a measure aims at partitioning the internal market along national borders and consequently it is not necessary to define the geographic relevant market – it follows naturally that such partitioning affects trade with other Member States.[305]

b) Having the "Object or Effect"

An infringement of Article 101(1) TFEU occurs only if the agreement, concerted practice or decision in question aims at or causes a restriction of competition within the internal market.[306] As it has been established that the kinds of behaviour patterns caught by Article 101(1) TFEU (agreements, concerted practices and decisions) differ only in their intensity and form of expression, all three activities are subject to the same criteria in determining whether they have as their object or effect a restriction of competition.[307] Additionally, the cumulative effects of any potentially anti-competitive agreements (both the effects on the parties to the agreements as well as effects on third parties) should be taken into account.

A measure *aims at* a restriction of competition if it has the potential to have a negative impact on competition.[308]

Key when analysing whether a restriction of competition was intended or did occur, are both the objects which the measure was intended to attain, as well as the economic and legal context in which such measure was agreed.[309] Whilst the Commission can take into account the intentions of the parties when they entered into the agreement,[310] a lack of anti-competitive intention does not absolve the parties of liability under Article 101(1) TFEU if the effect of the measure was nonetheless potentially anti-competitive.[311] Thus

---

304 Case T-213/00, *CMA CGM*, [2003] ECR II-913, paras. 215, 219 et seq., 223.

305 Case T-62/98, *Volkswagen*, [2000] ECR II-2707, para. 231.

306 Case C-209/07, *Beef Industry Development Society and Barry Brothers*, para. 15; Case C-8/08, *T-Mobile Netherlands*, [2009] ECR I-4529, para. 28.

307 Case C-8/08, *T-Mobile Netherlands*, [2009] ECR I-4529, paras. 23 et seq.

308 Case C-8/08, *T-Mobile Netherlands*, [2009] ECR I-4529, para. 31; Opinion of Advocate General Kokott, Case C-8/08, *T-Mobile Netherlands*, [2009] ECR I-4529, para. 46. Whether and to what extent anti-competitive effects actually occur can at most be of relevance for determining the amount of any fine and in relation to claims for damages.

309 Case C-8/08, *T-Mobile Netherlands*, [2009] ECR I-4529, paras. 27, 43; Joined Cases C-501/06 P, C-513/06 P, C-515/06 P and C-519/06 P, *GlaxoSmithKline*, [2009] ECR I-9291, para. 58; Opinion of Advocate General Kokott, Case C-8/08, *T-Mobile Netherlands*, [2009] ECR I-4529, para. 39.

310 Case C-8/08, *T-Mobile Netherlands*, [2009] ECR I-4529, paras. 27, 31, 43.

311 Opinion of Advocate General Kokott, Case C-8/08, *T-Mobile Netherlands*, [2009] ECR I-4529, para. 47; Case 19/77, *Miller*, [1978] ECR 131, para. 7.

agreements, decisions and concerted practices between undertakings are prohibited *per se*, regardless of their effect, when they have an anti-competitive object.[312] Only in cases where an agreement does not aim to restrict trade is it necessary to consider the actual and potential effects of that agreement on competition.[313] To measure this, it is necessary to analyse what would – hypothetically – have been the course of competition in the market had the agreement not existed.[314] Actual as well as potential effects are considered.[315] A restriction of competition can only be ascertained under Article 101(1) TFEU if the relevant agreement has actually had effects of that nature. Additionally, there must be a causal link between the anti-competitive measure and the actual restriction of competition that has occurred; however, the circumstances in which anti-competitive effects on a market are not imputable to undertakings who have engaged in anti-competitive behaviour are extremely limited.

aa) Example: Anti-Competitive Purpose of an Exchange of Information

It can be recalled that the case of *T-Mobile Netherlands* involved one meeting of representatives of Dutch mobile telecommunications operators at which they discussed, *inter alia*, the reduction of standard dealer remunerations for certain telephone subscriptions and exchanged certain confidential information. This case raised a question regarding the circumstances in which the exchange of information between competitors is aimed at, or has the effect of, causing a restriction of competition.

The Court of Justice stated that a concerted practice pursues an anti-competitive object for the purpose of Article 101(1) TFEU where it is capable of resulting in the prevention, restriction or distortion of competition within the common market.[316] Further, "[i]t is not necessary for there to be actual prevention, restriction or distortion of competition or a direct link between the concerted practice and consumer prices. An exchange of information between competitors is tainted with an anti-competitive object if the exchange is capable of removing uncertainties concerning the intended conduct of the participating undertakings."[317]

> An exchange of information between horizontal competitors contravenes the independence postulate when such information is capable of removing uncertainties

---

312 Case C-235/92 P, *Montecatini*, [1999] ECR I-4539, para. 124; Opinion of Advocate General Kokott, Case C-8/08, *T-Mobile Netherlands*, [2009] ECR I-4529, paras. 42 et seq.

313 Joined Cases 56/64 and 58/64, *Consten & Grundig*, [1966] ECR 322, 390; Case C-209/07, *Beef Industry Development Society and Barry Brothers*, para. 16; Case C-8/08, *T-Mobile Netherlands*, [2009] ECR I-4529, paras. 28–30.

314 Case C-7/95 P, *Deere*, [1998] ECR I-3111, para. 76; Case T-328/03, *O2 (Germany)*, [2006] ECR II-1231, paras. 68, 71 et seq., 77.

315 Case C-7/95 P, *Deere*, [1998] ECR I-3111, paras. 76, 77; Case T-328/03, *O2 (Germany)*, [2006] ECR II-1231, para. 71.

316 Case C-8/08, *T-Mobile Netherlands*, [2009] ECR I-4529, para. 43.

317 Case C-8/08, *T-Mobile Netherlands*, [2009] ECR I-4529, para. 43.

between market participants as regards the timing, extent and details of an under-taking's activities in the market.[318]

The Court of Justice also did not require that the exchange of information has an imme-diate anti-competitive effect in the market, stating that Article 101(1) TFEU "is designed to protect not only the immediate interests of individual competitors or consumers but also to protect the structure of the market and thus competition as such".[319] Finally, there is no need to consider the effects of a concerted practice where its anti-competitive object has been established.[320]

bb) Example: Restriction of Competition by Impediment of Parallel Trade – Cars

The case of *Peugeot* concerned a remuneration system implemented by Peugeot subsidiar-ies in the Netherlands that rewarded automobile dealerships for reaching or exceeding their sales targets for cars sold and registered in the Netherlands. The Commission was of the view that this system, as it excluded export sales, had an anti-competitive effect on parallel imports.

The Court of Justice held that such an agreement has an anti-competitive effect "if it clearly manifests the will to treat export sales less favourably than national sales and thus leads to a partitioning of the market in question".[321] Both direct restrictions on imports as well as indirect measures which operate as export restraints (i.e. measures which penal-ise export sales by excluding them from a bonus system) are caught.[322]

Notably, the Court confirmed that an agreement can be considered as having the ob-ject of restricting competition even if such restriction is not its sole aim, and the agree-ment also pursues other legitimate objectives.[323]

c) Coordination of Competitive Parameters

Article 101(1) TFEU mentions specifically that the coordination of certain market param-eters constitutes a restriction of competition. In order to avoid restricting competition, the entirety of competition must not be limited and the internal market must be allowed to operate freely.

Examples:
– Product price: meetings between undertakings in which they agree price increases, minimum prices and moratorium (non-competition) periods fall within the scope of

---

318   Cf. Case C-8/08, *T-Mobile Netherlands,* [2009] ECR I-4529, paras. 35, 41, 43; cf. also Case C-7/95 P, *Deere,* [1998] ECR I-3111, para. 90.

319   Case C-8/08, *T-Mobile Netherlands,* [2009] ECR I-4529, paras. 38 et seq.

320   Case C-8/08, *T-Mobile Netherlands,* [2009] ECR I-4529, para. 30.

321   Case T-450/05, *Peugeot,* [2009] ECR II-2533, para. 46.

322   Case T-450/05, *Peugeot,* [2009] ECR II-2533, para. 47.

323   Case T-450/05, *Peugeot,* [2009] ECR II-2533, para. 56.

the prohibition in Article 101(1) TFEU, as such behaviour seeks to organise artificially the operation of the market and therefore pursues an anti-competitive purpose.[324]

- Market share: meetings amongst competitors to split a national market or the whole of the European market constitute concerted practices with the aim of restricting competition. Simple participation in such meetings is sufficient to constitute an infringement of competition rules, even if an undertaking did not proceed to implement any of the measures agreed in those meetings. Additionally, behaviour such as boycotting a competitor not involved in the cartel also infringes Article 101(1) TFEU, as it seeks to regulate the market artificially and restrict competition.[325]
- Import and export: in principle, agreements aimed at prohibiting parallel trade have as their object the prevention of competition.[326]
- Resale: several Luxembourgish breweries agreed not to sell any beer to a reseller who was already tied to another beer supplier. This agreement was held to have as its purpose the objective of impeding the entry of foreign brewers into the Luxembourg market,[327] which amounted to a restriction of competition.[328]

d) Standardisation

A frequent topic of debate in European competition law is the extent to which binding standardisation agreements amongst market competitors amount to an infringement of Article 101(1) TFEU. Such agreements have as their primary objective "the definition of technical or quality requirements with which current or future products, production processes, services or methods may comply".[329] Standards can be set by trade associations, national standards institutes or even by individual undertakings. Standardisation agreements can cover various topics, such as standardisation of different grades or sizes of a particular product or technical specifications in product or services markets. Agreements may also set out standards on the environmental performance of products or production processes.[330]

On the one hand, standardisation often brings with it positive effects for the market and for consumers – innovation, cost reductions and increased compatibility and interoperability. On the other hand, however, standardisation agreements can also have negative effects on competition which bring them into the realm of the prohibition set out in

---

324 Case T-303/02, *Westfalen Gassen Nederland*, [2006] ECR II-4567, para. 75.

325 Joined Cases C-189/02 P, C-202/02 P, C-205/02 P to C-208/02 P and C-213/02 P, *Dansk Rørindustri A/S*, [2005] ECR I-5425, para. 145.

326 Joined Cases C-501/06 P, C-513/06 P, C-515/06 P and C-519/06 P, *GlaxoSmithKline*, [2009] ECR I-9291, para. 59.

327 Joined Cases T-49/02 to T-51/02, *Brasserie nationale SA, Brasserie Jules Simon et Cie SCS and Brasserie Battin SNC*, [2005] ECR II-3033, para. 91.

328 Joined Cases T-49/02 to T-51/02, *Brasserie nationale SA, Brasserie Jules Simon et Cie SCS and Brasserie Battin SNC*, [2005] ECR II-3033, para. 97.

329 Commission, Guidelines on the applicability of Article 101 of the Treaty on the Functioning of the European Union to horizontal co-operation agreements, [2011] OJ C11/1, para. 257 (amended by Corrigenda [2011] OJ C33/20).

330 Commission, Guidelines on the applicability of Article 101 of the Treaty on the Functioning of the European Union to horizontal co-operation agreements, [2011] OJ C11/1, para. 257 (amended by Corrigenda [2011] OJ C33/20).

Article 101(1) TFEU. For example, a third party who does not have access to the agreed standard can become excluded from the market – in such cases, access to the standard becomes a precondition to market entry.

The Commission, recognising that such agreements can have both significant advantages as well as disadvantages, has issued guidelines regarding horizontal cooperation agreements designed to enable standardisation agreements which comply with certain requirements to remain outside the realm of the prohibition contained in Article 101(1) TFEU. Key is that an agreement does not have as its object or effect the restriction of competition. This is achieved if the agreed standard is:

- voluntary, with no obligation on an undertaking to comply;
- non-discriminatory, open (unrestricted participation) and transparent; and *either*
- the standard agreement is part of a wider agreement to ensure compatibility of products; *or*
- there is no set obligation to comply with the standard, and there is no restriction on the development of alternative standards or products that do not comply with the standard.[331]

In order to ensure effective access to the standard, an agreement would need to require participants wishing to have their standard included in the agreed standard to provide an irrevocable commitment in writing to offer to license their essential intellectual property to all third parties on *fair, reasonable and non-discriminatory* terms (a 'FRAND commitment').[332]

Agreements regarding environmental standards are generally considered desirable. As the protection of the environment is a fundamental non-economic aim of the Union, the positive effects often outweigh the restrictive effects on competition (in the form of increased costs) for the purposes of Article 101(3) TFEU.[333]

Example: X/Open Group

The Commission applied these criteria in the case of X/Open Group[334] in which a number of computer manufacturers formed an association to benefit from the use of and further improvements to the Unix operating system. Two key areas analysed by the Commission were the exchange of information amongst competitors and the composition of the group.

aa) Exchange of Information

The regulation of standards by a group of horizontal competitors assumes that an exchange of information between undertakings will have to occur. Whether such informa-

---

331 For further detail see Commission, Guidelines on the applicability of Article 101 of the Treaty on the Functioning of the European Union to horizontal co-operation agreements, [2011] OJ C11/1, paras. 257 et seq.

332 Commission, Guidelines on the applicability of Article 101 of the Treaty on the Functioning of the European Union to horizontal co-operation agreements, [2011] OJ C11/1, para. 285.

333 Commission, Guidelines on the applicability of Article 101 of the Treaty on the Functioning of the European Union to horizontal co-operation agreements, [2011] OJ C11/1, para. 329.

334 *X/Open Group* (Case IV/31.458), Commission Decision, [1987] OJ L35/36.

tion exchange infringes Article 101(1) TFEU must be analysed in the context of European jurisprudence on "confidential competition".

In the case of the X/Open Group, the exchange of information was limited to information needed by the members to agree standards and maintain compatibility between different systems in the event of future changes and updates to the source software – i.e. technical information and data regarding user requirements only.[335] Details of prices, customer information, market position, production plans or other relevant market data about the parties' products was not communicated.

As the information exchanged was limited to that needed to implement the group's standardisation objectives, and did not limit the parties in their freedom to determine their market behaviour independently, the Commission concluded that the exchange of information in this case did not have the object or effect of restricting competition in the sense of Article 101(1) TFEU.[336]

bb) Membership of the Group

There is a danger when agreeing standards that non-participants in the decision-making will be at a disadvantage, with their ability to operate in the market made more difficult, or new participants' ability to enter the market hindered.

In the case of the X/Open Group, membership (decided upon by majority decision) was available to information technology manufacturers who met a turnover threshold, as well as other applicants who possessed special attributes which would contribute to the aims of the group. Members could withdraw at any time and were not obliged to produce products in accordance with the agreed standards. Finally, the standards were made available publicly free of charge (known as 'open industry standards').

The Commission noted that the industry in question was highly time-sensitive, in that obtaining information earlier could result in a substantial competitive advantage. Clearly, members of the group would benefit from earlier access to information regarding standards (even when they were only a work in progress), whereas non-members would only have access to the standard once it was made public. Additionally, the rules regarding membership were such that an undertaking could be rejected for membership, even if it technically fulfilled all specified criteria.

The Commission acknowledged that the group's membership structure could lead to "an appreciable distortion of competition within the meaning of Article 101(1)",[337] but nonetheless concluded that, on the overall balance of advantages and disadvantages, the advantages of the group's work easily outweighed the distortions of competition entailed in the rules governing the group's membership.[338]

---

335   *X/Open Group* (Case IV/31.458), Commission Decision, [1987] OJ L35/36, para. 37.

336   *X/Open Group* (Case IV/31.458), Commission Decision, [1987] OJ L35/36, para. 38.

337   *X/Open Group* (Case IV/31.458), Commission Decision, [1987] OJ L35/36, para. 32.

338   *X/Open Group* (Case IV/31.458), Commission Decision, [1987] OJ L35/36, para. 42.

3. An Exception to Article 101(1) for the Functioning of the Market?

Following the decision of the Court of Justice in the case of *Wouters,* Article 101(1) TFEU has not been applied in certain cases where a restriction of competition exists, if such restriction is necessary for the basic functioning of the market. *Wouters* concerned the ban imposed by the Dutch law society on the operating of mixed partnership between members of the Dutch Bar and auditors.[339]

The Court of Justice expressly confirmed that such a decision appeared to be anti-competitive and also affected trade between Member States. However, the Court declined to apply the prohibition contained in Article 101(1) TFEU on the basis that the anti-com-petitive effects resulting from the ban were necessary to guarantee the proper exercise of the solicitors' occupation. Jurisprudence has confirmed that no restriction of competition under Article 101(1) TFEU exists when such restriction is *necessary for the proper func-tioning of the market.*

Such a test of necessity should not be equated with a rule of reason.[340] Rather, this line of logic resembles the reasoning used by the Court of Justice regarding the right of free movements of goods developed in *Cassis de Dijon* – obstacles to the free movements of goods were acceptable insofar as they related to certain key issues of public policy.[341] The Court of Justice's analysis in *Wouters* was not a consideration of the competition-related advantages and disadvantages of the ban (as would be the case in applying a rule of reason), but instead considered the implied non-economic boundaries existent in Article 101(1) TFEU.

However, such an examination of barriers inherent to the Article 101(1) TFEU prohibi-tion does not accord with the semantics of this Article on its face: on a strict reading of the text of Article 101(1) TFEU, all measures which are intended to be or which in effect are anti-competitive are prohibited. Consideration of the non-economic advantages and disadvantages of anti-competitive measures as well as an analysis of their necessity to the functioning of the market is relegated to the justification provisions of Article 101(3) TFEU.

a) Example: Protecting the Integrity of the Market

In the Luxembourgish breweries[342] case, the breweries argued that their agreement that no brewery would provide beer to a customer who had entered into a supply agreement with another brewery was justified by the need to protect trading (i.e. by ensuring that existing supply contracts were honoured).[343]

---

339   Case C-309/99, *Wouters,* [2002] ECR I-1577, paras. 94 et seq.

340   See Chapter 3, Section III(1) (*Enabling Entry into the Market and Stimulation of the Market – a Rule of Reason Test?*).

341   See also Case 120/78, *Cassis de Dijon,* [1979] ECR 649.

342   Joined Cases T-49/02 to T-51/02, *Brasserie nationale SA, Brasserie Jules Simon et Cie SCS and Brasserie Battin SNC,* [2005] ECR II-3033.

343   Joined Cases T-49/02 to T-51/02, *Brasserie nationale SA, Brasserie Jules Simon et Cie SCS and Brasserie Battin SNC,* [2005] ECR II-3033, para. 52.

The General Court rejected this argument and held that the agreement was nonetheless intended to restrict competition, as it allocated customers to the breweries party to the agreement.[344] The situation was held not to be analogous to *Wouters*, with the General Court confirming that a restriction of competition could not be excused under a rule of reason, on the basis that the agreement also pursued other aims which did not restrict competition.[345]

IV. "TRADE BETWEEN MEMBER STATES"

Under Article 101(1) TFEU only anti-competitive agreements, decisions or concerted practices which may affect trade between Member States are prohibited. Thus the ranges of application of national competition law and European competition law are differentiated on the basis of whether the competition infringement exists only within an individual Member State, or across the borders of Member States (thus endangering the realisation of the internal market).[346]

The key criterion in identifying an effect on trade between Member States is whether the effects of anti-competitive behaviour have been felt in the internal market, notwithstanding that activities may have been carried out by an entity only within a single national market. Article 101(1) TFEU also catches all agreements, decisions and concerted practices of undertakings situated *outside* the European Union, if the effects of those agreements, etc. are felt *within* the Union.[347] An agreement or concerted practice is likely to affect trade between Member States if it is possible "to foresee with a sufficient degree of probability on the basis of a set of objective factors of law or of fact that the agreement in question may have an influence, direct or indirect, actual or potential, on the pattern of trade between Member States".[348]

Every influence on cross-border trade is included in this definition, whether positive or negative,[349] or even only a potential and not an actual influence.[350] Additionally, cross-

---

344 Joined Cases T-49/02 to T-51/02, *Brasserie nationale SA, Brasserie Jules Simon et Cie SCS and Brasserie Battin SNC,* [2005] ECR II-3033, para. 85.

345 Joined Cases T-49/02 to T-51/02, *Brasserie nationale SA, Brasserie Jules Simon et Cie SCS and Brasserie Battin SNC,* [2005] ECR II-3033, para. 85.

346 Commission, Guidelines on the effect on trade concept contained in Articles 81 and 82 of the Treaty, [2004] OJ C101/81, 82.

347 Case 28/77, *Tepea,* [1978] ECR 1391, paras. 48–51; Joined Cases C-89/85, C-104/85, C-114/85, C-116/85, C-117/85 and C-125/85 to C-129/85, *Ahlström,* [1988] ECR 5193, paras. 16–18; Commission, Guidelines on the effect on trade concept contained in Articles 81 and 82 of the Treaty, [2004] OJ C101/81, 93.

348 Case 5/69, *Völk,* [1969] ECR 295, para. 5; Case 56/65, *L.T.M./M.B.U.,* [1966] ECR 281, 303; Commission, Guidelines on the effect on trade concept contained in Articles 81 and 82 of the Treaty, [2004] OJ C101/81, 83.

349 Case T-2/89, *Petrofina,* [1991] ECR II-1087, para. 226.

350 This can be seen from the wording of Article 101(1) TFEU, which requires only that an agreement or concerted practice *can* affect (i.e. has the potential to restrict or distort) trade. Cf. Case 19/77, *Miller,* [1978] ECR 131, para. 15; Joined Cases C-215/96 and 216/96, *Bagnasco,* [1999] ECR I-135, para. 48; Joined Cases T-24/93 to T-26/93 and T-28/93, *Compagnie maritime belge,* [1996] ECR II-1201, para. 201; Commission, Guidelines on the effect on trade concept contained in Articles 81 and 82 of the Treaty, [2004] OJ C101/81, 83, 85.

border trade is affected simply if commercial activity between Member States would have developed differently in the absence of the agreement or concerted behaviour.[351]

For example, an agreement prohibiting the sale of products outside the EU does not affect trade between Member States, but if an agreement intends to prevent a distributor from re-exporting products to the EU which the distributor has undertaken to sell in non-member countries, then that prohibition could affect trade between Member States.[352]

Agreements or concerted practices affect cross-border trade if the *potential* effect of a behaviour stretches beyond the territory of an individual Member State.[353] Thus, for example, import and export bans, restrictions or other measures which insulate a national market (delivery or distribution agreements) and divisions of markets between manufacturers are all caught by the prohibition in Article 101(1) TFEU.[354] The nature of the commercial stream affected is irrelevant – the broad scope of Article 101(1) TFEU applies to any cross-border trade, whether in goods, services or capital.[355]

Finally, when analysing the effects of anti-competitive behaviour, a wide analysis should be undertaken, considering not only the nature of the relevant anti-competitive agreement, but also the effect of such agreement both on the parties involved and on third parties.[356] The cumulative effects of any potentially anti-competitive agreements should be taken into account as well.[357]

V. THE *DE MINIMIS* RULE

Not every agreement or concerted practice which restricts competition and is likely to affect trade between Member States is prohibited by Article 101(1) TFEU. The unwritten '*de minimis* condition' (recognised by the Commission) requires that the alleged infringement be significant enough to warrant attention. This condition applies both to restriction of competition and cross-border trade requirements of Article 101(1) TFEU.[358]

---

351   Cf. Joined Cases 40-48, 50, 54-56, 111, 113 and 114/73, *Suiker university*, [1975] ECR 1663, paras. 196–198; Case T-2/89, *Petrofina*, [1991] ECR II-1087, para. 226.

352   Case C-306/96, *Javico*, [1998] ECR I-1983.

353   Commission, Guidelines on the effect on trade concept contained in Articles 81 and 82 of the Treaty, [2004] OJ C101/81, 83.

354   Commission, Guidelines on the effect on trade concept contained in Articles 81 and 82 of the Treaty, [2004] OJ C101/81, 88 et seq.

355   Commission, Guidelines on the effect on trade concept contained in Articles 81 and 82 of the Treaty, [2004] OJ C101/81, 83.

356   Commission, Guidelines on the effect on trade concept contained in Articles 81 and 82 of the Treaty, [2004] OJ C101/81, 86.

357   Case C-234/89, *Delimitis*, [1991] ECR I-935, paras. 14 et seq.; Case T-7/93, *Langnese-Iglo*, [1995] ECR II-1533, para. 120; Case T-77/94, *Vereniging van Groothandelaren in Bloemkwekerijproducten*, [1997] ECR II-759, para. 140; Commission, Guidelines on the effect on trade concept contained in Articles 81 and 82 of the Treaty, [2004] OJ C101/81, 86.

358   Cf. Commission, Notice on agreements of minor importance which do not appreciably restrict competition under Article 81(1) of the Treaty establishing the European Community (de minimis), [2001] OJ C368/13.

The effect of the infringement on the market must be more than "insignificant".[359] Whether such is the case depends on an undertaking's position in the relevant market as well as its turnover derived from the relevant product according to the Commission's *de minimis* guidelines.[360]

1. An Appreciable Effect on Trade between Member States

The Commission has given as a basic guideline that "the stronger the market position of the undertakings concerned, the more likely it is that an agreement or practice capable of affecting trade between Member States can be held to do so appreciably".[361] Jurisprudence has indicated that a market share of 5 % or more indicates that an undertaking is "of sufficient importance for its behaviour to be, in principle, capable of affecting trade [between Member States]".[362] In circumstances where an undertaking's share of the market is less than 5 %, but nonetheless high in comparison to its competitors or the absolute amount of its turnover is a relatively high figure, the *de minimis* threshold may also be met.[363] It is irrelevant whether an undertaking's anti-competitive behaviour has actually had an appreciable effect on trade between Member States; it is sufficient that the restrictions on competition in which the undertaking was a participant were likely to distort trade between Member States.[364]

As regards small and medium size enterprises,[365] the Commission has indicated it is unlikely that these kinds of undertakings will have an appreciable effect on trade between Member States, as their activities are usually aimed at a local or regional market.[366] The Commission also announced in 2004 that in principle, as regards horizontal agreements, such agreements are not capable of appreciably affecting trade between Member States if the aggregate market share of the undertakings involved does exceed 5 % of the relevant market but the aggregate annual Union turnover of the undertakings involved

---

359 Case 5/69, *Völk,* [1969] ECR 295, para. 7; Commission, Guidelines on the effect on trade concept contained in Articles 81 and 82 of the Treaty, [2004] OJ C101/81, 85.

360 Case T-65/89, *BPB Industries,* [1993] ECR II-389, para. 138; Commission, Guidelines on the effect on trade concept contained in Articles 81 and 82 of the Treaty, [2004] OJ C101/81, 85 et seq.

361 Commission, Guidelines on the effect on trade concept contained in Articles 81 and 82 of the Treaty, [2004] OJ C101/81.

362 Case 19/77, *Miller,* [1978] ECR 131, paras. 8 et seq.; Case 107/82, *Allgemeine Elektrizitäts-Gesellschaft AEG-Telefunken AG,* [1983] ECR 3151, para. 58.

363 Joined Cases 100 to 103/80, *SA Musique Diffusion française and others,* [1983] ECR 1825, para. 86.

364 Case T-2/89, *Petrofina,* [1991] ECR II-1087, para. 227; Commission, Guidelines on the effect on trade concept contained in Articles 81 and 82 of the Treaty, [2004] OJ C101/81.

365 Undertakings with fewer than 250 employees and a maximum annual turnover of EUR 40 million or maximum total assets of EUR 27 million, as per the annex to the Commission Recommendation 96/280/EC of 3 April 1996 concerning the definition of small and medium-sized enterprises, [1996] OJ L107/4.

366 Commission, Notice on agreements of minor importance which do not appreciably restrict competition under Article 81(1) of the Treaty establishing the European Community (de minimis), [2001] OJ C368/13; Commission, Guidelines on the effect on trade concept contained in Articles 81 and 82 of the Treaty, [2004] OJ C101/81.

does not exceed EUR 40 million.[367] Notably however, these thresholds have been agreed by the Commission only, and do not bind national authorities, national courts or the European Courts.

Finally, it should be noted that measures such as market share and turnover are not definitive in determining whether an agreement is likely to affect trade between Member States – they are starting points for a full analysis taking account all facts of each case.[368]

2. An Appreciable Restriction of Competition

De minimis criteria also apply to the requirement under Article 101(1) TFEU that anti-competitive behaviour prevents, restricts or distorts competition. To clarify its position on this point the Commission issued a notice on agreements of minor importance which do not appreciably restrict competition under Article 101(1) TFEU, setting out the circumstances in which it will not institute proceedings for anti-competitive infringements.[369]

A restriction of competition is not appreciable according to the Commission if, in the case of undertakings which are competitors on a relevant market, the aggregate market share of undertakings party to the agreement is less than 10 %; or in the case of undertakings which are not competitors on the relevant market, no undertaking party to the agreement holds more than a 15 % market share.[370] In circumstances where relevant market competition has been restricted by the effect of a cumulative series of agreements amongst various competitors, the market share thresholds are reduced to 5 %.[371]

Certain agreements are always prohibited regardless of the market shares of the undertakings concerned; these include hardcore restrictions such as price fixing or the allocation of markets or customers.[372]

However, as per the *de minimis* conditions relating to trade between Member States, criteria agreed by the Commission for *de minimis* conditions for market share are not binding on national authorities, national courts or the European Courts, so in each case only an individual analysis of the full facts of the case can be definitive.[373]

---

367 Commission, Guidelines on the effect on trade concept contained in Articles 81 and 82 of the Treaty, [2004] OJ C101/81.

368 Commission, Guidelines on the effect on trade concept contained in Articles 81 and 82 of the Treaty, [2004] OJ C101/81.

369 Commission, Notice on agreements of minor importance which do not appreciably restrict competition under Article 81(1) of the Treaty establishing the European Community (de minimis), [2001] OJ C368/13.

370 Commission, Notice on agreements of minor importance which do not appreciably restrict competition under Article 81(1) of the Treaty establishing the European Community (de minimis), [2001] OJ C368/13, para. 7.

371 Commission, Notice on agreements of minor importance which do not appreciably restrict competition under Article 81(1) of the Treaty establishing the European Community (de minimis), [2001] OJ C368/13, para 8.

372 Commission, Notice on agreements of minor importance which do not appreciably restrict competition under Article 81(1) of the Treaty establishing the European Community (de minimis), [2001] OJ C368/13, para. 11.

373 Commission, Notice on agreements of minor importance which do not appreciably restrict competition under Article 81(1) of the Treaty establishing the European Community (de minimis), [2001] OJ C368/13.

VI. THE EXCEPTION UNDER ARTICLE 101(3) TFEU

Article 101(3) TFEU states that if certain conditions are met, an agreement, decision or concerted practice which would otherwise infringe Article 101(1) may be exempt from that prohibition. Although the precise text of Article 101(3) TFEU implies otherwise, an agreement as per Article 101(1) no longer needs to be "declared" exempt under Article 101(3). Following Council Regulation (EC) No 1/2003, an agreement meeting the conditions set out in Article 101(3) TFEU is automatically (i.e. with no further decision or approval by the Commission required) exempt from the prohibition contained in Article 101(1).[374]

Council Regulation (EC) No 1/2003 set up a system of *legal exemption*, with the Commission no longer responsible for designating exemptions.

The justification behind Article 101(3) TFEU lies in the fact that even though certain agreements between undertakings may have anti-competitive effects, they can also contain aims worth pursuing. Non-economic aims in particular can be considered worthwhile, provided that they are supported by, or at least compatible with, the objectives of the European Union.[375] Thus the Commission has considered, for example, environmental protection within the context of Article 101(3) TFEU and exempted anti-competitive behaviour which also had an aim of reducing carbon emissions from the prohibition in Article 101(1).[376]

1. The Application of the Exemption

Anti-competitive agreements which would normally be prohibited under Article 101(1) TFEU can benefit from the exemption in Article 101(3) if they meet the cumulative conditions contained therein:

- the agreement must contribute to improving the production or distribution of the goods or services, or to promoting technical or economic progress;
- consumers must be allowed a fair share of the resulting benefit;
- the agreement must not impose any non-essential restrictions on the participating undertakings; and
- the agreement must not afford them the possibility of eliminating competition in respect of a substantial part of the products or services in question.[377]

The risk in assessing whether an agreement satisfies the (somewhat vague) criteria of Article 101(3) TFEU lies firmly with the undertaking making that assessment. As a legal exemption, there is no input from the Commission – for example in the form of a letter of

---

374   Article 1(2) of Council Regulation (EC) No 1/2003.

375   In particular in terms of Article 3 TEU.

376   *CECED*, Commission Decision 2000/475/EC, [2000] OJ L187/47, paras. 55 et seq.

377   Case C-238/05, *Asnef-Euqifax*, [2006] ECR I-11125, para. 65.

comfort to give an undertaking confidence that its assessment of an agreement's exemption is correct.[378]

The risk associated with this self-assessment can be minimised if an agreement satisfies the more specific criteria of a (general) block exemption issued by the Commission. Block exemptions add substance to the conditions of Article 101(3) TFEU in the cases of special kinds of agreements and are binding on the European Courts and the Commission. However, it should also be noted that such exemptions can be withdrawn in individual cases, for example when an agreement has certain effects which are incompatible with Article 101(3) TFEU.[379]

If an agreement falls under the general subject matter of a block exemption but does not fully meet the relevant conditions, an individual exemption under the more vague conditions of Article 101(3) TFEU is still possible. The Commission has issued guidelines setting out its interpretation of the conditions for exception contained in Article 101(3) TFEU.[380] However, it should also be emphasised that each case must be assessed on its own facts and that the guidelines must be applied "reasonably and flexibly".[381]

2. Block Exemption Regulations

A number of block exemption regulations play a special role in the application of the Article 101(3) TFEU exemption.[382] Secondary legislative instruments exempt certain categories of agreements (e.g. licensing agreements) from the prohibition set out in Article 101(1) TFEU and confirm that such agreements benefit from the Article 101(3) exemption.

The older style of European block exemption regulations was highly specific and prescribed on the one hand certain clauses which had to be contained in every agreement capable of exemption (known as 'white clauses') and on the other hand prohibited certain other clauses (known as 'black clauses'). The newer block exemption regulations contain stronger, more abstract and more general rules. Systematically they define first the possible scope of application of the exemption, in particular for example maximum turnover and market share thresholds of the undertakings involved. The block exemption regula-

---

378   This term dates back to the time when Article 101(3) TFEU was not yet regarded as a legal exemption. Prior to the coming into force of Council Regulation (EC) No 1/2003, an exemption to the prohibition on cartels under Article 101(1) TFEU was only allowed for if "confirmed" by the Commission. Such "confirmation" was usually given either by means of a compulsory decision (today simply known as "decision" within the meaning of Article 288 TFEU) or by means of a letter of comfort being an atypical action of the Commission. It may be the case that the latter was not of the same binding nature as a decision, cf. Joined Cases 253/78, 1 to 3/79, *Giry and Guerlain*, [1980] ECR 2327, para. 12; Case 99/79, *Lancôme*, [1980] ECR 2511, para. 10. However, for protection of confidence reasons, the Commission was generally bound to its statement made in the letter of comfort, cf. Case T-7/93, *Langnese*, [1995] ECR II-1533, para. 36.

379   Article 29 of Council Regulation (EC) No 1/2003.

380   Commission, Guidelines on the application of Article 81(3) of the Treaty, [2004] OJ C101/97 (the "Commission Guidelines on the application of Article 81(3)"); Kjølbye, ECLR 2004, 566.

381   Commission Guidelines on the application of Article 81(3).

382   Examples currently include: the Vertical Agreement Block Exemption Regulation and Commission Regulation (EC) No 772/2004 of 27 April 2004 on the application of Article 81(3) of the Treaty to categories of technology transfer agreements, [2004] OJ L123/11.

tions then identify certain especially serious kinds of restrictions of competition (*hardcore restrictions*) which, if contained in an agreement, render the entire agreement (not just the relevant provision(s)) incapable of benefiting from a block exemption. The block exemption regulations also set out individual kinds of clauses to which the exemption cannot apply. Should an agreement contain one of those provisions, only that provision is rendered void while the remainder of the agreement remains in force and can benefit from the block exemption.

Sector-specific block exemption regulations are particularly important in certain industries – for example Commission Regulation (EU) No 461/2010 which applies to the motor vehicle sector.[383]

In order for the exemption contained in Article 101(3) TFEU to apply (as set out in the block exemption), the agreement must first have met the criteria set out in Article 101(1).[384] The scope of a block exemption is interpreted narrowly, the General Court having confirmed that a regulation allowing for categories of exemptions from the prohibition contained in Article 101(1) TFEU "cannot be interpreted widely or so as to extend the effects of the regulation further than is necessary for the protection of the interests which [the regulations] are intended to safeguard".[385] Thus block exemption regulations are to be interpreted teleologically restrictively.

As is often the case in the realm of European competition law, each case must be considered individually on its facts. However, if an agreement does not satisfy the conditions of a block exemption regulation, exemption under Article 101(3) TFEU may still be possible. Equally, even if an agreement does meet the conditions of a block exemption regulation, the Commission may in certain cases (e.g. if it finds that the agreement has certain effects which are incompatible with Article 101(3) TFEU), withdraw the benefit of such an exemption.[386]

a) Vertical Agreements

The block exemption regulation applying to categories of vertical agreements applies to agreements in all economic sectors.[387]

Commission Regulation (EU) No 330/2010 (the "Vertical Agreement Block Exemption Regulation") covers 'vertical agreements', i.e. agreements or concerted practices entered into between two or more undertakings each of which operates at a different level of the production or distribution chain and which relate to the conditions under which the parties may purchase, sell or resell certain goods or services.[388] The Guidelines on Vertical

---

383 Commission Regulation (EU) No 461/2010 of 27 May 2010 on the application of Article 101(3) of the Treaty on the Functioning of the European Union to categories of vertical agreements and concerted practices in the motor vehicle sector (the "Motor Vehicle Block Exemption Regulation").

384 Whish, Competition Law, (6th edn. 2008), pp. 167 et seq.; on the restrictive interpretation of the Article's wording: Case C-234/89, *Delimitis*, [1991] ECR I-935, paras. 36, 39.

385 Case T-9/92, *Peugeot*, [1993] ECR II-494, para. 37.

386 Cf. Article 29 of Commission Regulation (EC) No 1/2003 as well as individual block exemption regulations.

387 The Vertical Agreement Block Exemption Regulation.

388 Cf. Article 1(1)(a) of the Vertical Agreement Block Exemption Regulation.

Restraints issued by the Commission illustrate the application of the block exemption regulation in more detail.[389]

A variety of kinds of vertical agreements fall within the scope of the Vertical Agreement Block Exemption Regulation, including for example, anti-competitive distribution systems. As well as anti-competitive restrictions relating to the sale or purchase of goods, restrictions on the use, processing, resale or servicing of goods are also caught, provided that the agreement is concluded between undertakings active at different levels of the production or distribution chain.

The Vertical Agreement Block Exemption Regulation exempts vertical agreements which *prima facie* infringe Article 101(1) TFEU provided certain conditions are met:

- none of the undertakings involved has a total annual overall turnover of more than EUR 50 million;[390]
- none of the undertakings involved has more than 30 % of the market share on the relevant market;[391] and
- the agreement contains no hardcore restrictions (e.g. price setting or market sharing provisions).[392]

Additionally, exemption is not available to any obligations in an agreement which provide for long term non-compete obligations, prohibit a party from acting freely after the termination of the agreement or oblige members of a selective distribution system not to sell the products of competing suppliers.[393]

Finally, the Vertical Agreement Block Exemption Regulation applies only to vertical agreements which are not covered by the application of another, industry-specific block exemption regulation.[394] Thus, for example, vertical agreements relating to the distribution of automobiles are dealt with pursuant to Commission Regulation (EU) No 461/2010 which applies specifically to the motor vehicles sector, rather than under the more general Vertical Agreement Block Exemption Regulation (though it should be noted that in certain cases an agreement is only exempted if it fulfils conditions under both Regulation 461/2010 as well as the Vertical Agreement Block Exemption Regulation).

Examples:
The Vertical Agreement Block Exemption Regulation applies to, for example, the following kinds of agreements:
- Single branding: a buyer is obliged or induced to concentrate its orders for a particular type of product with one supplier.[395]

---

389 Commission, Guidelines on Vertical Restraints, [2010] OJ C130/1 (the "Guidelines on Vertical Restraints").

390 Article 2(1)-(2) of the Vertical Agreement Block Exemption Regulation.

391 Article 3 of the Vertical Agreement Block Exemption Regulation.

392 Article 4 of the Vertical Agreement Block Exemption Regulation.

393 Article 5 of the Vertical Agreement Block Exemption Regulation.

394 Article 2(5) of the Vertical Agreement Block Exemption Regulation.

395 Guidelines on Vertical Restraints, paras. 129–150.

- Exclusive distribution and exclusive customer allocation: a supplier agrees to sell its products only to one distributor (in a particular territory) and/or that distributor is obliged to resell only in one particular territory or to one particular group of customers.[396]
- Selective distribution agreements which restrict the number of authorised distributors on the one hand and the possibilities of resale on the other. Such agreements differ from exclusive distribution agreements in that the restriction on the number of dealers does not depend on the number of territories but on selection criteria linked to the nature of the product.[397]
- Exclusive supply: a supplier is obliged or induced to sell a certain product or service only or mainly to one buyer.[398]
- Upfront access payments: suppliers pay fixed fees to distributors at the beginning of a relevant period in order to obtain access to their distribution network and remunerate services provided to the supplier by the distributor.[399]
- Category management agreements: within a distribution agreement, a distributor entrusts a supplier with the marketing of a category of products – not only the supplier's products, but also those of its competitors. The danger of such agreements lies in the possibility of the supplier giving preferential treatment to its own products through the marketing strategy he employs (e.g. product placement or product promotion).[400]
- Tying: a supplier makes the sale of one of its products dependent upon the purchase of another product.[401]
- Retail price restrictions: price fixing is generally considered a hardcore restriction, but an exemption may be granted when the benefits of efficiencies are sufficient to justify the restriction.[402]

b) Horizontal Agreements

Horizontal agreements – agreements between undertakings active on the same level of the production or distribution chain – can be exempt from the provisions of Article 101(1) TFEU pursuant to block exemption regulations on a number of grounds, including e.g.

---

396 Guidelines on Vertical Restraints, paras. 151–173.
397 Guidelines on Vertical Restraints, paras. 174–188.
398 Guidelines on Vertical Restraints, paras. 192–202.
399 Guidelines on Vertical Restraints, paras. 203–208.
400 Guidelines on Vertical Restraints, paras. 209–213.
401 Guidelines on Vertical Restraints, paras. 214–222.
402 Guidelines on Vertical Restraints, paras. 223–229.

research and development[403] or specialisation agreements.[404] The Commission has also issued guidelines on horizontal agreements in general.[405]

aa) Research and Development Agreements

Commission Regulation (EU) No 1217/2010 (the "R&D Block Exemption Regulation") covers agreements pursuant to which parties engage in joint research and development ("R&D") and/or jointly exploit the results of that R&D. Research and development includes the acquisition of know-how, the carrying out of theoretical analysis, systematic study or experimentation, the establishment of the necessary facilities and the obtaining of intellectual property rights for the results.[406]

Cooperation in R&D and in the exploitation of the results of that research often promotes technical and economic progress if the parties contribute complementary skills, assets or activities to the co-operation.[407] Additionally, R&D tends to be financially intensive and therefore an undertaking may not be able to invest in a project alone. Consumers generally benefit from the increased volume and effectiveness of R&D through the introduction of new or improved products or services, a quicker launch of those products or services, or the reduction of prices brought about by new or improved technologies or processes.[408] In order to justify the exemption, the joint exploitation should relate to products, technologies or processes for which the use of the results of the R&D is essential.

In general, the exemption granted under the R&D Block Exemption Regulation is limited to a duration of 7 years. In cases where the parties are not actual competitors, the R&D agreement is exempt without limitation but the agreement on joint exploitation afterwards may not last longer than 7 years. After this period of time, the exemption only continues to apply as long as the combined market share of the parties does not exceed 25 % on any relevant markets.[409]

In essence, all the parties to the agreement must agree that each party will have full access to the final results of the joint R&D, including any intellectual property rights and know-how which results from the R&D.[410] Only research institutes, academic bodies, or undertakings which supply R&D as a commercial service may agree to confine their use of the results for the purposes of further research without exploitation of the results.[411]

---

403   Commission Regulation (EU) No 1217/2010 of 14 December 2010 on the application of Article 101(3) of the Treaty on the Functioning of the European Union to certain categories of research and development agreements, [2010] OJ L335/36 (the "R&D Block Exemption Regulation").

404   Commission Regulation (EU) No 1218/2010 of 14 December 2010 on the application of Article 101(3) of the Treaty on the Functioning of the European Union to certain categories of specialisation agreements, [2010] OJ L335/43 (the "Specialisation Block Exemption Regulation").

405   Commission, Guidelines on the applicability of Article 101 of the Treaty on the Functioning of the European Union to horizontal co-operation agreements, [2011] OJ C11/1.

406   Article 1(c) of the R&D Block Exemption Regulation.

407   Recital 8 of the R&D Block Exemption Regulation.

408   Recital 10 of the R&D Block Exemption Regulation.

409   Article 4 of the R&D Block Exemption Regulation.

410   Recital 11 of the R&D Block Exemption Regulation.

411   Article 3(2) of the R&D Block Exemption Regulation.

Additionally, the R&D Block Exemption Regulation does not apply to agreements which include hardcore restrictions (e.g. restrictions on R&D in a field unconnected to that to which the agreement relates, the limiting of output or sales (with some exceptions) or certain restrictions on sales).[412] Any obligation forbidding a challenge to property rights after the expiry of the R&D agreement or an obligation not to grant licences to third parties to manufacture the contract products is null and void.[413]

Examples:

The R&D Block Exemption Regulation applies to the following agreements:

– A small research company (A) which does not have its own marketing division has discovered and patented a pharmaceutical substance based on new technology that will revolutionise the treatment of a certain disease and is likely to create an entirely new market. Company A enters into an R&D agreement with a large pharmaceutical producer Company B, who is a manufacturer of products which, up until now, have been used in treating the relevant disease. Company A lacks any similar production and distribution expertise and would not be able to build such expertise within a relevant timeframe. The two companies agree to cooperate, with Company B providing considerable funding and know-how for product development, as well as future access to the market. In return, Company A grants Company B a licence for the exclusive production and distribution of the resulting product for the duration of the patent. It is expected that the product could be brought to market in five to seven years. The parties bring complementary resources and skills to the co-operation, and the likelihood of the product coming to the market increases substantially. The exploitation rights are likely to be necessary for Company B to make the considerable investments needed and Company A has no marketing resources of its own.[414] In this kind of situation the R&D Block Exemption Regulation will apply.

– Two engineering companies that produce vehicle components agree to set up a joint venture to combine their R&D efforts to improve the production and performance of an existing component. The production of that component would also have a positive effect on the environment. The companies pool their existing technology licensing businesses in the area, but will continue to manufacture and sell the components separately. The product life cycle for the component is typically two to three years. To the extent that the joint venture has restrictive effects on competition within the meaning of Article 101(1) TFEU, it is likely that it would fulfil the criteria of the R&D Block Exemption Regulation as long as consumers will benefit from the results.[415]

---

412 Article 5 of the R&D Block Exemption Regulation.

413 Article 6 of the R&D Block Exemption Regulation.

414 Commission, Guidelines on the applicability of Article 101 of the Treaty on the Functioning of the European Union to horizontal co-operation agreements, [2011] OJ C11/1, para. 147.

415 Commission, Guidelines on the applicability of Article 101 of the Treaty on the Functioning of the European Union to horizontal co-operation agreements, [2011] OJ C11/1, para. 149.

bb) Specialisation Agreements

Agreements relating to the specialisation of production often contribute to improving the production or distribution of goods because the parties can concentrate on the manufacture of certain products only and thus operate more efficiently and supply the products more cheaply; by analogy this also applies to the provision of services.

If such advantages for the consumer outweigh the anti-competitive effect of a specialisation agreement, the agreement will be exempt from Article 101 TFEU pursuant to Commission Regulation (EU) No 1218/2010 (the "Specialisation Block Exemption Regulation").

The Specialisation Block Exemption Regulation covers the following kinds of agreements between two or more parties active on the same product market:
– One or more parties agree(s) to cease producing (in full or in part) certain (different) products or to refrain from producing those products and to purchase them from the other party, who in turn agrees to produce and supply those products.
– Two or more parties agree to produce certain products jointly.[416]

Such specialisation agreements are exempt from the prohibition set out in Article 101(1) TFEU if the combined market share of the parties involved does not exceed 20 % on the relevant market[417] and no hardcore restrictions are included in the agreement (e.g. fixing of prices, limitation of output sales (with some exceptions) or the allocation of markets or customers).[418]

cc) Horizontal Guidelines

The Commission has also issued guidelines on the applicability of Article 101 TFEU to horizontal cooperation agreements.[419] Whilst not generally binding, these guidelines nonetheless provide important guidance as to how the Commission will apply Article 101 TFEU. The Guidelines provide detailed information on the competitive assessment of information exchange, R&D agreements, production and purchasing agreements, agreements on commercialisation and standardisation agreements.

c) Technology Transfer Agreements

Technology transfer agreements are covered by Commission Regulation (EC) No 772/2004 (the "Technology Block Exemption Regulation").[420] As in the case of the R&D Block Exemption Regulation, the Technology Block Exemption Regulation seeks to protect incentives for innovation.[421]

---

416 Article 1 of the Specialisation Block Exemption Regulation.
417 Article 3 of the Specialisation Block Exemption Regulation.
418 Article 4 of the Specialisation Block Exemption Regulation.
419 Commission, Guidelines on the applicability of Article 101 of the Treaty on the Functioning of the European Union to horizontal co-operation agreements, [2011] OJ C11/1.
420 Commission Regulation (EC) No 772/2004 of 27 April 2004 on the application of Article 81(3) of the Treaty to categories of technology transfer agreements, [2004] OJ L123/11 (the "Technology Block Exemption Regulation").
421 Cf. recital 14 of the Technology Block Exemption Regulation.

Technology transfer agreements under the Technology Block Exemption Regulation are agreements between two undertakings regarding the sale and purchase, licensing, assignment or other use of productions protected by intellectual property rights.[422]

In contrast to the R&D Block Exemption Regulation, the primary focus of the Technology Block Exemption Regulation lies not in the development of new products, but in the protection of products which are already in existence and are protected by intellectual property rights.

Technology transfer agreements may be exempt from the prohibition contained in Article 101(1) TFEU if they are related to a permitted (i.e. contractually agreed) use of technology which is protected by intellectual property rights. Where the undertakings party to the agreement are competitors, their combined market share may not exceed 20 %; where they are not competitors, no party should have more than a 30 % market share on the relevant market.[423] Additionally, the agreement must not contain any provisions relating to a limitation of product output or the fixing of prices,[424] and it may not impose restrictions on the owner of the relevant technology prohibiting him from licensing, assigning or otherwise dealing with its property.[425]

Examples:
The Technology Regulation applies to, for example, the following kinds of agreements:
– A biotechnology undertaking develops a new product X and protects this property with a patent. However, for commercial reasons the undertaking chooses not to produce and sell product X. However, it enters into a licensing agreement with another undertaking permitting the second undertaking to produce and distribute product X.[426]
– Two undertakings are active in the same relevant market for a chemical product. Each owns a patent for different production procedures relating to the same chemical product. The two undertakings conclude a licensing agreement which entitles each to use the other's production procedures.[427]

d) Automobile Sector

Vertical agreements relating to the motor vehicle sector are dealt with by Commission Regulation (EU) No 461/2010 (the "Motor Vehicle Block Exemption Regulation"). This Regulation aims at promoting competition amongst dealers and repair workshops, as well as encouraging the development of the internal market to make easier the cross-border

---

422 See the detailed definition in Article 1(1)(b) of the Technology Block Exemption Regulation. Products protected by industrial property rights, copyrights or other intellectual property rights are covered, cf. Article 1(1)(g) of the Technology Block Exemption Regulation.

423 Article 2 and Article 3 of the Technology Block Exemption Regulation.

424 Article 4 of the Technology Block Exemption Regulation.

425 For further detail see Article 5 of the Technology Block Exemption Regulation.

426 Commission, Notice on Guidelines on the application of Article 81 of the EC Treaty to technology transfer agreements, [2004] OJ C101/2, para. 73.

427 Commission, Notice on Guidelines on the application of Article 81 of the EC Treaty to technology transfer agreements, [2004] OJ C101/2, para. 73.

purchase of new vehicles. Additionally, an agreement has to fulfil the conditions of the Vertical Block Exemption Regulation to be exempted.[428]

In contrast to the former motor vehicle block exemption regulation (Commission Regulation (EC) No 1400/2002), the new Motor Vehicle Block Exemption Regulation draws a distinction between agreements for the distribution of new motor vehicles and agreements for the provision of repair and maintenance services and distribution of spare parts.

As regards the distribution of new motor vehicles, in the view of the Commission there are no significant competition shortcomings which would distinguish this sector from other economic sectors and which could require the application of rules different from and stricter than those set out in the Vertical Block Exemption Regulation. With effect from 1 July 2013 the Vertical Block Exemption Regulation will apply to those agreements only.[429]

As regards agreements for the distribution of spare parts and for the provision of repair and maintenance services, there are still special competition shortcomings. A separate aftermarket can be defined.[430] Effective competition on the markets for the purchase and sale of spare parts, as well as for the provision of repair and maintenance services for motor vehicles, depends on the degree of competitive interaction between authorised repairers as well as between authorised and independent operators. The latters' ability to compete depends on unrestricted access to essential inputs such as spare parts and technical information.[431] Therefore the Motor Vehicle Block Exemption Regulation includes some hardcore restrictions that go beyond those specified in the Vertical Block Exemption Regulation. For example, sales of spare parts for motor vehicles by members of a selective distribution system to independent repairers which use those parts for the repair and maintenance of a motor vehicle may not be restricted at all.[432]

The Commission has issued guidelines that set out principles for assessing particular issues arising in the context of vertical restraints in agreements for the sale and repair of motor vehicles and for the distribution of spare parts under Article 101 TFEU.[433]

e) Other Sector-Specific Block Exemption Regulations

In addition to the block exemption regulations applying to the motor vehicle sector, exemptions for other sectors also exist, including those for:

---

428   Article 4 of the Motor Vehicle Block Exemption Regulation.

429   Recital 10 and Article 3 of the Motor Vehicle Block Exemption Regulation.

430   At least in most cases, there is likely to be a brand-specific aftermarket for repair and maintenance services and spare parts that is separate from the market for the sale of new motor vehicles; cf. Commission, Notice on supplementary guidelines on vertical restraints in agreements for the sale and repair of motor vehicles and for the distribution of spare parts for motor vehicles, [2010] OJ C138/16, para. 57.

431   Recitals 11 and 13 of the Motor Vehicle Block Exemption Regulation.

432   Article 5 of the Motor Vehicle Block Exemption Regulation.

433   Commission, Notice on supplementary guidelines on vertical restraints in agreements for the sale and repair of motor vehicles and for the distribution of spare parts for motor vehicles, [2010] OJ C138/16.

- Agreements between agricultural producers;[434]
- Agreements between undertakings in the insurance sector;[435]
- Agreements between maritime shipping undertakings;[436] and
- Agreements regarding technical cooperation in the areas of railway, road and ship transport, as long as the undertakings involved are solely small or medium sized enterprises.[437]

3. Individual Exemption

If an agreement is not exempted by a block exemption, there is still the possibility that it can benefit from individual exemption pursuant to Article 101(3) TFEU.

An agreement is not prohibited by Article 101(1) TFEU if it contributes to improving the production or distribution of goods or to promoting technical or economic progress, while allowing consumers a fair share of the resulting benefit, and which does not impose restrictions which are not indispensable to the attainment of these objectives. Furthermore, the agreement may not afford the possibility of eliminating competition in respect of a substantial part of the products in question.

a) Gains in Efficiency

An agreement, decision or concerted practice can only benefit from the Article 101(3) TFEU exemption if it leads to gains in efficiency: the anti-competitive agreement must contribute to "improving the production of goods or to promoting technical or economic progress"; by analogy this requirement also applies to services.[438]

Efficiencies are not assessed from the point of view of the parties; rather, objective criteria must be applied. For example, cost savings may constitute an efficiency for a manufacturer, but they cannot be considered gains in efficiency for the purposes of the Article 101(3) TFEU exemption as they merely allow the relevant undertakings to increase their profits without producing any pro-competitive effects in the market.[439] There also must exist a causal link between the efficiency gains and the anti-competitive behaviour. In

---

434 Article 2 Council Regulation (EC) No 1184/2006 of 24 July 2006 applying certain rules of competition to the production of, and trade in, agricultural products, [2006] OJ L214/7; Article 176 of Council Regulation (EC) No 1234/2007 of 22 October 2007 establishing a common organisation of agricultural markets and on specific provisions for certain agricultural products, [2007] OJ L299/1.

435 Commission Regulation (EU) No 267/2010 of 24 March 2010 on the application of Article 101(3) of the Treaty on the Functioning of the European Union to certain categories of agreements, decisions and concerted practices in the insurance sector, [2010] OJ L83/1.

436 Commission Regulation (EC) No 906/2009 of 28 September 2009 on the application of Article 81(3) of the Treaty to certain categories of agreements, decisions and concerted practices between liner shipping companies (consortia), [2009] OJ L256/31.

437 Council Regulation (EC) No 169/2009 of 26 February 2009 applying rules of competition to transport by rail, road and inland waterway, [2009] OJ L61/1.

438 Commission Guidelines on the application of Article 81(3), para. 48.

439 Commission Guidelines on the application of Article 81(3), para. 49.

most cases, the anti-competitive behaviour will need to be the source of the gains in efficiency.[440]

b) Consumers Must Share the Benefits

A "fair share" of the benefits resulting from the anti-competitive behaviour should be passed on to consumers. The analysis required in determining if sufficient benefit will indeed be passed on to consumers requires a balancing of the negative and positive effects of an agreement on consumers.[441] "Consumers" are all direct or indirect users of the products covered by the agreement, including producers who use the product as a component in the production of a further product.[442] Ultimately the positive and negative effects of anti-competitive behaviour on consumers have to be considered in the context of all relevant commercial circumstances.

Consumers must not be placed in a worse position than they would have been if the agreement were not in place. The positive effects of the anti-competitive agreement must at least offset any negative effects on consumers.[443] It is not necessary that consumers benefit from each and every efficiency gain; it is sufficient for consumers to obtain a fair share of the benefits overall.[444]

If a restrictive agreement is likely to lead to higher prices, consumers must be compensated through increased quality or other benefits.[445] Essentially, the greater the restriction of competition under Article 101(1) TFEU, the greater must be the efficiencies passed on to consumers.[446]

c) Indispensability of the Restrictions of Competition

The third condition to the applicability of the Article 101(3) TFEU exemption is that the restrictions of competition must be indispensable to the achievement of the efficiency profits. This condition is analysed in two steps.

Firstly, the restrictive agreement must be reasonably necessary in order to achieve the efficiencies.[447] There must be no financially feasible or less anti-competitive means than the agreement to achieve the efficiency profits.[448] To fulfil this criterion undertakings

---

440 Commission Guidelines on the application of Article 81(3), paras. 53 et seq.

441 The Commission will not analyse whether sufficient benefit has been passed on to consumers before having examined the indispensability of a measure because the analysis of the "fair share" of the benefits demands a weighting of the negative and the positive effects of the measure. However, as effects which are not indispensable are prohibited under Article 101 TFEU, such effects should not be allowed for. Cf. Commission Guidelines on the application of Article 81(3), para. 39.

442 Commission Guidelines on the application of Article 81(3), para. 84.

443 Commission Guidelines on the application of Article 81(3), para. 85.

444 Commission Guidelines on the application of Article 81(3), para. 86.

445 Commission Guidelines on the application of Article 81(3), para. 86.

446 Commission Guidelines on the application of Article 81(3), para. 90.

447 Commission Guidelines on the application of Article 81(3), para. 73.

448 Commission Guidelines on the application of Article 81(3), para. 75.

must explain why any "seemingly realistic and significantly less restrictive alternatives to the agreement would be significantly less efficient".[449]

Secondly, the individual restrictions of competition that flow from the agreement must also be reasonably necessary for the attainment of the efficiencies.[450] It is decisive whether the anti-competitive agreement makes it possible to perform the activity in question more efficiently than would likely have been the case in the absence of the agreement.[451] Thus a restriction of competition is essential if "its absence would eliminate or significantly reduce the efficiencies that follow from the agreement or make it significantly less likely that they will materialise".[452]

Additionally, the more the restriction limits competition, the stricter the test of indispensability.[453]

d) No Elimination of Competition

The anti-competitive agreement must not allow the undertakings concerned the possibility of eliminating competition in respect of a substantial part of the products concerned. On the basis that "rivalry between undertakings is an essential driver of economic efficiency" (including e.g. innovation), priority is given to protecting the competitive process.[454] If competition in a particular market were to be eliminated, any short term efficiency gains would be outweighed by longer term losses stemming from a lack of checks on the market incumbent(s).[455]

Whether competition is restricted depends on "a realistic analysis of the various sources of competition in the market, the level of competitive constraint that they impose on the parties to the agreement and the impact of the agreement on competitive constraint".[456]

Impacts on both actual as well as potential competition should be considered. The anti-competitive agreement must not, in particular, eliminate the most important parameters of competition which may be more relevant in future (e.g. price competition or innovation).[457] Finally, an assessment of potential competition requires an analysis of barriers to entry facing undertakings not already operating in the market.[458]

---

449 Commission Guidelines on the application of Article 81(3), para. 75.
450 Commission Guidelines on the application of Article 81(3), para. 73.
451 Commission Guidelines on the application of Article 81(3), para. 74.
452 Commission Guidelines on the application of Article 81(3), para. 79.
453 Commission Guidelines on the application of Article 81(3), para. 79.
454 Commission Guidelines on the application of Article 81(3), para. 105.
455 Commission Guidelines on the application of Article 81(3), para. 105.
456 Commission Guidelines on the application of Article 81(3), para. 108.
457 Commission Guidelines on the application of Article 81(3), para. 110.
458 Commission Guidelines on the application of Article 81(3), para. 114.

Chapter Four

ABUSE OF A DOMINANT POSITION
UNDER ARTICLE 102 TFEU

Article 102 TFEU provides that every undertaking in a dominant position is subject to controls on anti-competitive behaviour.

Article 102 TFEU
"Any abuse by one or more undertakings of a dominant position within the internal market or in a substantial part of it shall be prohibited as incompatible with the internal market in so far as it may affect trade between Member States.

Such abuse may, in particular, consist in:
  (a) directly or indirectly imposing unfair purchase or selling prices or other unfair trading conditions;
  (b) limiting production, markets or technical development to the prejudice of consumers;
  (c) applying dissimilar conditions to equivalent transactions with other trading parties, thereby placing them at a competitive disadvantage;
  (d) making the conclusion of contracts subject to acceptance by the other parties of supplementary obligations which, by their nature or according to commercial usage, have no connection with the subject of such contracts."

This Article reflects the recognition that as the market power of undertakings increases, the self-regulating forces of the market decrease. Undertakings in a dominant position are able unilaterally to influence competitive conditions such as price through supply and demand side management on the basis of their market strength. The supervision of market behaviour provided for by Article 102 TFEU is intended to counteract such abuses of market power.

Notably, Article 102 TFEU does not forbid an undertaking from holding a dominant position; rather, it forbids only the *abuse* of such a position.

European jurisprudence has indicated that a dominant undertaking has a *special responsibility* not to allow its conduct to impair genuine undistorted competition on the internal market.[459]

---

459   Case 322/81, *Michelin*, [1983] ECR 3461, para. 57; Case T-83/91, *Tetra Pak*, [1993] ECR II-755, para. 114; Case T-111/96, *ITT Promedia NV*, [1998] ECR II-2937, para. 139; Case C-280/08 P, *Deutsche Telekom*, para. 176; Case T-228/97, *Irish Sugar*, [1999] ECR II-2969, para. 112; Case T-203/01, *Michelin*, [2003] ECR II-4071, para. 97; Case T-271/03, *Deutsche Telekom*, [2008] ECR II-477.

I. DOMINANT POSITION

In contrast to Article 101 TFEU, Article 102 does not catch all undertakings operating in the European Union; it applies only to those holding a "dominant position" in (a part or the whole of) the internal market.

A dominant position can exist on a specific, substantively, geographically- and possibly temporally-defined market.[460] Therefore determining whether an undertaking holds a dominant position requires two steps. First, the relevant market must be identified in order for the relevant competition law provisions to be applied to the specific facts of a case. Second, the status of the undertaking in question that acts on the relevant market must be ascertained, with reference to the abusive behaviours described in Article 102 TFEU.

> An undertaking enjoys a dominant position if it is able to prevent effective competition being maintained on the relevant market and has the power to behave, to an appreciable extent, independently of its competitors, customers and ultimately its consumers.[461]

Such independent behaviour is indicated by the fact that a dominant undertaking needs to show no consideration for the actions and reactions of its customers and competitors when determining its course of action.[462] This analysis is made on the basis of the economic circumstances in existence at the time of the allegedly abusive behaviour.

1. Market Share

The first indication of the market power of an undertaking is its market share.[463] A high market share – the Commission starts from a threshold value of approx. 40 %[464] and the General Court and Court of Justice from approx. 50 %[465] – will usually indicate a dominant position.[466] If an undertaking possesses a market share of more than 70 %, it is deemed to be in a dominant position with no further analysis required.[467]

---

460   Case 27/76, *United Brands,* [1978] ECR 207, paras. 10 et seq.

461   Case 27/76, *United Brands,* [1978] ECR 207, para. 65; Case 85/76, *Hoffmann-La Roche,* [1979] ECR 461, para. 38.

462   Commission, Guidance on the Commission's enforcement priorities in applying Article 82 of the EC Treaty to abusive exclusionary conduct by dominant undertakings, [2009] OJ C45/7, para. 10.

463   Case 85/76, *Hoffmann-La Roche,* [1979] ECR 461, paras. 39–41; Case C-62/86, *Akzo,* [1991] ECR I-3359, para. 60; Case T-30/89, *Hilti,* [1991] ECR II-1439, paras. 90–92; Case T-340/03, *France Télécom,* [2007] ECR II-107, para. 100.

464   Commission, Guidance on the Commission's enforcement priorities in applying Article 82 of the EC Treaty to abusive exclusionary conduct by dominant undertakings, [2009] OJ C45/7, para. 14.

465   Case C-62/86, *Akzo,* [1991] ECR I-3359, para. 60; Case T-395/94, *Atlantic Container Line,* [2002] ECR II-875, para. 223; Case T-340/03, *France Télécom,* [2007] ECR II-107, para. 100.

466   Case 85/76, *Hoffmann-La Roche,* [1979] ECR 461, paras. 39 et seq. On the link between market share and the finding of an abuse see Joined Cases C-395/96 P and C-396/96 P, *Compagnie maritime belge transports,* [2000] ECR I-1365, para. 119; Case Rs. T-228/97, *Irish Sugar,* [1999] ECR II-2969, para. 186.

467   *Microsoft* (COMP/C-3/37.792) Commission Decision, para. 435.

However, in less unequivocal circumstances, neither a high nor a low market share is definitive in classifying an undertaking as dominant, or excluding it from being so. This is because an ultimate determination of market dominance depends on an undertaking's capacity for independent behaviour, not only on simple market share. Additionally, it is possible for a high market share not to constitute a dominant position as well, if, for example, the demand power of purchaser X is sufficient to constrain the behaviour of supplier Y.[468] This is the case in particular in situations of countervailing power – i.e. when purchaser X in relevant market A is also a significant supplier in relevant market B, purchaser X is in a position to exercise its dominance over undertaking Y. As Y is also a significant supplier, each company deters the other from exercising its dominance. Thus neither X nor Y is in a dominant position pursuant to Article 102 TFEU (i.e. being capable of behaving independently of its customers).

2. Decisive Criteria for Determining a Dominant Position

Determining whether an undertaking holds a dominant position in a market depends upon a number of factors.[469] These can include but are not limited to: the market share of an undertaking's competitors, the existence of barriers to entry to the market, the buying power of purchasers and the price regulation of an undertaking or its capital strength.[470]

a) Market Shares of Competitors

Market share provides a useful first indication of the state of the relevant market and of the relative importance of the various undertakings active on that market.[471] A number of undertakings all holding smaller market shares will enable more economic independence than a larger market share concentrated in the hands of one undertaking. Additionally, relative market share, i.e. an undertaking's market share as compared to that of its principle competitor(s),[472] is a key factor.

An undertaking holding a 40 % market share may well not be able to act independently of its purchasers or competitors if its two nearest competitors hold, for example, 30 % market share each. In contrast, in the case relating to HB Ice Cream, that undertaking held a market share of over 75 % in the market for wrapped ice cream products, with its nearest competitors Mars and Nestlé possessing only very small market shares in the relevant market. Not only was HB's absolute share of the market very high, but in addi-

---

468   See Case T-228/97, *Irish Sugar*, [1999] ECR II-2969, para. 98.

469   Case 27/76, *United Brands*, [1978] ECR 207, paras. 65, 66; Case C-250/92, *Gøttrup-Klim e.a. Grovvar-eforeninger/Dansk Landbrugs Grovvareselskab AmbA*, [1994] ECR I-5641, para. 47; Case T-30/89, *Hilti*, [1991] ECR II-1439, para. 90.

470   Cf. Commission, Guidance on the Commission's enforcement priorities in applying Article 82 of the EC Treaty to abusive exclusionary conduct by dominant undertakings, [2009] OJ C45/7, para. 12.

471   Commission, Guidance on the Commission's enforcement priorities in applying Article 82 of the EC Treaty to abusive exclusionary conduct by dominant undertakings, [2009] OJ C45/7, para. 13.

472   Joined Cases T-24/93, T-25/93, T-26/93 and T-28/93, *Compagnie maritime belge transports*, [1996] ECR II-1201, para. 78.

tion there was a considerable distance between its market share and that of its nearest competitors.[473]

b) Profit Margin

An undertaking which is capable of increasing its prices above the competitive level for a significant period of time (and still remaining profitable) does not face effective constrains on competition and can thus generally be regarded as dominant.[474] In contrast, an undertaking which is compelled by its' competitors' price reductions to lower its own prices is, in general, evidence that the undertaking is not capable of acting independently in the market and therefore is not in a dominant position.[475]

Additionally, market share should not be confused with profitability. An undertaking selling products at a loss can still hold a dominant position on a market if its levels of sales are high; low (or no) profits can arise in a position of dominance, as equally, high profits can arise in a situation of effective competition where undertakings benefit from efficiency gains such as cost reductions and innovation.[476]

c) Barriers to Entry

High barriers to entry in a market are indicative of a dominant position. Low barriers to entry mean that an undertaking active on a market must always be wary of new market entrants, and therefore the incumbent is unlikely to be able to act financially independently in the market.[477]

– A dominant position is more likely if, for example, an undertaking can protect its market share through favourable technology protected under intellectual property laws, an especially strong position as regards research and development or a strong and well organised marketing system.[478]
– However, the simple fact of possessing favourable intellectual property rights is not itself sufficient evidence of a dominant position.[479] An exclusive intellectual property right, relating to e.g. an innovative production technique, is not to be equated with the product produced with that technology, as the product sold on the market can nonetheless face high competitive pressure from other products on the market which are still

---

473 Case T-65/98, *Van den Bergh Foods*, [2003] ECR II-4653, paras. 155 et seq. The fact that Mars and Nestlé were well represented in the neighbouring markets for sweets and chocolate and sold these products at the same points of sale as the ice cream products was irrelevant.

474 Commission, Guidance on the Commission's enforcement priorities in applying Article 82 of the EC Treaty to abusive exclusionary conduct by dominant undertakings, [2009] OJ C45/7, para. 11.

475 Case 85/76, *Hoffmann-La Roche*, [1979] ECR 461, para. 71.

476 See to the latter Case 27/76, *United Brands*, [1978] ECR 207, paras. 126–128.

477 Cf. Commission, Guidance on the Commission's enforcement priorities in applying Article 82 of the EC Treaty to abusive exclusionary conduct by dominant undertakings, [2009] OJ C45/7, para. 17.

478 Case T-30/89, *Hilti*, [1991] ECR II-1439, paras. 19, 93; cf. also Joined Cases T-24/93, T-25/93, T-26/93 and T-28/93, *Compagnie maritime belge transports*, [1996] ECR II-1201, para. 78.

479 Joined Cases C-241/91 P and C-242/91 P, *Magill*, [1995] ECR I-743, para. 46.

produced in a conventional way. Such is the case, for example, as regards competition between hybrid and conventional vehicles in the automobile industry.

- High barriers to entry can exist in several ways and are most typical in network industries. For example, any costs or impediments which consumers must tolerate if they wish to change to a new supplier encourage customers to stay with existing market providers rather than switch to new entrants. Long-term contracts that have appreciable costs upon termination can also lead to a restriction of viable new entrants to the market, given that customers are tied to existing providers for longer periods of time and it is therefore difficult for new entrants to win these customers.[480]
- High barriers to entry can also originate from so-called sunk costs (costs which an undertaking is unlikely to recover fully upon exiting the market). Such costs exist in particular in transmission-oriented infrastructure markets in which the construction of an infrastructure is possible only with significant financial and time investment.

d) Buying Power of Purchasers

Whether a dominant position exists also depends on whether the purchasers of a potentially dominant undertaking's products can exert pressure on that undertaking. Even an undertaking with a high market share may not be able to act independently in a market if its customers possess sufficient bargaining strength.[481] If purchasers' power is of a sufficient magnitude, it may deter or defeat an undertaking's attempt to profitably increase prices. However, a strong demand side in a relevant market does not definitively exclude the existence of an undertaking with a dominant position; rather it is one of a number of indicators.[482]

3. Collective Market Dominance

Article 102 TFEU also prohibits the abuse by multiple undertakings possessing a collectively dominant position on a market. In certain circumstances, multiple undertakings, rather than a single undertaking, can be the targets of an investigation of abuse of a dominant position.

a) Criteria

Multiple undertakings together can be considered to be collectively dominant on a market if they act – or choose not to act – collectively such that no real competition exists.[483] If two or more (legally independent) undertakings in a market act together and appear

---

480   Cf. Commission, Guidance on the Commission's enforcement priorities in applying Article 82 of the EC Treaty to abusive exclusionary conduct by dominant undertakings, [2009] OJ C45/7, para. 17.

481   Case T-228/97, *Irish Sugar*, [1999] ECR II-2969, paras. 93–104; cf. Commission, Guidance on the Commission's enforcement priorities in applying Article 82 of the EC Treaty to abusive exclusionary conduct by dominant undertakings, [2009] OJ C45/7, para. 18.

482   Case 85/76, *Hoffmann-La Roche*, [1979] ECR 461, para. 120.

483   Case C-96/94, *Centro Servizi Spediporto*, [1995] ECR I-2883, paras. 33, 34.

as one economic unit in that particular market, their actions can be analysed in the same way as if such behaviour patterns came from one single dominant undertaking.[484]

Article 102 TFEU refers to abuses of a dominant position by "one or more undertakings", so in cases where more than one undertaking is involved, in order to establish abusive behaviour for the purposes of Article 102, it is necessary that the multiple undertakings be connected in some way such that from an economic point of view, they present themselves as a *collective entity* with the power to act independently of their competitors, customers or consumers.[485] Therefore a collective dominant position requires the undertakings to be sufficiently "linked" to each other to adopt the same conduct on the market.

A link between undertakings can be legal or financial, however, the precise form of link necessary between undertakings to constitute collective dominance is not clear.[486]

- The Court of Justice has stated that the mere fact that two or more undertakings are linked by an agreement, a decision of an association of undertakings or a concerted practice within the meaning of Article 101 TFEU does not, of itself, constitute a sufficient basis for finding that a collective dominant position under Article 102 exists.[487]
- On the other hand, such behavioural coordination may, where it is implemented, result in the undertakings concerned being so linked as to their conduct on a particular market that they present themselves on that market (i.e. to competitors, trading partners and consumers) as a collective entity.[488]
- However, the existence of behavioural coordination, whilst it may be indicative of a collective dominant position, is not a decisive factor in making a final determination. Such a finding can also occur in the absence of behavioural coordination as described under Article 101 TFEU, and in each case the specific facts must be analysed in the context of the structure of the relevant market.[489]
- A collectively dominant position does not necessarily exist on the basis that all undertakings active in a relevant market must calculate their prices in accordance with a State-imposed fee system.[490]

Although most cases relating to collective dominance relate to the field of merger control, the criteria for assessing collective dominance are also applicable to cases falling under Article 102 TFEU. In one sense, both merger control and the prohibition of abuse of a dominant position are concerned with the same issue – undertakings accumulating such

---

484   The Court of Justice does not state these criteria explicitly, but they can be interpreted from a number of judgements: Case C-393/92, *Almelo*, [1994] ECR I-1477, para. 42; Case C-96/94, *Centro Servizi Spediporto*, [1995] ECR I-2883, para. 33; Joined Cases C-395/96 P and C-396/96 P, *Compagnie maritime belge transports*, [2000] ECR I-1365, para. 36.

485   Cf. Opinion of Advocate General Léger, Case C-309/99, *Wouters*, [2002] ECR I-1577, para. 147.

486   Cf. Opinion of Advocate General Léger, Case C-309/99, *Wouters*, [2002] ECR I-1577, para. 148.

487   Joined Cases C-395/96 P and C-396/96 P, *Compagnie maritime belge transports*, [2000] ECR I-1365, para. 43.

488   Joined Cases C-395/96 P and C-396/96 P, *Compagnie maritime belge transports*, [2000] ECR I-1365, para. 44; cf. also Case T-193/02, *Laurent Piau*, [2005] ECR II-209, para. 113.

489   Joined Cases C-395/96 P and C-396/96 P, *Compagnie maritime belge transports*, [2000] ECR I-1365, para. 45.

490   Case C-96/94, *Centro Servizi Spediporto*, [1995] ECR I-2883, para. 34.

market power that they can behave independently. However, there are still differences between merger control and the application of Article 102 TFEU which should be kept in mind. Within the scope of merger control, consideration of the creation (or strengthening) of possible collective dominance effects is undertaken from an *ex ante* point of view – a 'best guess' as to what the future effects of the proposed merger would be. Such analysis is necessarily speculative and imprecise, with the possibility that approval for the proposed merger might lead to a situation of collective dominance (and to negative impacts on market structure as well as consumers). In contrast, the prohibition of abuse of a dominant position under Article 102 TFEU is an *ex post* tool to address collective dominance which has, in fact, occurred.

Allowing for the differences between merger control and abuse of a dominant position, European jurisprudence has developed a consistent approach in analysing whether collective dominance does, or is likely, to exist.

b) Example: an Economic Unit Consisting of Multiple Undertakings

The requirements for two or more undertakings to be "linked" for the purposes of identifying collective dominance on a relative market are not clear.[491] Such links can exist through the use of common supply terms,[492] shareholdings in a joint venture, the use of a common market strategy or marketing policy[493] or even in situations of family ties or other personal relationships such as friendships between business owners or directors of competing undertakings.

Regardless of the nature of the connection between two or more undertakings, the key factor in determining if they exhibit collective dominance is whether they appear on the relevant market as one unit.[494]

4. Substantial Part of the Internal Market

In order to fall within the prohibition contained in Article 102 TFEU, an undertaking or group of undertakings must hold a dominant position in the whole of the internal market or a substantial part of it. Only after the relevant product and geographical markets have been identified can it be assessed whether a substantial part of the internal market is affected by the alleged abuse.

Additionally, in order to qualify as 'a *substantial part of the internal market*' it is not necessary for the geographic market to cross national boundaries of Member States. The whole or a substantial part of an individual Member State can be sufficient to constitute

---

491   Cf. Depoortere/Motta, The Doctrine of Collective Dominance: All Together Forever?, GCP 10/2009, pp. 1, 2.

492   Case C-393/92, *Almelo*, [1994] ECR I-1477, paras. 40–42, 38.

493   Case 30/87, *Bodson*, [1988] ECR 2479, paras. 28 et seq.

494   Opinion of Advocate General Fennelly, Joined Cases C-395/96 P and C-396/96 P, *Compagnie maritime belge transports,* [2000] ECR I-1365, para. 28.

a substantial part of the internal market (e.g. the City of London, the Région Parisien, the state of Bavaria, etc.).[495]

5. "Trade between Member States"

As in the case of the prohibition on cartels set out in Article 101 TFEU, Article 102 also specifies that only actions which "affect trade between Member States" are caught by its provisions. It can be recalled[496] that this requirement is satisfied if it is possible "to foresee with a sufficient degree of probability" that the abusive behaviour "may have an influence, direct or indirect, actual or potential, on the pattern of trade between Member States".[497]

II. ABUSE OF A DOMINANT POSITION

Article 102 TFEU does not prohibit an undertaking from holding a dominant position in a market – it only prohibits the abuse of such a position. The concept of "abuse of a dominant position" can be unclear and so needs to be clarified somewhat. Primary legislation (the TFEU) sets out a basic description of the concept, while Commission guidance and European jurisprudence have added to the development of the concept over time.[498]

In the interests of legal certainty, particularly for undertakings who need clarity as to what behaviours are or are not permitted, potentially abusive behaviour is first identified as falling generally within certain categories of abuse as developed in particular by Commission guidance and European jurisprudence. This does not mean, however, that the list of behaviours classified at any one point in time as abusive is static; rather, new types of abusive behaviour are each analysed on their facts and potentially integrated into the existing conception of abuse of a dominant position, taking particular account of judicial, economic and socio-political developments.

In the same way that holding a dominant position on a market is not in and of itself prohibited, equally an undertaking is free to seek to strengthen its market position on an ongoing basis – provided of course that the undertaking complies with competition rules. Significantly, however, it is not sufficient for an undertaking to adhere only to the latter of these rules; the European courts have made clear that a dominant undertaking bears a

---

495   Case 322/81, *Michelin*, [1983] ECR 3461, paras. 23 et seq; Joined Cases 40 to 48, 50, 54 to 56, 111, 113
      and 114/73, *Suiker Unie*, [1975] ECR 1663, para. 448.

496   See Chapter 3, Section IV (*"Trade between Member States"*).

497   Case 5/69, *Völk*, [1969] ECR 295, para. 5; Case 56/65, *L.T.M./M.B.U.*, [1966] ECR 281, 303;
      Commission, Guidelines on the effect on trade concept contained in Articles 81 and 82 of the
      Treaty, [2004] OJ C101/81, 83.

498   As early as 1979, the Court of Justice ruled that today's Article 102 TFEU is clear and precise enough
      in spite of the use of imprecise legal terms, cf. Case 85/76, *Hoffmann-La Roche*, [1979] ECR 461, para.
      130.

special responsibility for the maintenance of effective competition in a market in which it is dominant.[499]

Therefore, 'abusive' behaviour is behaviour which differs from normal competition in the market and affects the competitive structure of the market negatively. The use of a *per se* rule (i.e. that certain behaviours, such as price discrimination, product bundling or refusing to deal, always constitute abuse) has lately come under fire. Recently the Commission has adopted an approach of using a more economic analysis (as in the case of restraints of trade)[500] to analyse the effects of an undertaking's behaviour on a market. Moving away from a more formal approach and towards a more economic approach seeks to ensure a more consistent treatment of undertakings suspected of abuse of a dominant position.

1. Specific Behaviour to Which Article 102 TFEU Applies

Article 102 TFEU identifies a list of behaviours which are specifically identified as constituting 'abuse' of a dominant position, though this list is not exhaustive.[501] These include:
- imposing unfair prices or other unfair trading conditions (Article 102(a) TFEU);
- limiting production, markets or technical development to the prejudice of consumers (Article 102(b));
- applying dissimilar conditions to equivalent transactions to disadvantage one party as compared to another (Article 102(c)); and
- making the conclusion of contracts subject to acceptance by the other party of supplementary obligations which have no relationship to the subject matter of the original contract (Article 102(d)).

2. Categorisation of Abuses: Exploitative and Exclusionary Conduct

Abuses of a dominant position can be organised into two broad categories: exploitative abuse and exclusionary abuse. These categories are not set in stone; rather they provide an easy first-stage classification of kinds of abuse so that the details of each set of circumstances do not have to be detailed fully (a helpful method often used in literature relating to Article 102 TFEU).

> *Exploitative abuse* relates to the unfair treatment by one undertaking of other undertakings which sit on the downstream or upstream market (above or below it in the value added chain). A primary example of exploitative abuse is the imposition of unfair purchase or selling prices.

---

499   Case 322/81, *Michelin*, [1983] ECR 3461, para. 57; Case T-83/91, *Tetra Pak*, [1993] ECR II-755, para. 114; Case T-111/96, *ITT Promedia NV,* [1998] ECR II-2937, para. 139; Case T-228/97, *Irish Sugar,* [1999] ECR II-2969, para. 112; Case T-203/01, *Michelin*, [2003] ECR II-4071, para. 97.

500   See Chapter 1, Section II(2) (*The Investigation of Restraints of Trade*).

501   See for example Case 6/72, *Continental Can,* [1973] ECR 215, para. 26; Case C-95/04 P, *British Airways,* [2007] ECR I-2331, para. 57; Case T-201/04, *Microsoft,* [2007] ECR II-3601, para. 860.

Exclusionary abuse relates to 'anti-competitive foreclosure' which occurs when a dominant undertaking restricts the access of actual or potential competitors to supplies or a market with negative effects for consumers, i.e. higher prices, limited product availability or reduced customer choice.

III. TYPES OF ABUSE OF A DOMINANT POSITION

1. Price Abuse

One of the most obvious kinds of abuse in which a dominant undertaking may engage relates to pricing. Courtesy of its dominant position, such an undertaking can infringe Article 102 TFEU by setting unreasonably high prices, using predatory pricing or engaging in a price margin squeeze.

a) Unreasonably High Prices – Der Grüne Punkt (the 'Green Dot')

Price abuse exists if an undertaking imposes prices which it can enforce only because of its dominant position and which do not correspond reasonably to its costs of production.[502] For the purposes of Article 102 TFEU, an undertaking's price setting is abusive where it charges for its services fees which are disproportionate to the economic value of the service provided.[503]

> Is a licence fee to use a trademark abusive if the fee charged is disproportionate to the services provided by the trademark-holder?

In the interests of preventing and reducing the impact of packaging waste on the environment, German law required manufacturers and distributors to take back and recover used sales packaging outside the public waste disposal system. This obligation could be met in two ways: (i) by taking back packaging from customers near the original point of sale (the "self-management system") and/or (ii) by participating in a system which guaranteed the regular collection of packaging waste throughout the manufacturer or distributor's sales territory (the "exemption system"). Participating in the exemption system absolved manufacturers and distributors from further responsibility for recovering any packaging covered by that system.

The only exemption system which operated throughout Germany was known as Der Grüne Punkt and was operated by Duales System Deutschland GmbH (DSD). DSD held the trademark for Der Grüne Punkt. For a fee paid to it by manufactures and distributors, DSD agreed to allow the Der Grüne Punkt symbol to be placed on relevant packaging materials, which were then recovered in accordance with German law (and thereby absolved participating manufacturers and distributors from further obligations under Ger-

---

502   Case 27/76, *United Brands*, [1978] ECR 207, paras. 248–252.
503   Case C-385/07, *Der grüne Punkt*, [2009] ECR I-6155, para. 142.

man law). DSD itself did not collect the relevant packaging material, but sub-contracted this task to other undertakings.[504]

It was undisputed that DSD held a dominant position in the market for Germany-wide exemption services. At issue in this case was whether the fee charged by DSD for the use of its trademark was disproportionate to the services provided.

The abuse of a dominant position was alleged based on the fact that the fee which DSD charged participants in the exemption system was not conditional upon the actual use of that system; instead the fee was calculated on the basis of the amount of packaging bearing the Der Grüne Punkt logo which participating manufacturers and distributors put into circulation in Germany, meaning that participants had to affix the logo to every piece of packaging notified to DSD and intended for consumption in Germany. Thus, the Commission claimed, DSD abused its dominant position by not linking the fee payable under the Agreement to the actual use of the DSD system.[505] The General Court, and later the Court of Justice, held that DSD's behaviour was indeed abusive, as the fees it charged for its services were disproportionate to the economic value of the service provided.[506]

Additionally, both the General Court as well as the Court of Justice dismissed DSD's claim for exemption from Article 102 TFEU on the grounds that it provided a service of a general economic interest as described under Article 106(2). The Courts noted that Article 106(2) TFEU made clear that undertakings entrusted with the provision of a service of a general economic interest were still subject to European competition law, and that any exemption could only apply if such rules were to obstruct the performance of the tasks assigned to the relevant undertaking.[507] It was debatable whether DSD actually did provide services of general economic interest, but in any case, even if it did, nothing in the Commission's decision would interfere with DSD carrying out its activities.[508]

b) Predatory Pricing

Predatory pricing involves an undertaking deliberately incurring losses or foregoing profits in the short term so as to be able to force one or more of its actual or potential competitors out of the market.[509] Such a pricing strategy can be abusive if its purpose is to eliminate a competitor, or to prevent new competitors from entering the market.[510]

> Is a dominant undertaking guilty of predatory pricing if it merely adjusts (lowers) its price levels to those of its competitors?

WIN, an undertaking active on the French telecommunication market, engaged in predatory conduct by deliberately incurring losses or foregoing profits in the short term – a

---

504 For the facts of the case see Case T-151/01, *Der Grüne Punkt,* [2007] ECR II-1607, paras. 12–19.

505 Case T-151/01, *Der Grüne Punkt,* [2007] ECR II-1607, para. 48.

506 Case T-151/01, *Der Grüne Punkt,* [2007] ECR II-1607, para. 121.

507 Case T-151/01, *Der Grüne Punkt,* [2007] ECR II-1607, para. 207.

508 Case T-151/01, *Der Grüne Punkt,* [2007] ECR II-1607, paras. 206 and 210.

509 Commission, Guidance on the Commission's enforcement priorities in applying Article 82 of the EC Treaty to abusive exclusionary conduct by dominant undertakings, [2009] OJ C45/7, para. 63.

510 Cf. Case T-83/91, *Tetra Pak,* [1994] ECR II-755, paras. 147, 151 et seq., 173.

strategy to strengthen its own market position and to exclude its competitors from the market.[511]

However, WIN contended that it had not intended to engage in predatory pricing and had only adjusted its prices in response to its competitors' actions. WIN's argument was that every undertaking engaging in economic activity had a right to adapt itself (in good faith) to its competitors' behaviour, including in the area of prices. The fact that the prices offered by WIN's competitors would lie below WIN's costs in providing the service in question was irrelevant.[512]

The Commission took the view that, in principle, nothing prevented a dominant undertaking from adapting its prices to its competitors'. However, that freedom was restricted if the price for the relevant service lies below the dominant undertaking's variable costs of providing that service. Such was the case for WIN, who, when matching its competitors' price was doing so below variable cost, and in such a situation, a dominant undertaking aligning its prices to those of a non-dominant competitor was not justified.[513]

The General Court held (and the Court of Justice confirmed) in the WIN case that a dominant undertaking's right to align its prices to those of its competitors is not absolute – it cannot be invoked to justify the use of predatory pricing which would otherwise be prevented by European competition law. Although a dominant undertaking is entitled to protect its own commercial interests and take reasonable steps to protect those interests, equally such behaviour may not serve to strengthen the undertaking's dominant position and amount to abuse of that dominant position. The General Court noted that it was established case law that, ultimately, in specific circumstances, undertakings in a dominant position may be deprived of the right to adopt a certain course of conduct or take measures which are not in themselves abuses, even if such behaviours or measures would be unobjectionable if adopted or taken by non-dominant undertakings.[514]

c) Price Margin Squeeze

As discussed in Chapter 2,[515] a price margin squeeze takes place when a dominant undertaking applies inappropriate (abusive) pricing schemes for a product offered on both the wholesale and the consumer (retail) markets. Under price margin squeeze conditions, the dominant undertaking's competitors (often non-vertically integrated newcomers) who have to buy the (access or raw) product from the vertically integrated dominant undertaking on the upstream wholesale market in order to compete on the downstream retail market will not be able (profitably) to match the price offered by the dominant undertaking to final consumers on the retail market.[516] Therefore, price margin squeeze conditions

---

511   For the facts of the case see Case T-340/03, *France Télécom*, [2007] ECR II-107, in particular paras. 1–11.

512   Case T-340/03, *France Télécom*, [2007] ECR II-107, in particular para. 171.

513   Case T-340/03, *France Télécom*, [2007] ECR II-107, in particular para. 174.

514   Case T-340/03, *France Télécom*, [2007] ECR II-107, in particular paras. 182, 185–186 (upheld in Case C-202/07 P, *France Télécom*, [2009] ECR I-2369).

515   See Chapter 2, Section IV(2)(a) (*Example: Deutsche Telekom*).

516   See e.g. Case T-5/97, *Industrie des poudres sphériques*, [2000] ECR II-3755, para. 178; *Deutsche Telekom AG* (Case COMP/C-1/37.451, 37.578, 37.579) Commission Decision 2003/707/EC, [2003] OJ L263/9, para. 102.

often lead to large-scale market exits and insolvencies of newcomers, as has been seen in the telecommunications and postal markets.

For the purposes of Article 102 TFEU, a price margin squeeze is abusive if wholesale prices exceed, or are only very slightly lower, than those offered to final consumers. The 'margin test' consists essentially of the following equation:

downstream consumer price

= or >

all fixed and variable costs of producing and marketing the relevant goods or services for final consumers on the retail market, including the upstream wholesale price paid.

In other words (for those less mathematically inclined), the difference between upstream wholesale and downstream consumer prices has to be enough to cover all fixed and variable costs of producing the goods or services for final consumers on the retail market efficiently.[517] Otherwise, although the competitors may be as efficient as the dominant undertaking, they may be able to operate on the retail market only at a loss or at artificially reduced levels of profitability.[518]

In the case of *Deutsche Telekom*, although its prices on the wholesale market were regulated and its prices on the consumer market were reactive to competitors' behaviour, the Court of Justice (upholding the General Court's decision) still held that an abusive price margin squeeze existed.

Deutsche Telekom was dominant in the relevant market(s) and its competitors had no option but to purchase services from it on a wholesale basis. On account of prices at the wholesale level, it was very difficult, if not impossible, for them to offer their products to final consumers and make a profit.[519] The decision in this case is noteworthy, as the prices offered by the dominant undertaking were approved by the national regulator, and the scope for Deutsche Telekom to amend those prices was rather limited. The Courts nonetheless held that Deutsche Telekom was under an obligation to take active steps (e.g. applying for new, more appropriate price approvals) to avoid imposing an abusive price margin squeeze on its competitors.[520]

2. Refusal to Supply

Article 102 TFEU specifies that limiting production, markets or technical development to the prejudice of consumers can constitute an abuse of a dominant position. This provision is key to the functioning of the internal market – cross-border competition can only exist effectively when production is free to occur, is unhindered and undergoes continuous improvement. Thus a dominant undertaking is prohibited from influencing this "free play of the competitive strengths" to its benefit and to the detriment of consumers. Such

---

517 *Deutsche Telekom AG* (Case COMP/C-1/37.451, 37.578, 37.579) Commission Decision 2003/707/EC, [2003] OJ L263/9, para. 107; Case C-52/09, *TeliaSonera*, para. 32.

518 Case C-52/09, *TeliaSonera*, para. 33.

519 Case T-271/03, *Deutsche Telekom*, [2008] ECR II-477 (upheld in Case C-280/08 P, *Deutsche Telekom*).

520 For details see Chapter 2, Section IV(2)(a) (*Example: Deutsche Telekom*).

behaviour could include, in particular, restricting supply to drive up prices or refusing to supply other undertakings with goods they require for production at a different level in the product chain or the provision of services.

The Commission starts from the perspective that, generally, every undertaking has a right to choose its trading partners and deal freely with its property. However, in certain circumstances it is appropriate to restrict this right – i.e. to impose an obligation on a dominant undertaking to supply another undertaking. Given the significance of this kind of intervention, applying Article 102 TFEU in such circumstances must be considered carefully. The existence of such an obligation (even for a fair remuneration) has the potential to undermine undertakings' incentives to invest and innovate, and thereby ultimately harm consumers.[521]

The following kinds of behaviour have been considered abusive refusals to supply:

– The arbitrary refusal to supply independent motor vehicle repair workshops with spare parts, the fixing of prices for spare parts at an unfair level or the decision no longer to produce spare parts for a particular model even though many cars of that model are still in circulation.[522]
– GVL was the only undertaking in Germany which dealt with the protection of copyright and other rights of performers. Its primary task was to collect royalties on behalf of artists and then distribute them to the artists appropriately. GVL restricted its services to artists who lived in Germany, and excluded all other artists. Such behaviour was held to be abusive, as GVL could not exclude the possibility that artists living in other Member States might be entitled to royalties.[523]
– A dominant undertaking abuses its position if it obliges dealers supplied by it to channel products to specific consignees or destinations, which has the effect of limiting sales.[524]

a) Ambulance Transportation

In the case of *Ambulanz Glöckner*, the undertaking in question was licensed by the State to provide public emergency ambulance services in a specific geographic area. At issue was whether an undertaking to whom a monopoly for such services had been granted by the State was capable of infringing European competition law.

– The mere fact that an undertaking has been placed in a dominant position through the granting to it of special or exclusive rights does not necessarily infringe Article 102 TFEU. However, such an undertaking can be caught by Article 102 TFEU if it uses those special or exclusive rights in an abusive manner.[525]
– In this case, Ambulanz Glöckner reserved to itself the market for transporting non-emergency patients, which went beyond its statutory obligation to transport emergency

---

521   Cf. Commission, Guidance on the Commission's enforcement priorities in applying Article 82 of the EC Treaty to abusive exclusionary conduct by dominant undertakings, [2009] OJ C45/7, para. 75.

522   Case 238/87, *AB Volvo v Erik Veng,* [1988] ECR 6211, para. 9.

523   Case 7/82, *GVL v Commission,* [1983] ECR 483, paras. 54–56.

524   Joined Cases 40 to 48, 50, 54 to 56, 111, 113 and 114/73, Suiker Unie, [1975] ECR 1663, paras. 398–399.

525   Case C-41/90, *Höfner and Elser,* [1991] ECR I-1979.

patients. The Court of Justice held that Ambulanz Glöckner had reserved to itself an ancillary activity which could actually have been carried out by another undertaking operating in the market for transporting non-emergency patients. Such behaviour had the potential to eliminate all competition from the alternative undertaking and therefore constituted abusive behaviour.[526]

b) GlaxoSmithKline

The Greek subsidiary of GlaxoSmithKline (GSK) was responsible for the import, storage and distribution of GSK's pharmaceutical products in Greece. Over a period of years a number of Greek wholesalers of pharmaceutical products had purchased additional products from GSK so that they could export the excess beyond what was required for the Greek market to other Member States where prices for these products were higher (parallel trading). In October 2000 GSK altered its distribution system in Greece, citing a shortage of products, for which it denied responsibility. From November 2000 GSK began selling its products directly to Greek hospitals and chemists rather than selling to wholesalers. In December 2001, following discussions with the Greek competition authority, GSK agreed to supply wholesalers with products equivalent to national consumption plus 18 %.

At issue in this case was whether the refusal by GSK (who was dominant on the relevant market) to supply to wholesalers in an effort to prevent parallel trading was an abuse under Article 102 TFEU.[527]

> European jurisprudence indicates that refusal by a dominant undertaking to meet the orders of an existing customer constitutes abuse of that dominant position under Article 102 TFEU where, without any objective justification, such conduct is liable to eliminate a trading party as a competitor. As regards a refusal by an undertaking to supply products to wholesalers who export those products to other Member States, the effect of eliminating a competitor can occur in the original Member State, but also if the conduct leads to the elimination of effective competition in the distribution of the products on the markets of the other Member States.[528]

GSK argued that the general logic behind protecting competition does not function in the pharmaceutical sector, where State regulation prevents manufacturers of medicines from engaging in normal competitive activities. In this sector prices are regulated by the State and pharmaceutical undertakings are legally obliged to deliver products in Member States in which they are licensed. In contrast, parallel importers are free to shift their activities between products or markets if doing so offers higher profits – potentially resulting in shortfalls in some exporting Member States.[529] GSK further argued that its refusal to supply the quantities of products requested by the wholesalers was not abusive, as the

---

526 Case C-475/99, *Ambulanz Glöckner*, [2001] ECR I-8089, paras. 39 et seq., 42.

527 Joined Cases C-468/06 to C-478/06, *GlaxoSmithKline*, [2008] ECR I-7139, paras. 9–27.

528 Joined Cases C-468/06 to C-478/06, *GlaxoSmithKline*, [2008] ECR I-7139, paras. 34, 35.

529 Joined Cases C-468/06 to C-478/06, *GlaxoSmithKline*, [2008] ECR I-7139, paras. 41–43.

wholesalers (i) had still been supplied with sufficient quantities to meet national needs (and indeed some excess) and (ii) were free to acquire those products from suppliers in other Member States. Ultimately, GSK said, it had not put the wholesalers at risk of being eliminated from the market, since its supplies had been sufficient for market needs.[530]

The Greek wholesalers as well as the Commission contended that Article 102 TFEU could apply to the pharmaceutical sector as the prices set by the State had been subject to negotiations with the relevant pharmaceutical undertaking.[531] The Court of Justice also pointed out in its judgement that where a medicine is protected by a patent which confers a monopoly on its holder, until the expiry of that patent, the only price competition which could exist would exist between a producer and its distributors, or between parallel traders and national distributors.[532]

The Court of Justice held that although national regulatory regimes did exercise control over e.g. the sale prices of medicines, the pharmaceutical industry nonetheless was still subject to the effects of supply and demand as there was an element of negotiation in the original setting of the price. Therefore the pharmaceutical sector should be subject to Article 102 TFEU. However, the Court also noted that the system of State regulation of medical product prices itself contributes to the creation of opportunities for parallel trade. Consequently, if, due to competition law, an undertaking was unable to defend its own commercial interests (i.e. in attempting to prevent parallel trading), the only choice left for a pharmaceutical company in a dominant position would be not to place its medicines on the market at all in a Member State where the prices of those products are set at a relatively low level.[533] Ultimately, although a pharmaceutical company in a dominant position in a Member State where prices are relatively low cannot be allowed to cease to honour the ordinary orders of an existing customer for the sole reason that the customer, in addition to supplying the market in that Member State, exports part of the quantities ordered to other Member States with higher prices, it is nonetheless permissible for that pharmaceutical company to counter in a reasonable and proportionate way the threat to its own commercial interests potentially posed by the activities of an undertaking which wishes to be supplied in the first Member State with significant quantities of products that are essentially destined for parallel export.[534]

In conclusion, a dominant undertaking must be able to defend its commercial interests adequately. Such refusal to supply crosses the threshold into abuse if it relates to long-standing customers and if the supply orders are not out of the ordinary.[535]

3. Discrimination

Article 102(c) TFEU provides that "applying dissimilar conditions to equivalent transactions with other trading parties [and] thereby placing them at a disadvantage" constitutes

---

530 Joined Cases C-468/06 to C-478/06, *GlaxoSmithKline,* [2008] ECR I-7139, para. 30.

531 Joined Cases C-468/06 to C-478/06, *GlaxoSmithKline,* [2008] ECR I-7139, para. 47.

532 Joined Cases C-468/06 to C-478/06, *GlaxoSmithKline,* [2008] ECR I-7139, para. 64.

533 Joined Cases C-468/06 to C-478/06, *GlaxoSmithKline,* [2008] ECR I-7139, paras. 67 et seq.

534 Joined Cases C-468/06 to C-478/06, *GlaxoSmithKline,* [2008] ECR I-7139, para. 69.

535 Joined Cases C-468/06 to C-478/06, *GlaxoSmithKline,* [2008] ECR I-7139, paras. 49, 70, 71.

'abuse' for the purposes of Article 102. Such discrimination potentially could occur between a dominant undertaking and its trading partners at other stages of the value added chain.

> Discrimination exists if one undertaking is treated differently to another, in the absence of justification for such differentiation.

Examples
– It is not discrimination to treat one's regular customers and one's occasional customers differently during the period of a goods shortage; in such situations, even a dominant undertaking is permitted to treat the two categories of customers differently.[536]
– The Finnish Civil Aviation Administration imposed a system of differentiated landing charges (higher charges for intra-EEA flights) which was found to have the effect of applying dissimilar conditions for equivalent landing and take-off services for airlines. Certain airlines were thereby placed at a competitive disadvantage, constituting an abuse of a dominant position within the meaning of Article 102(c) TFEU.[537]

4. Exclusive Dealing

An undertaking can also abuse its dominant position by locking its customers into exclusive arrangements, and thereby edging its competitors out of the market.[538] Such exclusive arrangements can consist, for example, of exclusive purchasing agreements or linking purchase quantities to price discounts (beyond any discounts which might be justified by the marginal cost advantage to the undertaking of selling large quantities).

a) BPB Industries

> Does an undertaking making a payment to its customers in return for entry by those customers into an exclusive purchasing agreement amount to an abuse of a dominant position?

In the case of *BPB Industries,* the Commission argued that BPB's policy of paying rebates to purchasers who agreed to source plaster boards solely from BPB was an abuse of BPB's dominant position in that market.[539] BPB operated a system through which wholesale purchasers who purchased certain products exclusively from BPB received regular contributions by BPB to those customers' advertising and promotional expenses.[540]

---

536 Case 77/77, *Benzine en Petroleum Handelsmaatschappij BV and others*, [1978] ECR 1513, in particular para. 32.

537 Cf. *Ilmailulaitos/Luftfartsverket* (Case IV/35.767, notified under document number C(1999)239), Commission Decision 1999/198/EC, [1999] OJ L69/24, para. 42.

538 Cf. Commission, Guidance on the Commission's enforcement priorities in applying Article 82 of the EC Treaty to abusive exclusionary conduct by dominant undertakings, [2009] OJ C45/7, para. 32.

539 For the facts of the case cf. Case T-65/89, *BPB Industries Plc and British Gypsum*, [1993] ECR II-389, paras. 1–10.

540 Case T-65/89, *BPB Industries Plc and British Gypsum*, [1993] ECR II-389, para. 39.

The Court of Justice determined that BPB's behaviour was indeed abusive:

– The Court noted that whilst the arrangement provided benefits for both parties (BPB benefited from having certainty about its sales and the purchasers could rely on security of supply as well as additional funding for marketing activities), such behaviour can nonetheless constitute an abuse of a dominant position, depending on the specific qualities of the relevant market – in particular, whether a market is highly concentrated or characterised by lively competition.

– An exclusive purchasing agreement in favour of a dominant undertaking is likely to be abusive, as it can edge out competitors and hinder other undertakings entering the market.

– Even if, as BPB argued, the system in question served to promote the marketing of certain products generally, the Court held that the essence of the payments made by BPB was to ensure its purchasers entered into exclusive purchasing agreements.

– The fact that purchasers could discontinue their contractual relations with BPB at any time did not negate the existence of abuse (the abuse would exist up until the point of the contracts being terminated). Additionally, if an undertaking is dominant enough to require its customers to enter into and maintain such contracts, the possibility of termination is, in reality, illusory.[541]

b) Michelin

The French subsidiary of Michelin (a manufacturer of vehicle tyres) established "The Michelin Friends Club" – aimed at dealers of tyres who wished to enter into a closer cooperation with Michelin. In return for contributions to training and investment and a financial payment amounting to 0.75 % of the annual 'Michelin Service' turnover, dealers were obliged, *inter alia*, to provide Michelin with financial information and sales statistics and to promote Michelin products. Dealers were also not permitted to divert customers who had asked for Michelin products to other brands.[542]

The General Court considered the structure of the Club to be abusive, as its entire purpose was to support the position of Michelin and limit competition from other brands. Additionally, membership of the Club brought with it numerous disadvantages, the logic being that Michelin would need to use its dominant position to induce dealers into the group, as they would not otherwise join.[543]

5. Refusal of Access or to License

Another form of abuse under Article 102 TFEU occurs when an undertaking unfairly refuses access to essential infrastructure equipment (so-called "essential facilities") or unfairly restricts the use of its protected intellectual property.

---

541   Case T-65/89, *BPB Industries Plc and British Gypsum*, [1993] ECR II-389, paras. 65–77.

542   For the facts of the case cf. Case T-203/01, *Michelin*, [2003] ECR II-4071, paras. 1–4, 21.

543   Case T-203/01, *Michelin*, [2003] ECR II-4071, para. 210.

> A refusal to allow access to or use of certain products can be abusive if that conduct is likely to eliminate all of the undertaking's competition.[544]

The *Microsoft*[545] case is highly important in assessing this kind of abuse of a dominant position, with the Commission's Decision setting out in detail the criteria for judging such cases. In its Decision, the Commission considered that Microsoft had withheld certain key information regarding its operating system from competitors, and that that information (in particular regarding interfacing with the Windows operating system) was key for competitors to develop products which could operate on Windows-based computers. The Commission contended that Microsoft's behaviour was part of a strategy to maintain its dominant position in the market for computer operating systems and certain related software and was therefore an abuse of its dominant position under Article 102 TFEU. The Commission ordered Microsoft, for a reasonable license fee, to make public its interoperability specifications to enable the development of compatible software by other undertakings.

The General Court upheld the essential points of the Commission's Decision in 2007, thereby bringing to an end one of the most protracted competition disputes in European history. For lawyers, this case also stands out for the use of the "more economic approach" to competition regulation in Europe as well as highlighting the tensions between competitive supervision and the protection of intellectual property rights in the Union.

Microsoft had argued that the Commission's order for Microsoft to share its intellectual property infringed copyright and patent law as well as exposed business secrets to its rivals. However, the Commission and General Court looked to prior jurisprudence from the European Courts (in particular *Magill*,[546] *Bronner*[547] and *IMS Health*[548]) which had found that dominant undertakings do not possess an absolute right to use their intellectual property unrestrictedly. Thus a refusal by a dominant undertaking to license its software to its competitors for a reasonable fee could amount to an abuse of a dominant position under Article 102 TFEU. Notably as well, *Microsoft* is one of the rare cases where an undertaking was not permitted the right to choose its competitors and deal with its property freely – usually a key tenant in European law.[549]

a) When is a Refusal of Access or to Licence an Abuse?

> A refusal of access or to licence can, under "exceptional circumstances", constitute an abuse of power when:
> (1) the use or licensing is essential for access to a neighbouring (downstream) market;

---

544 Case C-7/97, *Bronner*, [1998] ECR I-7791, para. 38.

545 Case T-201/04, *Microsoft*, [2007] ECR II-1491; *Microsoft* (Case COMP/C-3/37.792) Commission Decision.

546 Joined Cases C-241/91 P and C-242/91 P, *Magill*, [1995] ECR I-743.

547 Joined Cases C-7/97, *Bronner*, [1998] ECR I-7791.

548 Case C-418/01, *IMS Health*, [2004] ECR I-5039.

549 Commission, Guidance on the Commission's enforcement priorities in applying Article 82 of the EC Treaty to abusive exclusionary conduct by dominant undertakings, [2009] OJ C45/7, para. 75.

(2) the refusal in essence excludes any effective competition on a neighbouring market; and

(3) the refusal would prevent a "new" product for which there is a potential consumer demand from entering the market (for which there is a potential consumer demand – the *Microsoft* provision).

If these three conditions are satisfied, then the refusal to supply or license is abusive if the refusal is not justified objectively.[550]

In the earlier cases of *Magill* and *IMS Health,* the Court of Justice had held that it was necessary for a dominant undertaking's competitor to want to offer a new product in the downstream market. However, in *Microsoft*, the General Court dropped this requirement tacitly, as Microsoft's competitors were not seeking to offer a new product, but rather a similar product competing with Microsoft's software. The General Court found justification for this shift in Article 102(b) TFEU, which refers not only to "limiting production" of products, but also to "limiting ... technical development to the prejudice of consumers" (i.e. Microsoft's refusal to license would limit the ability of its competitors to develop improved products).[551]

As in the case of a refusal to license, corresponding criteria exist for determining when a refusal to allow access to essential infrastructure equipment is abusive.

b) IMS Health

IMS compiled data regarding the sales of pharmaceutical and healthcare products in Germany, with the data broken down into set geographic areas (called 'bricks'); this data was then sold to pharmaceutical companies. IMS provided this technology to pharmacies and doctors' surgeries free of charge, which helped this technology to become the industry standard to which IMS's clients (pharmaceutical companies) adapted their information and distribution systems. IMS's data gathering technology (its specific 'brick structure') was held by national courts to be a database, and therefore protected by intellectual property rights.

The issue in this case arose when a competitor of IMS called NDC attempted to market its own brick structure form of technology for data gathering, but was prevented from doing so on the basis that its brick structure would infringe IMS's intellectual property rights. As IMS also refused to licence its intellectual property to NCD, the Commission argued that such refusal to license was an infringement of Article 102 TFEU and ordered IMS to licence its product to NDC for a reasonable fee.

As IMS Health was before the Court of Justice as a preliminary reference from a German court, it fell to the Court of Justice to indicate to the German court how to determine whether "exceptional circumstances"[552] existed – i.e. how to determine if IMS's refusal to license was abusive.

---

550   Cf. Case C-418/01, *IMS Health*, [2004] ECR I-5039, in particular paras. 35, 38, 52.

551   Case T-201/04, *Microsoft*, [2007] ECR II-3601, paras. 643–665.

552   See Chapter 4, Section III(4)(a) (*BPB Industries*).

Firstly, the Court of Justice commented that it was for the national court to establish whether the use of property protected by intellectual property rights was indispensable for enabling an undertaking to carry on business in a particular market – i.e. whether there are products or services which constitute alternative solutions, even if they are less advantageous, and whether there are technical, legal or economic obstacles capable of making it impossible or at least unreasonably difficult for any undertaking seeking to operate in the market to create alternative products or services.[553] Secondly, it was for the national court to determine whether IMS's brick structure constituted, upstream, an indispensable factor in the downstream supply of German regional sales data for pharmaceutical products.[554] Finally, would the effect of IMS refusing to license its property to competitors be that no new products or services would be able to develop which might benefit consumers?[555] If so, and if potential demand for such products or services exists, then in conjunction with the first two criteria, IMS's refusal to license would have to be found to be abusive.

6. Protection of Intellectual Property and Abuse of Legal Rights

The tension between the protection of intellectual property and the application of European competition law has been the subject of a number of controversial discussions in the pharmaceutical sector. In 2005 the Commission determined that AstraZeneca had infringed Article 102 TFEU by giving misleading representations to the patent offices in various Member States. The consequence of this behaviour was that it was impossible for other undertakings to produce medicines containing the patented substance (known as generic medicines) and to enter into competition with AstraZeneca, as the production of such medicines would have infringed patent law.[556] Decisive in this case was that AstraZeneca had acted dishonestly and therefore also infringed patent law.[557] In other circumstances in which a dominant undertaking acts honestly (and does not infringe patent law), protection of intellectual property may not constitute an abuse (the Court did not rule on this precise issue in *AstraZeneca*).

The General Court held that AstraZeneca also acted abusively regarding registration data it was required by law to provide to government authorities to market the relevant medical product (or a generic version of it).[558] Although AstraZeneca no longer intended to market the particular product, certain registration data was still required to be provided. The Court was of the view that the main reason for AstraZeneca withdrawing the relevant information was to hinder its competitors' ability to market a generic version of the medicine in question. Thus AstraZeneca hindered its competitors' entry into the

---

553   Case C-418/01, *IMS Health*, [2004] ECR I-5039, paras. 28–30.

554   Case C-418/01, *IMS Health*, [2004] ECR I-5039, para. 46.

555   Case C-418/01, *IMS Health*, [2004] ECR I-5039, paras. 48–50.

556   *AstraZeneca* (Case COMP/A-37.507/F3) Commission Decision. The main points were upheld by Case T-321/05, *AstraZeneca* (appeal brought on 16 September 2010 by AstraZeneca, Case C-457/10 P).

557   Case T-321/05, *AstraZeneca*, para. 361.

558   This registration data (e.g. clinical studies) is needed to market the original pharmaceutical or a generic version of it.

market.[559] This ruling established – similarly to the case of *Deutsche Telekom*[560] – that dominant undertakings bear a special responsibility in caring for their competitors.

The Commission conducted a sector inquiry into the pharmaceutical sector and found a number of types of abuse were occurring, particularly in relation to the registration and enforcement of patents. Some of these abuses included: registering a succession of (slightly different) patents to prohibit or delay competitors from producing generic versions of medicines; making representations to national courts regarding the state of patents held whilst knowing that those patents were invalid; and shortly before the expiry of patent protection, entering into exclusive arrangements with individual manufacturers of generic medicines which contain some disadvantageous conditions for the latter and hinder other competitors' entry into the market.[561] The Commission has initiated a number of formal investigation procedures because of suspicions of abuse, including possible unilateral behaviour by the pharmaceutical producer Servier which may have the object or effect of hindering the market entry of certain generic medicine[562] and thereby infringing Article 102 TFEU, and Lundbeck possibly engaging in abusive measures to prevent competitors from producing a generic version of its product Citalopram.[563]

7. Product Tying, Bundling and Discounts

Article 102(d) TFEU specifies that making the conclusion of contracts subject to acceptance by the other party of supplementary obligations which, by their nature or according to commercial usage, have no connection with the subject matter of the original contract constitutes abuse of a dominant position. A number of commonly-used business techniques can fall into this category – i.e. making the purchase of one product dependent on the purchase of another (tying) or offering the sale of one product on better terms if a second product is also purchased (grouping). If a dominant undertaking engages in these kinds of behaviours, they can lead to an abuse of a dominant position – a hindering of competition in the market.[564] In addition to abuse of a dominant position in the original product market, such tying or bundling can also constitute an abuse on the second market (that of the coupled or bundled product) as well.

a) Market Power Transference

An undertaking which holds a dominant position on one market can also be held to be abusive on a neighbouring market.[565] An undertaking which enjoys a quasi-monopoly on

---

559   Case T-321/05, *AstraZeneca*, in particular paras. 666 et seq.

560   For details see Chapter 2, Section IV(2)(a) (*Example: Deutsche Telekom*).

561   Executive Summary of the Pharmaceutical Sector Inquiry Report, 8 July 2009, in particular pp. 9–17, available on the Internet at <http://ec.europa.eu/competition/sectors/pharmaceuticals/inquiry/index.html> (last accessed on 19 April 2011).

562   Commission, MEMO/09/322 of 7 August 2009.

563   Commission, IP/10/8 of 1 July 2010.

564   Commission, Guidance on the Commission's enforcement priorities in applying Article 82 of the EC Treaty to abusive exclusionary conduct by dominant undertakings, [2009] OJ C45/7, para. 49.

565   Joined Cases 6/73 and 7/73, *Commercial Solvents*, [1974] ECR 223, para. 25.

a particular market and a leading position on a distinct, though closely associated, market is placed in a situation comparable to that of holding a dominant position on those markets as a whole, and therefore abusive behaviour on the second, related market may also be caught by the prohibition contained in Article 102 TFEU.[566]

In the case of *Microsoft*, the Commission argued (and the General Court upheld) that Microsoft's tying of its media streaming player (Windows Media Player ("WMP")) to its Windows operating system was abusive, as Microsoft was dominant on the market for computer operating systems.[567] As a consequence the Commission required that Microsoft offered a version of Windows which does not include WMP and to refrain from using other means which would have the equivalent effect of tying WMP to Windows operating system – i.e. including WMP for a discount price, or making it easier for customers to choose WMP over another media player.[568]

Various other examples of market power transference also exist. An undertaking in a dominant position may not restrict the use of spare parts manufactured by another undertaking in the dominant undertaking's main products, e.g. by itself refusing to supply parts, applying discriminatory policies to customers whom it suspects of using the other manufacturer's parts or refusing to honour guarantees for its products when they have been used in conjunction with other manufacturers' spare parts.[569] A tying bundle rebate, i.e. the granting of a rebate following the purchase of several products from the same manufacturer, can be abusive if it is so large that equally efficient competitors who offer only one of the products cannot compete with the discounted product bundle.[570] Finally, a refusal to supply can be abusive, even in the absence of a product grouping, if the supply of the products or services in question is essential for competitive activity in a neighbouring market.

b) Discount Practices – Intel

In the summer of 2009, the Commission imposed one of its highest fines ever (EUR 1.06 billion) on Intel for Intel's infringement of Article 102 TFEU. The Commission found two elements of the infringement: (i) the granting of hidden rebates to computer manufacturers who purchased all, or almost all, of their computer processing units from Intel and (ii) the making of payments by Intel to computer manufacturers to stop or delay the launch of products containing Intel's competitors' components and to limit the sales channels available for these products.[571]

---

566 Case C-333/94 P, *Tetra Pak II*, [1996] ECR I-5951, para. 31.

567 *Microsoft* (Case COMP/C-3/37.792), Commission Decision, paras. 979–984; main points upheld in Case T-201/04, *Microsoft*, [2007] ECR II-1491; cf. also the rejection of Microsoft's request for provisional legal protection by the General Court, Case T-201/04, *Microsoft*, [2007] ECR II-1491.

568 *Microsoft* (Case COMP/C-3/37.792), Commission Decision, paras. 1101–1014.

569 Cf. Case T-30/89, *Hilti*, [1991] ECR II-1439, para. 68 where the General Court states that generally "any independent producer is quite free, as far as Community competition law is concerned, to manufacture consumables intended for use in equipment manufactured by others, unless in doing so it infringes a patent or some other industrial or intellectual property right".

570 Commission, Guidance on the Commission's enforcement priorities in applying Article 82 of the EC Treaty to abusive exclusionary conduct by dominant undertakings, [2009] OJ C45/7, para. 59.

571 *Intel* (Case COMP/C-3/37.990), Commission Decision, paras. 917, 1640, 1737.

European case law had clearly established that the granting of discounts which related to an undertaking purchasing all or a substantial share of its products from a dominant undertaking were abusive under Article 102 TFEU.[572] Such was held to be the case here, as the Commission found that Intel's practice of granting rebates to computer manufacturers was conditional upon those companies purchasing all or nearly all of their computer processing units from Intel, and thereby restricting those companies' freedom to choose their suppliers.[573] In addition, Intel's restriction of the development of products containing its competitors' components and the narrowing of sales channels available to those products infringed Article 102 TFEU, as it limited competition on the final user market and had the potential to edge other suppliers out of the market – clearly abusive behaviour according to European case law.[574]

8. Predatory Behaviour

Infringements of Article 102 TFEU can include a variety of behaviours by dominant undertakings beyond price-setting. Predatory behaviour can include, for example, as in the case of *Tetra Pak*:
- obtaining an agreement from a supplier not to use machines which the supplier had acquired from competitors of Tetra Pak;
- edging out almost all packaging machines of a certain type in Italy which had been developed by a competing undertaking; and
- appropriating advertising media by obtaining an oral exclusive rights agreement for the largest specialist journal on the dairy industry in Italy.[575]

The case of *AKZO* highlighted one difference between normal competitive behaviour and predatory behaviour. AKZO obtained information from its customers regarding the terms and prices of offers made by other suppliers of flour additives and then itself offered a price just below the lowest competing offer. In addition, AKZO sometimes required that the customer obtained its total product requirements from AKZO. This behaviour served to displace competitors and went beyond normal competitive conduct, thereby constituting abuse for the purposes of Article 102 TFEU.[576]

---

572   Case 85/76, *Hoffmann-La Roche*, [1979] ECR 461, para. 89.

573   *Intel* (Case COMP/C-3/37.990), Commission Decision, para. 924.

574   See for example Case T-228/97, *Irish Sugar*, [1999] ECR II-2969, para. 233.

575   Case T-83/91, *Tetra Pak*, [1994] ECR II-755, paras. 212 et seq.

576   Case C-62/86, *Akzo*, [1991] ECR I-3359, paras. 147 et seq.

IV. THE RELATIONSHIP BETWEEN ARTICLES 101 AND 102 TFEU

Articles 101 and 102 TFEU stand shoulder to shoulder – they apply independently of each other and are complementary. As such, the fact that an undertaking's behaviour is capable of exemption under Article 101(3) TFEU does not mean that such behaviour is not capable of infringing Article 102.[577] Article 101 TFEU operates to identify whether an infringement of competition law has occurred and then, once an infringement has indeed been identified, to establish whether such infringement is capable of benefiting from the Article 101(3) TFEU exemption. In contrast, Article 102 TFEU only seeks to identify the existence of abuse, with no further analysis of exceptionality. However, in practice, both the Commission and the European courts undertake a *de facto* analysis of exemption, as the analysis of infringing behaviour also includes a consideration of any positive effects.[578]

---

577 Case T-51/89, *Tetra Pak*, [1990] ECR II-309, paras. 25, 29, 30.
578 Cf. Case T-193/02, *Laurent Piau*, [2005] ECR II-209, para. 119.

Chapter Five

THE ARTICLE 106(2) TFEU EXEMPTION

Article 106 TFEU

"1. In the case of public undertakings and undertakings to which Member States grant special or exclusive rights, Member States shall neither enact nor maintain in force any measure contrary to the rules contained in the Treaties, in particular to those rules provided for in Article 18 and Articles 101 to 109.

2. Undertakings entrusted with the operation of services of general economic interest or having the character of a revenue-producing monopoly shall be subject to the rules contained in the Treaties, in particular to the rules on competition, in so far as the application of such rules does not obstruct the performance, in law or in fact, of the particular tasks assigned to them. The development of trade must not be affected to such an extent as would be contrary to the interests of the Union.

3. The Commission shall ensure the application of the provisions of this Article and shall, where necessary, address appropriate directives or decisions to Member States."

Article 106(2) TFEU limits the application of the rules contained in the TFEU and TEU (and in particular, competition rules) to certain kinds of undertakings. This provision is in addition to any other exclusions (e.g. those contained in Articles 36, 51 and 52 TFEU), however, it applies *after* other exclusions – i.e. if Article 36 applies, then Article 106(2) is not necessary. Only if no other exclusionary provision is applicable, does Article 106(2) TFEU become relevant.

The scope of the Article 106(2) TFEU exemption has grown rapidly over recent years. In the early 1990s some commentators claimed that this exemption provision was "obsolete",[579] however, in the years following Article 106(2) TFEU has been the subject of renewed consideration. In particular, the European Union has tried to balance the economic and socio-political objectives of its Member States on the one hand, and the Union-wide benefits of protecting genuine competition in the internal market on the other hand.[580] The starting point for a resolution of these two priorities has been the question of the scope of the European prohibition on State aid – the realm within which Article 106(2) TFEU plays its greatest role.

---

579   Pappalando, Sleeping Beauty, ECLRev. 1991, p. 29 (30).

580   See Case C-202/88, *France v Commission,* [1991] ECR I-1223, paras. 11 et seq; Case C-67/96, *Albany International,* [1999] ECR I-5751, para. 103; Case T-289/03, *BUPA-Ireland,* [2008] ECR II-81, para. 163.

I. "UNDERTAKINGS" IN ARTICLE 106(2) TFEU

Article 106(2) TFEU favours certain types of undertakings above others: specifically, undertakings which (i) have been entrusted by a State with the provision of services of general economic interest or (ii) have the character of a revenue-producing monopoly. Here, the concept of an "undertaking" is the same as applies in relation to the rest of European competition law, and in particular Articles 101 and 102 TFEU.[581]

In order to determine whether an undertaking can benefit from the Article 106(2) TFEU exemption, a two-step analysis is required. First, it must be determined whether an undertaking does provide or did provide services of general economic interest or possesses the character of a revenue-producing monopoly. Second, and of paramount importance, is whether the Member State has entrusted the operation of the relevant services to the undertaking (an 'entrusting act'). Furthermore, the exemption may only hinder the application of the rules of competition set out in the Treaties to the extent that restrictions on competition, or even the exclusion of all competition by other economic operators, is necessary to ensure the performance of the particular tasks assigned to the undertaking holding the exclusive rights.[582]

II. SERVICES OF GENERAL ECONOMIC INTEREST

The first condition for the applicability of Article 106(2) is that an undertaking must now, or have in past, provided services of general economic interest. The concept of "services of general economic interest" is therefore a Union rather than national concept.[583] Though Member States possess a wide discretion as to the definition of the *content* of such services, the act of entrustment must nonetheless define the *scope* of entrusted services rather precisely.

> The Commission takes the approach that this concept refers to "services of an economic nature which the Member States or the Community [following the Lisbon Treaty, the Union] subject to specific public service obligations by virtue of a general interest criterion".[584]

Such services include in particular those relating to water supply and disposal, transport services, healthcare systems (in particular the provision of sufficient hospitals as well as transportation of ill persons and rescue services), universal postal services, waste management and disposal, environmental protection and public housing.

---

581 On the concept of an "undertaking" see Chapter 2, Section II (*Elements of an Infringement: an Undertaking's Actions*) – Section IV (*Member States*).

582 Case C-475/99, *Ambulanz Glöckner*, [2001] ECR I-8089, para. 56.

583 See Case 41/83, *Italy v Commission*, [1985] ECR 873, para. 30; Case T-260/94, *Air Inter*, [1997] ECR II-997, para. 135.

584 Commission, White Paper on services of general interest, COM(2004) 374 final, Annex 1, p. 22; Commission, Green Paper on services of general interest, COM(2003) 270 final, para. 17.

The concept of "services of general economic interest" appears not only in Article 106(2) TFEU but also in Article 14 TFEU and Article 36 of the Charter of Fundamental Rights, where their role in promoting social and territorial cohesion is noted. Article 14 TFEU highlights the importance of such services generally, whilst Article 36 of the Charter of Fundamental Rights goes further and states that the Union "recognises and respects access to services of general economic interest as provided for in national laws and practices" in accordance with European primary law.

1. Services of Economic Interest

The concept of *services* is well defined in European law. Article 57 TFEU sets out that services "shall be considered to be 'services' within the meaning of the Treaties where they are normally provided for remuneration ... where such services do not relate to the freedoms of movement for goods, capital and persons".

The requirement of specifically economic activity derives from both the text of Article 106(2) TFEU as well as from the system of EU competition law generally and the internal market freedoms. In particular the definition of an undertaking within the context of European competition law assumes such market-related activity; indeed in the absence of such activity, the relevant entity is not considered an undertaking at all and consequently cannot be subject to European competition law rules.

Article 106(2) TFEU focuses most often on exempting certain economic activity from competition rules on account of non-economic aims. On this basis, the Article 106(2) TFEU exemption does not apply merely in cases of an economic interest, but rather on the basis of politically-determined public objectives. It is incorrect to see competition rules and services of a general economic interest as opposing each other. Instead, in most cases, the existence of such services and the rules of competition law interact successfully, given the existence of a legal framework for excluding such services from competition rules in desirable circumstances.[585]

Because few relevant activities contain really no element of an economic character, the scope of application of Article 106(2) TFEU is broad – it frequently applies to fulfil charitable, public welfare-related, social and cultural purposes which are perhaps only partly (rather than fully) economic activity.

Examples:
Examples of economic services acknowledged by the European courts include environmental protection in the area of waste disposal,[586] the guarantee of public security in harbours,[587] compulsory affiliation with a sectoral pension fund[588] and the universal supply of electricity and gas at the lowest possible cost and in a socially responsible man-

---

585 See also Chapter 5, Section III (*'Entrustment' of an Undertaking*) and Chapter 8, Section IV(3) (*Article 106(2) TFEU in the Context of State Aid*).

586 Case C-209/98, *FFAD*, [2000] ECR I-3743, para. 75.

587 Case C-266/96, *Corsica Ferries*, [1998] ECR I-3949; Case 10/71, *Luxembourg public prosecutor*, [1971] ECR 723, paras. 8, 12.

588 Case C-67/96, *Albany International*, [1999] ECR I-5751, para. 98.

ner.[589] Thus, for example, the provision of a universal service for a non-economic purpose which, by necessity, is accompanied by economic activity in a relevant market can still be considered a service of general economic interest.[590]

The General Court recognised that a public law broadcasting company provides a service of general economic interest when it stressed that such classification is based on the *de facto* impact of public service broadcasting on the otherwise competitive and commercial broadcasting sector, rather than on the alleged commercial dimension to broadcasting.[591]

Therefore, the existence of economic activity is interpreted broadly. It does not exist solely in traditional economic activity, but rather also within the context of any economic effects of the provision of that service.

2. Services of General Interest

The service provided must also be in the public interest. No comprehensive definition currently exists for 'the public interest'; what qualifies as such is a question of fact in each individual case rather than an issue of technical classification.

It is clear that activities in the public interest do not include, in any case, purely private interests[592] which profit individual economic participants; activities in the public interest would include those which benefit the public generally. In light of Member States' freedom to act in their national interests, it is not necessary for a service to be in the interests of the Union as a whole; it is sufficient for the service to be in the interest of a particular region or segment of the population of a Member State.

> Services of general economic interest are those which are of direct benefit to the public.[593]

European jurisprudence indicates consistently that services which operate "on behalf of all users throughout the territory of the Member State concerned ... irrespective of the specific situations or the degree of economic profitability of each individual operation" are considered to be in the public interest.[594] Additionally, a service of limited territorial or material application, or one which benefits only a relatively limited group of users can still be a service of general economic interest.[595]

---

589   Case C-159/94, *EDF,* [1997] ECR I-5815, para. 58.

590   See Case C-475/99, *Ambulanz Glöckner,* [2001] ECR I-8089, para. 55; also Joined Cases T-528/93, T-542/93, T-543/93 and T-546/93, *Métropole television,* [1996] ECR II-649, para. 116.

591   Case T-442/03, *SIC,* [2008] ECR II-1161, paras. 3, 153.

592   Case 127/73, *BRT II,* [1974] ECR 313, para. 23; Case T-289/03, *BUPA-Ireland,* [2008] ECR II-81, paras. 178 et seq.

593   Opinion of Advocate General Van Gerven, Case C-179/90, *Porto di Genova,* [1991] ECR I-5889, para. 27; Opinion of Advocate General Darmon, Case C-393/92, *Almelo,* [1994] ECR I-1477, para. 137.

594   Joined Cases T-528/93, T-542/93, T-543/93 and T-546/93, *Métropole television,* [1996] ECR II-649, para. 116.

595   Case T-289/3, *BUPA-Ireland,* [2008] ECR II-81, para. 4.

3. Union-Level Regulation – Member State Discretion

Even if the concept of "services of general economic interest" is a Union-level concept, Member States still have a wide discretion in classifying services as being in the general economic interest.[596] Rather than delving into the details of a Member State's analysis, the Commission and the European courts limit themselves to examining whether the discretion left to Member States is being abused.[597] It is also the case that Member States have a greater degree of discretion in sectors which are not subject to Union-level harmonising regulation, than in sectors which are highly harmonised.[598]

This approach corresponds to the existing manner of interpreting Article 106(2) TFEU within the context of Article 14 as well as the Commission's Communication on Services of General Economic Interest.[599] Every Member State is obliged to ensure that providers of services of general economic interest are able to fulfil their missions, though it is not necessary that the State itself provides such services. Member States have a discretion in identifying when services are in the general interest, the conditions under which a supplier of such services operates and the extent to which the supplier is supported (e.g. financially) by the Member State.[600] In this way it is possible that the concept of services of general economic interest varies from Member State to Member State.

Following the Lisbon Treaty, Article 14 TFEU grants legislative competence to the European Parliament and the Council to establish the principles of and set conditions relating to services of general economic interest. However, that Article does not seek to impose comprehensive harmonisation in the realm of services of general economic interest – it does not affect the Member States' discretion. This is evident from the wording in that Article itself: Member States and the Union can only act "within the scope of their respective powers and within the scope of application of the Treaties".[601] The European Parliament and the Council are deemed to have legislative powers only as regards 'establishing principles' and 'setting conditions' "without prejudice to the competence of Member States ... to provide, to commission and to fund such services".

---

596 See Case 41/83, *Italy v Commission*, [1985] ECR 873, para. 30; Case T-260/4, *Air Inter*, [1997] ECR II-997, para. 135.

597 See Case C-67/96, *Albany International*, [1999] ECR I-5751, para. 107; Case C-202/88, *France v Commission*, [1991] ECR I-1223, para. 12; Case C-157/94, *Commission v Netherlands*, [1997] ECR I-5699, paras. 38 et seq.; Case T-17/02, *Olsen*, [2005] ECR II-2031, para. 216; Opinion of Advocate General Léger, Case C-309/99, *Wouters*, [2002] ECR I-1577, para. 162.

598 [2001] OJ C17/4.

599 Cf. [2001] OJ C17/4, para. 22.

600 Commission, Services of general economic interest in Europe, [2001] OJ C17/4, para. 22. See also Case C-265/08, *Federutility*, para. 29 for details of the application of Article 106(2) TFEU in a harmonised market.

601 See also Commission, White Paper on services of general interest, COM(2004) 374 final, where para. 2.3 states with regard to the new wording of Article 16 EC (which is the same as the one in the Treaty of Lisbon in this respect): "Nevertheless, it is primarily for the relevant national, regional and local authorities to define, organise, finance and monitor services of general interest. This shared responsibility is the concept underlying the provision of Article 16 of the EC Treaty."

4. Example: British United Provident Association Ltd. (BUPA)

> Does an obligation to make private health insurance universally available consti-
> tute a service of general economic interest?

The case of *BUPA* involved Irish legislation which imposed a risk equalisation scheme on
the Irish private insurance market. It was evident in Ireland that certain private insurers
(who offered insurance cover supplementary to the universal public health insurance system) had a disproportionate share of young, healthy subscribers whereas other insurers
had a disproportionate share of older people who are more prone to illness. An advisory
board to the Irish government proposed a risk equalisation scheme which would have the
effect of making individual insurance providers each bear the costs which it would have
had to bear if its own risk profile was equal to the average market risk profile. This was
done via a system of transfers of payments from insurers whose customers' risk profile
was healthier than the average market risk profile, to insurers whose customers' risk
profile was less healthy than the average market risk profile. In practice, BUPA would
be making payments to other private insurers and BUPA complained to the Commission
that the proposed risk equalisation scheme infringed European State aid law.

The Commission took the view that the risk equalisation scheme did not constitute
State aid, or that even if it did constitute State aid, that it could be declared compatible
with the common market pursuant to Article 106(2) TFEU as it related to undertakings
entrusted with the operation of a service of general economic interest.[602] BUPA contested
the decision that the services provided by private insurers constituted services of general
economic interest.

It fell to the General Court to consider whether the Commission's approval of the Irish
government's identification of services of general economic interest was manifestly incorrect.

Indicating services of general economic interest were present:	Indicating services of general economic interest were not present:
Private insurers were subject to open enrol-ment requirements – i.e. they were obliged to offer private insurance to any person request-ing such a contract, independently of his age, sex, health status, etc. (ensuring that even old or chronically ill persons were covered). Cover was also lifelong, meaning that insurers could not reject policy-holders when they became sick or old.[603]	BUPA argued that it was not correct to say that private insurers were obliged to accept any person for cover – they could actually exclude persons over 65 seeking cover for the first time and impose 'waiting periods' before cover was effective for pre-existing conditions.[604]

602   Case T-289/03, *BUPA-Ireland*, [2008] ECR II-81, paras. 39–41.

603   Case T-289/03, *BUPA-Ireland*, [2008] ECR II-81, para. 41.

604   Case T-289/03, *BUPA-Ireland*, [2008] ECR II-81, para. 106.

Indicating services of general economic interest were present:	Indicating services of general economic interest were not present:
Regulations on minimum benefits ensured certain minimum standards for all persons covered by private insurance.[605]	None of the relevant Irish legislation imposed an obligation on private insurers to provide services, much less a minimum level of those services. The legislation was simply regulatory oversight of the provision of a service.[606]
Insurers were obliged to apply the same premium to all policy-holders for the same type of product irrespective of their health status, age or sex, ensuring solidarity between the generations.[607]	Private insurers were free to set prices and offer products as they liked[608] and such prices and products were determined by market forces.[609] Ultimately, private medical insurance was in addition to universal public healthcare, and therefore did not constitute a service of general economic interest.[610]

The General Court noted that Member States possess a wide discretion to define what they regard as services of general economic interest and that the definition of such services can only be questioned by the Commission in the event of manifest error.[611] Further, it is not necessary that the service in question affect the whole of a population or the whole of the territory of a Member State – it must not be 'universal' in a narrow sense. The fact that a service has only a limited territorial or material application, or that the service is enjoyed by only a relatively limited group of users, does not necessarily call into question the universal nature of a service of general economic interest within the meaning of Union law. Nor is it necessary that the service be offered without an intention to make profit, or that the price of the service to consumers be capped.[612]

In this case, the General Court therefore held that the provision of supplementary private medical insurance constituted a service of general economic interest and thus remained outside the scope of Union State aid regulation.

III. "ENTRUSTMENT" OF AN UNDERTAKING

Another requirement of Article 106(2) TFEU is that an undertaking must have been *entrusted* specifically with the task of providing a service of a general economic interest. The entrustment must come from a sovereign act of the Member State which imposes certain public obligations. Such entrustment can take the form of, for example, legislation,

---

605   Case T-289/03, *BUPA-Ireland,* [2008] ECR II-81, para. 41.

606   Case T-289/03, *BUPA-Ireland,* [2008] ECR II-81, para. 105.

607   Case T-289/03, *BUPA-Ireland,* [2008] ECR II-81, para 41.

608   Case T-289/03, *BUPA-Ireland,* [2008] ECR II-81, para. 42.

609   Case T-289/03, *BUPA-Ireland,* [2008] ECR II-81, para. 107.

610   Case T-289/03, *BUPA-Ireland,* [2008] ECR II-81, para. 108.

611   Case T-289/03, *BUPA-Ireland,* [2008] ECR II-81, para. 172.

612   Case T-289/03, *BUPA-Ireland,* [2008] ECR II-81, paras. 4, 186–189.

the grant of a concession[613] or another act of public power. An instruction only, which the undertaking may or may not act upon, is insufficient.

The official act of entrustment with which a Member State entrusts an undertaking should be sufficiently precise to ensure that the conditions of Article 106(2) TFEU are met.

> The act must specify, in particular:
> (1) the nature and the duration of the public service obligations;
> (2) the undertaking and territory concerned;
> (3) the nature of any exclusive or special rights assigned to the undertaking;
> (4) the parameters for calculating, controlling and reviewing any compensation; and
> (5) the arrangements for avoiding and repaying any overcompensation.[614]

Example:
In the case of *GVL*, an undertaking which managed copyright in Germany, the General Court held that it had not been entrusted with a service of general economic interest. Although the copyright management activity it undertook required governmental authorisation, the relevant German legislation did not confer copyright-related rights on it specifically; rather, it defined in a general manner the rules which applied to the activities of undertakings engaging in this kind of work.[615]

1. Example: British United Provident Association Ltd. (BUPA)

The question of whether private insurers were 'entrusted' with the provision of a service of general economic interest for the purposes of Article 106(2) TFEU was also dealt with in *BUPA*. At issue was whether private insurers had been entrusted with a specific public mission or were merely subject to 'normal' regulatory obligations.[616]

BUPA argued that a distinction must be drawn between the creation of obligations relating to services of general economic interest and the control and regulation of the activities of undertakings.[617] The general or public interest which is purportedly the purpose of the relevant services must not be reduced to a need to subject commercial activity on a market to certain rules or authorisation by the State; the mere fact that an industry is regulated in some way does not in principle mean that the undertakings operating in that market are entrusted with the provision of services of general economic interest.[618] A legal measure which regulates, imposes constraints on or requires prior authorisation in

---

613 Case C-159/94, *EDF,* [1997] ECR I-5815, paras. 65 et seq.

614 Article 4 of the Commission Decision 2005/842/EC of 28 November 2005 on the application of Article 86(2) of the EC Treaty to State aid in the form of public service compensation granted to certain undertakings entrusted with the operation of services of general economic interest, [2005] OJ L312/67.

615 Case 7/82, *GVL,* [1983] ECR 483, paras. 29–32.

616 Case T-289/03, *BUPA-Ireland,* [2008] ECR II-81, paras. 177 et seq.; see also Chapter 5, Section II(4) (*British United Provident Association Ltd. (BUPA)*).

617 Case T-289/03, *BUPA-Ireland,* [2008] ECR II-81, para. 98.

618 Case T-289/03, *BUPA-Ireland,* [2008] ECR II-81, para. 178.

which to operate does not constitute entrustment. Rather, entrustment only occurs when a State body imposes a particular, fixed mission to be achieved by the provider of the relevant service. Additionally, the Irish legislation was concerned with transfers of payments between undertakings operating in the market – it imposed no new obligations relating to the carrying out of insurance services on those undertakings. Thus, BUPA contended, the State had not entrusted the insurers with any services of general economic interest.[619]

The General Court disagreed with BUPA's analysis and held that the relevant Irish legislation did not involve merely regulation or authorisation of private insurers, but instead could be characterised as an act of a public authority creating and defining a specific mission relating to the provision of private insurance services. As various pieces of Irish legislation defined in detail the obligations of private insurance suppliers, and those suppliers served approximately 50 % of the Irish population (being the persons in possession of private medical insurance), it was clear that the freedom of private insurers was restricted beyond ordinary conditions of authorisation to operate in a specific sector.[620] The General Court was satisfied that the Irish legislation fulfilled the condition of a clear and precise definition of obligations relating to services of general economic interest. It was also not essential that undertakings be entrusted individually; it was sufficient for all operators in a market to be entrusted with the achievement of a mission.[621] Thus the legislation relating to the risk equalisation scheme constituted an entrustment for the purposes of Article 106(2) TFEU.

2. Example: Postal Services' Exemption from Value Added Tax ("VAT")

Article 113 TFEU provides for the harmonisation of certain kinds of taxes in the Union to the extent that such harmonisation is necessary to ensure the establishment and functioning of the internal market and to avoid distortion of competition. The case of *TNT Post* raised the issue of how to apply a tax exemption provided for in European law to the liberalised UK postal sector.

Directive 97/67 contained a provision specifying that "the supply by the public postal services ... and the supply of goods incidental thereto" shall be exempt from VAT.[622] Of particular issue in this case was what precisely constituted "public postal services". In the UK postal service providers operate under licences granted by the State. As part of its licence, the Royal Mail was required to provide the UK with a nationwide, comprehensive and affordable postal system accessible to by every natural and legal person. TNT had a license to convey letters in the UK, but was not a universal service provider and was not subject to any specific service obligations.

The UK tax authority allowed Royal Mail to be exempt from paying VAT on all the services it provided, not just those it was obliged to provide as universal services. TNT was not permitted to claim VAT exemption for any of its services. TNT challenged this

---

619   Case T-289/03, *BUPA-Ireland,* [2008] ECR II-81, para.130.

620   Case T-289/03, *BUPA-Ireland,* [2008] ECR II-81, paras. 3, 182.

621   Case T-289/03, *BUPA-Ireland,* [2008] ECR II-81, paras. 3, 183.

622   Article 132(1)(a) of Council Directive 2006/112/EC of 28 November 2006 on the common system of value added tax, [2006] OJ L347/1.

decision in the English courts, arguing that either (a) none of the postal services provided by Royal Mail should be exempt or (b) all postal services should be exempt no matter who supplied them. TNT also argued that (c) if it was the case that the exemption applied only to Royal Mail as the universal service provider, it should apply only to the universal services it was obliged to supply, rather than to all the services it offered.

The Court of Justice held that the tax exemption should be construed restrictively, applying only to the Royal Mail in its capacity of universal service provider, on the basis that a universal service provider is under a special obligation to provide certain services and is therefore in a different position to a wholly commercial enterprise.[623] However, the exemption should also only apply to the services provided by Royal Mail pursuant to its special role as a universal service provider; any other services offered by Royal Mail should not benefit from the tax exemption as those additional services did not serve the objective of Directive 97/67, which was to promote activity in the public interest.[624]

IV. OBSTRUCTION OF PERFORMANCE

The exemption contained in Article 106(2) is subject to two additional provisos. First, an undertaking is only exempt from competition rules insofar as those rules obstruct the undertaking's performance of the tasks assigned to it. Second, there exists a proportionality test, in that the exemption applies only if the development of trade is not affected to such an extent as would be contrary to the interests of the Union.

1. Obstruction of an Undertaking's Assigned Tasks

An undertaking can be obstructed from fulfilling its assigned tasks in two ways: legally or factually. A legal hindrance occurs when, absent Article 106(2) TFEU, an undertaking which carried out its assigned tasks would infringe a provision of European or national law. A factual hindrance occurs when Union legislation would make the carrying out of the undertaking's assigned tasks financially impossible.

European jurisprudence has established that an undertaking is obstructed from fulfilling its assigned tasks if it is not possible to do so under economically acceptable conditions.[625] The starting point of such analysis as set out in *Corbeau* is that the obligation on the relevant undertaking to carry out its assigned tasks presupposes that it will be possible to offset less profitable business areas against the profitable ones, and hence a restriction of the competition provided by other undertakings in profitable areas is justified.[626] If it were not possible to restrict competition in order to protect the activities of the universal service provider, other undertakings would seize upon profitable business

---

623   Case C-357/07, *TNT Post UK*, [2009] ECR I-3025, paras. 39, 40.

624   Case C-357/07, *TNT Post UK*, [2009] ECR I-3025, para. 49.

625   Joined Cases C-147/97 and C-148/97, *Deutsche Post*, [2000] ECR I-825, paras. 49 et seq.; Case C-340/99, *TNT Traco*, [2001] ECR I-4109, para. 54; see Case C-320/91, *Corbeau*, [1993] ECR I-2533, paras. 16 et seq.

626   Case C-320/91, *Corbeau*, [1993] ECR I-2533, para. 17.

areas ('cherry picking') and be able to offer services at a lower price than the universal service provider, as those undertakings would not have to cross-subsidise activity in unprofitable areas.

The European courts have also considered the extent to which restricting competition is necessary to allow an undertaking to carry out its assigned tasks under economically acceptable conditions.[627] It is not necessary for the purposes of Article 106(2) TFEU that the very existence of the entrusted undertaking is endangered.[628] In a series of judgments the language used by the European Courts to describe the test of an undertaking being 'obstructed' from carrying out its assigned tasks has been weakened to the degree of an undertaking's performance of the relevant task simply being "jeopardised".[629] However, it should be noted that much of the case law in this area is related to the energy sector, where long-standing monopolies meant that converting the sector to open competition would have required extensive measures at both Union and Member State level – measures which simply were not practicable at the time of the Courts' decisions. On that basis, one should not draw a general conclusion from the Courts' use of weakened language in these cases.

Article 106(2) TFEU invokes the concept of "obstruction", so it is not sufficient for a legal measure only to complicate or hinder the undertaking's performance of its assigned tasks. Analysis in each case must be objective, rather than subjective – i.e. obstruction does not depend on whether it is possible for *this* individual undertaking to carry out its assigned task. Rather, it is necessary to consider whether, objectively, it is possible for *an* undertaking to carry out its tasks whilst observing the relevant European law.

a) Example: British United Provident Association Ltd. (BUPA)

The *BUPA* case also required the General Court to determine whether the introduction of the risk equalisation system was necessary to ensure adequate provision of private health insurance services. An insurance system operates on the basis that premiums paid by old and ill persons are subsidised by those paid by young and healthy persons, i.e. 'solidarity between the generations'. The Court found that there was a link between additional costs to an insurer from having a negative risk profile, and that the public objectives private insurers were seeking to fulfil (i.e. open enrolment) could only be achieved with the use of a corrective measure such as the risk equalisation system.[630]

b) Example: International Mail Spain

The case of *International Mail Spain* originated with the Spanish government penalising International Mail Spain for providing postal services reserved to the national universal

---

627   Case C-320/91, *Corbeau*, [1993] ECR I-2533, para. 16; Case T-266/02, *Deutsche Post*, ECR [2008] II-1233, para. 74.

628   Case C-159/94, *EDF*, [1997] ECR I-5815, paras. 59, 95.

629   Case C-67/96, *Albany International*, [1999] ECR I-5751, para. 107; Case C-219/97, *Maatschappij Drijvende Bokken*, [1999] ECR I-6121, para. 97; Joined Cases C-147/97 and C-148/97, *Deutsche Post*, [2000] ECR I-825, para. 50.

630   Case T-289/03, *BUPA-Ireland*, [2008] ECR II-81, paras. 291 et seq.

postal service provider without the latter's authorisation. *Inter alia*, the Court of Justice had to determine whether Member States could reserve cross-border postal services solely to the supplier of the national universal service.[631]

European law[632] specified that, in view of the gradual liberalisation of cross-border postal services in the Union, the survival of national universal service providers was to be ensured via, *inter alia*, the reservation of certain postal activities to the universal service provider.[633] Therefore the Court of Justice held that it was acceptable for a Member State to ensure a universal service provider had the resources available to it to carry out its assigned tasks. It was not necessary for the financial balance or the essential economic survival of the entrusted undertaking to be threatened; rather, it was sufficient that the carrying out of the assigned tasks be endangered.[634]

The Court held in this case that the reservation of cross-border post to the universal service provider was justified if (a) in the absence of such reservation it would be impossible to achieve universal service and (b) the reservation is necessary to enable the universal service provider's tasks to be carried out under economically acceptable conditions.[635]

2. The Development of Trade

The second stage of determining the applicability of Article 106(2) TFEU is to consider whether the proposed exclusion would affect the development of trade to such an extent as would be contrary to the interest of the Union. This provision is not synonymous with the concept of trade between Member States under Articles 101 and 102 TFEU. For the purposes of Article 106(2) TFEU, analysis of the effects of an exemption involves considering the frequently diverging interests of the Union and Member States. The Union prioritises the principles set out in the Treaties and the aim of establishing and maintaining an internal market. Indeed, as per the Treaties themselves (e.g. Article 14 TFEU) a high value is also placed on the provision of services of general economic interest, and such value is not diminished by the effects of Article 106(2) TFEU.

3. Proportionality

Finally, Article 106(2) provides for a proportionality test which limits the compensation provided to the entrusted undertaking (e.g. the degree to which competition is limited) to the minimum necessary for that undertaking to be capable of performing its assigned tasks in economically acceptable conditions. Inherent in a full analysis of an exemption falling under Article 106(2) TFEU is a limiting of measures which are not necessary for

---

631   Case C-162/06, *International Mail Spain*, [2007] ECR I-9911, para. 2.

632   Directive 97/67/EC.

633   Case C-162/06, *International Mail Spain*, [2007] ECR I-9911, para. 27.

634   Case C-162/06, *International Mail Spain*, [2007] ECR I-9911, paras. 32 et seq.

635   Case C-162/06, *International Mail Spain*, [2007] ECR I-9911, para. 50.

the achievement of the public aims or which can be substituted with milder regulations having an equivalent effect. European jurisprudence has consistently asked whether "maintenance of those rights is necessary to enable the holder of them to perform the tasks of general economic interest assigned to it under economically acceptable conditions".[636]

V. THE COMMISSION'S COMPETENCE UNDER ARTICLE 106 TFEU

Article 106(3) TFEU empowers the Commission with special competence regarding the application and enforcement of Articles 106(1) and (2). Article 106(3) TFEU effectively places the Commission in the role of secondary legislative arbiter of the primary law set out in the Treaties. The Commission is able to address appropriate directives or decisions directly to Member States, without needing to consult the Council or the European Parliament.

The competence provided to the Commission under Article 106(2) TFEU goes substantially further than its competence in the usual legislative procedures (Articles 239 et seq.). Usually, the Commission is only entitled to propose a directive or a regulation, with the measure then being adopted by the Council and the Parliament pursuant to the codecision procedure.

Under Article 106(2) TFEU, the Commission has a discretion to act via a directive or a decision. To date, the factor determining which kind of measure it used was the nature of the addressee. If the measure relates to a single offence in one or more Member States, the Commission uses primarily decisions, which are directly binding on Member States (Article 288(4) TFEU). In the absence of competence to act via a directive, when seeking to enforce Article 106(2) TFEU, the Commission would have to initiate onerous and time consuming proceedings for a Treaty infringement under Article 258. If a measure is to be addressed to all Member States, the Commission uses a directive, which is also binding upon each Member State to which it is addressed, but only as to the result to be achieved, leaving it to the national authorities to choice the form and method by which the measure is implemented in national law (Article 288(3) TFEU).[637]

The Commission has made particular use of its Article 106(3) TFEU competence following the Transparency Directive. That Directive obliges Member States to disclose details of their financial relationships with their public undertakings as well as to use transparent accounting (particularly in relation to public industries). Thus it is easier for the Commission to identify the circumstances in which the Article 106(2) TFEU exclusion should, or should not apply.

---

636   Case C-157/94, *Commission v Netherlands*, [1997] ECR I-5699, para. 53; Case T-289/03, *BUPA-Ireland*, [2008] ECR II-81, para. 222; Joined Cases T-125/96 and T-152/96, *Boehringer v Council and Commission*, [1999] ECR II-3427, paras. 73 et seq.

637   Case C-202/88, *France v Commission*, [1991] ECR I-1223, paras. 23 et seq.

Chapter Six

THE COMMISSION'S COMPETENCE

Article 105(1) TFEU tasks the Commission with supervising the enforcement of Articles 101 and 102.[638] Under Article 105(1) TFEU the Commission is authorised to carry out investigations of suspected infringements of Articles 101 and 102 and, in the event of finding an infringement of one of these provisions, to propose appropriate measures to bring the infringement to an end (including issuing a decision setting out the conditions and details which, in the Commission's view, are necessary to remedy the situation). The practical means by which the Commission exercises its powers to enforce European competition law are set out in Council Regulation (EC) No 1/2003[639] ("Regulation 1/2003") and Commission Regulation (EC) No 773/2004[640] ("Regulation 773/2004") The Commission is an administrative authority that must act in the public interest, so investigations can be initiated both on the Commission's own initiative or upon a complaint from a third party.

The path from the Commission initiating an investigation of certain behaviour to the issuing of administrative measures on the grounds of Articles 101 and 102 TFEU involves three stages: preliminary proceedings, a phase of preliminary assessment and the final decision.

I. PRELIMINARY PROCEEDINGS

The Commission can initiate investigations on the basis of a complaint made by natural or legal persons who can show a legitimate interest in the matter[641] or on the basis of evidence otherwise obtained which may indicate anti-competitive behaviour. The Commission's primary law competence to investigate the possibility of anti-competitive behaviour is set out in Chapter V of Regulation 1/2003. In addition, prior to the initiation of the formal investigation procedure, the Commission may make use of its investigative powers generally (though it must inform the parties concerned that it is doing so).[642]

---

638 As to the Commission's responsibilities cf. Case C-344/98, *Masterfoods/HB Ice Cream*, [2000] ECR I-11369, para. 46.

639 Council Regulation (EC) No 1/2003 of 16 December 2002 on the implementation of the rules on competition laid down in Articles 81 and 82 of the Treaty [2003] OJ L1/1 ("Regulation 1/2003"). The Commission has recently published a report on the functioning of Regulation 1/2003, Report on the functioning of Regulation 1/2003, COM(2009) 206 final.

640 Commission Regulation (EC) No 773/2004 of 7 April 2004 relating to the conduct of proceedings by the Commission pursuant to Articles 81 and 82 of the EC Treaty [2004] OJ L123/18 ("Regulation 773/2004").

641 Commission, Notice on the handling of complaints by the Commission under Articles 81 and 82 of the EC Treaty, [2004] OJ C101/65, para 26.

642 Article 2(3) of Regulation 773/2004.

The aim of preliminary proceedings is to clarify the facts regarding the market behaviour of one or more undertakings in order to assess whether certain behaviour does indeed infringe Article 101 or 102 TFEU.

1. Powers of Investigation

Three formal powers of investigation are available to the Commission pursuant to Regulation 1/2003: requests for information (Article 18), power to take statements (Article 19) and powers of inspection (Articles 20 and 21). Informal inquiries such as informal requests for information are also possible, though addressees of such requests are under no obligation to provide information, nor can the provision of false information be sanctioned. Consequently a lower evidentiary value is attributed to information obtained through such informal procedures.

a) Formal Powers of Investigation

Article 18 of Regulation 1/2003 gives the Commission the power to obtain all necessary information from undertakings. Under Article 18 of Regulation 1/2003, the Commission has the choice to issue either a simple request pursuant to Article 18(2) or to proceed immediately to a decision requiring that information be provided.[643] Pursuant to Article 19 of that Regulation, the Commission has the power to take statements. The Commission is authorised to require all information necessary for the clarification of an undertaking's behaviour as well as to question natural and legal persons to obtain information in connection with the relevant behaviour. Although the addressees of such inquiries are not obliged to answer the Commission's queries, if they do so, such responses may not be incorrect or misleading. In the case of incorrect or misleading information, Article 23 of Regulation 1/2003 permits the Commission to impose a fine if such information was provided intentionally or negligently. Given the scope for financial penalties in relation to information provided in this manner, a greater evidentiary weight is given to such information. An additional instrument of inquiry is a formal request for information issued pursuant to Article 18(3) of Regulation 1/2003. The Commission's investigatory powers are backed up by an ability to set fines or penalty payments pursuant to Articles 23 and 24 of Regulation 1/2003.

The Commission's investigatory instruments are complementary – they can be used independently or in conjunction with each other. The choice as to which instruments the Commission employs depends upon the purpose of the investigation and must also take into account the principle of proportionality.

---

643 Commission, Staff working paper accompanying the Communication from the Commission to the European Parliament and the Council, SEC(2009) 574 final, para. 81.

b) Conditions Governing the Commission's Investigatory Powers

The Commission may only employ its formal instruments of investigation when it has concrete evidence of a potential offence (i.e. an initial suspicion) to justify using inquiry instruments to interfere with an undertaking's freedom to operate as it determines fit. Inquiries without an initial cause for suspicion (so-called 'fishing expeditions') are not permitted. Third parties (persons who are not suspected of infringing Article 101 or 102 TFEU) may only be addressees of inquiry instruments if the Commission has concrete evidence that those persons possess relevant information.

The Commission's use of an investigatory instrument presumes the existence of an initial suspicion that such instrument is objectively necessary for the clarification of the factual circumstances surrounding the alleged infringement. There must be a sufficient link between the investigative action and the aim of the investigation as a whole, i.e. the Commission must, from an *ex ante* point of view, be of the opinion that the specific investigative tool must be of use in analysing the alleged offence.[644] Additionally, the specific investigative instrument used must be proportionate,[645] e.g. the amount of work generated for the undertaking being investigated must be in proportion to the purposes of the inquiry.[646] In making such a determination the Commission must consider, *inter alia*, the (alleged) involvement of the undertaking in the offence, the gravity of the offence,[647] the possible (financial) costs to the undertaking and the impact of the Commission's provisional findings.

Finally, the Commission is obliged to disclose the nature and purpose of its investigation to the undertaking under investigation[648] to enable a legal analysis of the Commission's actions as well as to afford legal protection to the undertaking[649] and to establish clearly the undertaking's rights and obligations.[650]

2. Undertakings under Investigation: Their Rights and Obligations

The Commission can oblige addressees of formal investigations to cooperate actively with the Commission's inquiries – failure to cooperate can result in the Commission imposing fines (Article 23(1) of Regulation 1/2003) and/or periodic penalty payments (Article 24(1)(d) and (e) of Regulation 1/2003). However, an undertaking of course retains a right to safeguard its defence[651] and cooperate only within the scope of what is mandatory.[652]

---

644   Case 374/87, *Orkem*, [1989] ECR 3283, para. 15; Case T-39/90, *SEP*, [1991] ECR II-1497, paras. 29 et seq.

645   Case 136/79, *National Panasonic*, [1980] ECR 2033, paras. 29 et seq.

646   Cf. Joined Cases 46/87 and 227/88, *Hoechst AG*, [1989] ECR 2859, para. 19, 35; Case T-39/90, *SEP*, [1991] ECR II-1497, para. 51; Case T-340/04, *France Télécom SAT.*, [2007] ECR II-573, para. 147.

647   Case T-145/06, *Omya AG*, [2009] ECR II-145, para. 34.

648   Case T-340/04, *France Télécom SAT.*, [2007] ECR II-573, paras. 49 et seq.

649   Joined Cases 46/87 and 227/88, *Hoechst AG*, [1989] ECR 2859, paras. 20, 29.

650   Cf. Joined Cases 46/87 and 227/88, *Hoechst AG*, [1989] ECR 2859, para. 29; Case T-99/04, *AC-Treuhand AG*, [2008] ECR II-1501, para. 56.

651   This right is recognised as a general principle of law, see Joined Cases C-204/00 P, C-205/00 P, C-211/00 P, C-213/00 P, C-217/00 P and C-219/00 P, *Aalborg Portland A/S and others*, [2004] ECR I-123, para. 64.

652   Cf. Article 27(2) of Regulation 1/2003.

Examples:
- The Commission may only carry out its competence in the context of existing suspicions which form the basis of the investigation; it may not compel an undertaking to provide it with answers which might involve an admission of its part in the existence of an infringement (a right against self-incrimination).[653] However, an undertaking does not have an absolute right to silence – such a right would go beyond what is necessary in order to protect the rights of defence of undertakings and would constitute an unjustified hindrance to the Commission's performance of its investigative duties.[654]
- Correspondence between a lawyer and his client regarding independent legal advice is protected (legal professional privilege), meaning that the Commission cannot access such advice in the course of its investigation.[655] However, it should be noted that legal professional privilege applies only to correspondence with independent lawyers and *not* to in house lawyers (i.e. those employed by the undertaking).[656]

3. Sector Inquiries

In addition to cases relating to individual instances of alleged anti-competitive behaviour, the Commission can use its investigative powers to inquire into the functioning of a sector or industry, even without a specific initial allegation of wrongdoing (Article 17 of Regulation 1/2003). Such 'sector inquiries' have been used to investigate, *inter alia*, the energy[657] and pharmaceutical[658] sectors.[659] In order to commence such an inquiry, the Commission must have a reasonable suspicion that competition in this economic area is restricted or distorted. In the case of the pharmaceutical sector, the Commission's suspicions were triggered by a decline in innovation (seen as a fall in the number of new medicines arriving on the market) and a delay in generic medicines[660] arriving on the market.[661]

---

653 Cf. Joined Cases C-204/00 P, C-205/00 P, C-211/00 P, C-213/00 P, C-217/00 P and C-219/00 P, *Aalborg Portland A/S and others,* [2004] ECR I-123, para. 65; Joined Cases T-236/01, T-239/01 to T-246/01, T-251/01 and T-252/01, *Tokai Carbon,* [2004] ECR II-1181, para. 412; Case T-446/05, *Amann & Söhne,* para. 325.

654 Case T-446/05, *Amann & Söhne,* para. 326.

655 See Case 155/79, *AM&S,* [1982] ECR 1575, para. 18.

656 Opinion of Advocate General Kokott, Case C-550/07 P, *Akzo Nobel,* in particular paras. 58, 69.

657 Commission, Inquiry pursuant to Article 17 of Regulation (EC) No 1/2003 into the European gas and electricity sectors (Final Report), COM(2006) 851 final.

658 Commission, Executive Summary of the Pharmaceutical Sector Inquiry Report, 8 July 2009, available on the Internet at <http://ec.europa.eu/competition/sectors/pharmaceuticals/inquiry/index.html> (last accessed on 19 April 2011).

659 Cf. the overview in Commission, Report on the functioning of Regulation 1/2003, COM(2009) 206 final, paras. 63–67.

660 Generic medicines are imitator products which "copy" new medicines after the expiry of patent protection.

661 *Pharmaceutical sector inquiry – Inspection sanofi aventis* (Case COMP/39.514) Commission Decision, 3rd recital.

II. PRELIMINARY ASSESSMENT

If a preliminary assessment yields enough evidence of anti-competitive behaviour, the Commission will initiate formal proceedings pursuant to Article 11(6) of Regulation 1/2003 or Article 2 of Regulation 773/2004. The preliminary assessment sets the basis for the further investigation including evidentiary hearings and statements whilst taking into account the rights of the affected undertakings (due process of law).[662]

On account of the presumption of innocence until the Commission proves otherwise, the Commission may not make a final decision finding an infringement until the affected undertaking and its legal representatives have been permitted to exercise all procedural avenues available to them within the scope of a normal judicial procedure.[663] These avenues include in particular those set out in Article 27(1) of Regulation 1/2003 regarding hearings of the parties and complaints.[664]

III. DECISION BY THE COMMISSION

An inquiry by the Commission involves a formal decision being issued pursuant to Chapter III of Regulation 1/2003. There are four forms of decision that the Commission can issue pursuant to Regulation 1/2003: (i) a finding of an infringement and an order to terminate it (Article 7); (ii) interim measures (Article 8); (iii) commitments (Article 9) and (iv) a finding of non-applicability (Article 10). In addition, the Commission can, in certain circumstances (i.e. when it finds that certain behaviour is contrary to Article 103(3) TFEU), issue a decision withdrawing the benefit of an block exemption regulation which would, under other circumstances, have exempted the undertaking's anti-competitive behaviour (Article 29 of Regulation 1/2003).

1. Behavioural and Structural Remedies

When an infringement of Article 101 or 102 TFEU has been found, Article 7(1) of Regulation 1/2003 permits the Commission to require that an undertaking cease the behaviour causing the infringement and if necessary to implement structural or behavioural remedies to cease or neutralise the effects of the relevant behaviour. Behavioural remedies are usually straightforward (i.e. to cease a certain activity) and structural remedies include, for example, ordering the sale of a subsidiary undertaking.[665] However, the Commission can only impose structural remedies where there is no equally effective behavioural remedy or where an equally effective behavioural remedy would be more burdensome for the undertaking than the structural remedy.

In the event that an undertaking does not comply with such a decision by the Commission, the Commission can impose penalty payments (Article 24 of Regulation 1/2003)

---

662 Cf. in particular Articles 10–16 of Regulation 773/2004.

663 Cf. Joined Cases T-22/02 and T-23/02, *Sumitomo Chemical*, [2005] ECR II-4065, para. 106.

664 Set out in Articles 10–16 of Regulation 773/2004.

665 Cf. Case T-102/96, *Gencor*, [1999] ECR II-753, para. 319.

until the undertaking has complied. Additionally, the Commission can impose a separate fine for failure to comply with a binding commitment set out in a Commission decision (Article 23(2) of Regulation 1/2003).

2. Commitments

When an undertaking has offered commitments to address the Commission's concerns and the Commission has formalised those commitments in a decision, such commitments are binding on the undertaking under Article 9 of Regulation 1/2003. An undertaking's giving of commitments does not include an admission of guilt regarding the alleged infringement. It is also possible that notwithstanding the Commission's acceptance of an undertaking's commitments, a further infringement of Article 101 or 102 TFEU may be found.

A number of investigations into the energy sector were halted on the basis of commitments given by the relevant undertakings, and those commitments likely went beyond what the Commission could have achieved through further formal procedures.[666] For example, the vertically integrated German energy giants E.ON and RWE undertook to dispose of shares in their distribution network operators, i.e. ownership unbundling.[667] The consequence of such commitments was that the Commission was able effectively to implement ownership unbundling – whereas previously such structural changes had been achieved only in part, through the normal legislative procedure amending the electricity and gas directives.[668]

IV. THE BURDEN OF PROOF

Article 2 of Regulation 1/2003 places the burden of proof for establishing an infringement of Article 101 or 102 TFEU on the Commission. If such a level of proof is met, it then falls to the undertaking in question to prove that the conditions of the Article 101(3) TFEU exemption apply. However, the Commission is also obliged to check whether any justifications for the undertaking's anti-competitive behaviour exist.

---

666   As to this (political) issue see von Rosenberg, ECLR 2009, pp. 237 et seq.

667   *E.ON* (Case COMP/39.388 and COMP/39.389) Commission Decision; *RWE* (Case COMP/39.402) Commission Decision.

668   In contrast to the Commission's original intention, the new common rules for the internal markets in electricity (Directive 2009/72/EC) and natural gas (Directive 2009/73/EC) include the unbundling of property as one of a set of options only, alongside other structural measures.

V. LIMITATION PERIODS

The ability of the Commission to levy fines or impose penalty payments for an infringement of Article 101 or 102 TFEU is five years, as set out in Article 25(1) of Regulation 1/2003.[669] However, there is no statute of limitations on the Commission's ability to investigate an infringement of Article 101 or 102 themselves.

Article 25(2) of Regulation 1/2003 specifies that the limitation period shall begin to run on the day on which the infringement is committed. However, given the nature of many infringements of Article 101 or 102 TFEU, it may not be possible to identify the demarcation of an isolated offence in the context of a pattern of behaviour. The Courts have held that the concept of a continuous infringement comprises "a pattern of unlawful conduct implementing a single infringement, united by a common subjective element".[670] Key is that various infringement behaviours were engaged in for the purpose of achieving a specific economic aim. In such cases, i.e. continuing or repeated infringements, the statute of limitations begins to run on the day on which the infringement ceases.

Any action taken by the Commission or a national competition authority for the purposes of investigating an infringement interrupts the limitation period for the imposition of fines or periodic penalty payments,[671] with the specific date of interruption being the date on which the action is notified to the undertaking which has participated in the infringement.[672] If more than one undertaking was involved in the infringement, notice to one undertaking interrupts the limitation period for all undertakings involved.[673] After every interruption the limitation period begins again, i.e. a new five year period starts to run once more. However, a maximum ten year limitation period in total applies.[674] Additionally, the limitation period for the imposition of fines or periodic penalty payments is suspended for as long as the Commission's decision is the subject of proceedings before the European Courts.[675]

VI. APPEALS AGAINST COMMISSION DECISIONS

1. Primary Legal Protection

Commission decisions issued on the basis of Regulation 1/2003 or Regulation 773/2004 are subject to legal review by the European courts as set out in Article 263 TFEU (including an ability to annul Commission decisions).

---

669 The powers of the Commission to impose fines and penalty payments because of infringements of provisions concerning requests for information or the conduct of inspections shall be subject to a limitation period of three years (Article 25(1)(a) of Regulation 1/2003).

670 Case C-235/92 P, *Montecatini*, [1999] ECR I-4539, para. 195.

671 Article 25(3) of Regulation 1/2003.

672 Article 25(3) of Regulation 1/2003.

673 Article 25(4) of Regulation 1/2003.

674 Article 25(5) of Regulation 1/2003.

675 Article 25(6) of Regulation 1/2003.

2. Secondary Legal Protection

In the event that a Commission decision has been annulled by a European court and a natural or legal person (i.e. an undertaking to whom the decision was addressed or a third party) has suffered damage as a result, the injured party has a cause of action for damages. This is not an action against the Commission itself *per se*, but rather an action against the Union for damages caused by one of its institutions in that institution's performance of its duty. A claim for the annulment of a Commission decision and a claim for damages can be made in the same proceedings.[676]

> European jurisprudence has established that a claim for damages pursuant to Article 340(2) TFEU relating to a Commission decision must satisfy the following conditions:
> (1) the Commission's behaviour must have been found to be unlawful;
> (2) the party making the claim must actually have suffered damage; and
> (3) there must exist a causal link between the Commission's actions and the damage incurred.[677]

Additionally, the unlawful measure must constitute a sufficiently serious breach of a rule of law intended to confer rights on individuals. The decisive criterion is whether the Commission manifestly and gravely disregarded the limits of its discretion. In circumstances where the Commission has only a considerably reduced (or even no) discretion, then the mere infringement of Union law may be sufficient to establish the existence of a sufficiently serious breach of Union law.[678]

The European Courts take account of the complexity of situations to be regulated by European institutions, difficulties in the application or interpretation of legislation and the margin of discretion available to the institution.[679] For example, in the case of merger control[680] where the Commission's assessment requires analysis of complicated economic and financial circumstances, a greater latitude is granted to the Commission. Nonetheless, the Courts have not ruled out the possibility that "manifest and serious defects affecting the economic analysis underlying competition policy decisions may constitute sufficiently serious breaches of a rule of law" and therefore cause the Union to incur non-contractual liability.[681]

---

676 Cf. Case T-452/05, *BST.*

677 Recently Case T-452/05, *BST*, para. 163; see also Case T-351/03, *Schneider Electric*, [2007] ECR II-2237, paras. 114–118.

678 Case T-351/03, *Schneider Electric*, [2007] ECR II-2237, paras. 114–118.

679 Case T-351/03, *Schneider Electric*, [2007] ECR II-2237, para. 116.

680 Merger control is discussed in Chapter 7 (*Main features of European Merger Control*).

681 Case T-351/03, *Schneider Electric*, [2007] ECR II-2237, para. 129; upheld in Case C-440/07 P, *Commission v Schneider Electric*, [2009] ECR I-6413, in particular para. 173.

Example: Schneider Electric

In the case of *Schneider Electric* the General Court annulled the Commission's decision to prohibit a merger between Schneider and another electrical products undertaking called Legrand.[682] Following that judgment Schneider brought an action for damages of more than EUR 1.5 billion.[683] The General Court held in favour of Schneider, ordering the Commission to pay an amount totalling 2/3 of the loss suffered by Schneider as a result of the Commission's original decision.[684] However, on appeal from the Commission the Court of Justice overruled the General Court on the grounds of a lack of evidence of causation between the Commission's decision and the loss suffered by Schneider.[685]

This case highlighted two key aspects relating to the Commission's non-contractual liability. Given that the initial decision was annulled, the first question related to whether the Commission's breaches of European law were sufficiently serious to merit an award of damages; the second question related to the existence of a causal link between the Commission's actions and the damage suffered by Schneider.

a) Breach of Law – Sufficiently Serious

Schneider cited a discrepancy between the statement of objections it received from the Commission and one of the Commission's final decisions, claiming that this discrepancy deprived it of the opportunity to assess the Commission's claims fully.[686] Such a breach, Schneider alleged, was a breach of a rule intended to confer rights on individuals[687] – i.e. that it was deprived of its right to have its views taken into account.[688]

The General Court noted the importance of an undertaking's right to respond to Commission's proceeding at each step of the investigatory process, as only then could an undertaking react to the Commission's concerns and suggest measures which might alleviate those concerns and allow the proposed merger to go ahead. As regards merger control, this right afforded to an undertaking by the Union is of particular importance.[689]

Thus the General Court held that the Commission's drafting of the statement of objections constituted a manifest and serious breach of Schneider's rights, as it prevented that undertaking from proposing proper corrective measures which could have changed the outcome of the investigation. Additionally, such a breach could not be excused on either the grounds of the complexity of an investigation or the requirement for the communication of preliminary findings.[690]

---

682 Case T-310/01, *Schneider Electric*, [2002] ECR II-4071.

683 Case T-351/03, *Schneider Electric*, [2007] ECR II-2237.

684 Case T-351/03, *Schneider Electric*, [2007] ECR II-2237, para. 352.

685 Case C-440/07 P, *Commission v Schneider Electric*, [2009] ECR I-6413, para. 227.

686 Case T-351/03, *Schneider Electric*, [2007] ECR II-2237, para. 139.

687 Case T-351/03, *Schneider Electric*, [2007] ECR II-2237, para. 151.

688 Case T-351/03, *Schneider Electric*, [2007] ECR II-2237, paras. 145–147.

689 Case T-351/03, *Schneider Electric*, [2007] ECR II-2237, paras. 148 et seq.

690 Case T-351/03, *Schneider Electric*, [2007] ECR II-2237, paras. 152–157; upheld by Case C-440/07 P, *Commission v Schneider Electric*, [2009] ECR I-6413, in particular para. 173.

b) Causal Link between Actions and Damage

In *Schneider*, prior to the Commission issuing a decision claiming the merger would be incompatible with European competition law, Schneider had already acquired 98.1 % of Legrand's share capital. Thus the Commission sent a second statement of objections relating to a proposed order by the Commission that Schneider divest itself of assets in Legrand such that it no longer held a significant position. Schneider arrived at its claim for damages by comparing the price it paid for the shares in Legrand with the price for which it could sell them within the time frame allotted by the Commission.[691] However, the General Court held that such analysis was incorrect, as it presumed that, had Schneider's rights not been breached, the proposed merger would indeed have been permitted to go ahead – and this would not necessarily have been the case. Rather, the correct determination of a causal link was to consider what damages Schneider had sustained as a result of the Commission not having behaved in a lawful manner – i.e. having failed to undertake the procedural investigation properly.[692]

The General Court did find that the causal link, whilst insufficient to relate to the total difference between the price Schneider paid for the Legrand shares and the price for which it sold them, was sufficiently close to entitle Schneider to compensation for two types of damage it incurred. These were (i) the costs incurred by Schneider in participating in the renewed Commission investigation and (ii) a reduction in the sale price of the Legrand shares which Schneider had to grant to the purchaser of those shares to secure an agreement that the date on which the sale was to take place could be deferred until the Community Courts had made their ruling. This flexibility in the sale contract came at a financial cost to Schneider in the form of a lower sale price than might otherwise have been achieved.[693]

Also contained in the sale contract was an option in Schneider's favour permitting it to cancel the sale (i.e. if the European Courts ruled in its favour).[694] However, even after the General Court handed down its ruling that the Commission's decision ordering the divestment of the Legrand shares was annulled, Schneider nonetheless decided not to exercise its option to cancel the sale. This decision seemed to be on the basis that Schneider could not be certain that the Commission would not re-open proceedings and, this time after following the correct procedure, again find that the merger breached competition rules and again order divestment of the Legrand shares.[695]

When the Commission appealed the amount of damages granted to Schneider by the General Court, the Court of Justice queried whether, in light of Schneider's unilateral decision not to cancel the sale, a causal link could indeed be found between the Commission's breach of Schneider's rights in the course of the investigation and the lower price Schneider received upon sale of the Legrand shares.

691　Case T-351/03, *Schneider Electric*, [2007] ECR II-2237, para. 262.

692　Case T-351/03, *Schneider Electric*, [2007] ECR II-2237, paras. 263–268.

693　Case T-351/03, *Schneider Electric*, [2007] ECR II-2237, para. 288.

694　Case C-440/07 P, *Commission v Schneider Electric*, [2009] ECR I-6413, para. 200.

695　Case C-440/07 P, *Commission v Schneider Electric*, [2009] ECR I-6413, para. 202.

Indicating a causal link between the Commission's actions and the damage sustained:	Indicating no causal link between the Commission's actions and the damage sustained:
The necessity to enter into a contract for the sale of the Legrand shares and the discounted price contained in that agreement were a direct result of the Commission's unlawful decision.[696]	The discounted sale price was not directly causally linked to the unlawful Commission decision: the General Court had already made its ruling annulling the Commission's decision and yet Schneider decided to continue with the sale anyway.[697]
Schneider only entered into negotiations for the sale of the Legrand shares as a result of the Commission's unlawful decision, and felt forced, even after the General Court's ruling, to proceed with the sale due to the Commission's previous ruling.[698]	Schneider determined of its own volition to proceed with the sale of the Legrand shares on the basis of its concern that a new Commission investigation would also result in a decision requiring divestment.[699] Such an outcome is always a risk in competition proceedings and does not indicate causality for the purposes of damages.

Ultimately, the Court of Justice held that no causal link existed between the Commission's unlawful decision and the loss suffered by Schneider in disposing of its shares in Legrand, as Schneider's decision to do so was taken independently, not at the order of the Commission.[700]

VII. PRIVATE ENFORCEMENT OF COMPETITION LAW

Any civil claims relating to an infringement of Article 101 or 102 TFEU are to be asserted before the national courts. Technically Article 6 of Regulation 1/2003 is merely declaratory, as Articles 101 and 102 TFEU are directly effective,[701] but for the avoidance of doubt Article 6 of Regulation 1/2003 makes this point clear.

Civil claims regarding infringements of competition law are particularly important for the way that they can put a monetary value on the damage suffered by the average person as a result of anti-competitive behaviour.[702] Such claims also serve to encourage undertakings not to infringe competition law for the risk of incurring liability for damages, and thereby help in maintaining effective competition in the Union.[703]

As no Union law regulates civil claims in this area, the procedure for pursuing such claims is set out individually by the Member States.[704] In England and Wales such cases are brought before the High Court or, since the Enterprise Act 2002, the Competition

---

696 Cf. Case T-351/03, *Schneider Electric*, [2007] ECR II-2237, para. 288.

697 Case C-440/07 P, *Commission v Schneider Electric*, [2009] ECR I-6413, para. 204.

698 Case T-351/03, *Schneider Electric*, [2007] ECR II-2237, paras. 304–312.

699 Case C-440/07 P, *Commission v Schneider Electric*, [2009] ECR I-6413, para. 203.

700 Case C-440/07 P, *Commission v Schneider Electric*, [2009] ECR I-6413, paras. 205 et seq.

701 Case C-282/95 P, *Guérin automobiles*, [1997] ECR I-1503, para. 39.

702 De Bronett, Kommentar zum EU-Kartellverfahrensrecht, 2005, Article 6, para. 3.

703 Case C-453/99, *Courage v Crehan*, [2001] ECR I-6297, paras. 26 et seq.

704 Case C-453/99, *Courage v Crehan*, [2001] ECR I-6297, para. 29.

Appeals Tribunal on the grounds of the tort of breach of statutory duty.[705] The choice of court depends on whether there exists an Office of Fair Trading or Commission decision. If such a decision exists, once the appeals process has been exhausted, a third party may bring a claim for damages before the Competition Appeals Tribunal. If no such decision exists, claims must be brought in the High Court.

The private enforcement of European competition law is seen broadly as a positive development, with the Commission examining further options such as collective actions for damages by e.g. consumer bodies or other groups.[706] However, there are also some concerns of potentially developing an 'Americanised' system of litigation, dominated by a 'claims culture' and characterised by the award of punitive damages,[707] so we must wait to see how this area develops.

VIII. SCOPE OF EUROPEAN COMPETITION LAW

1. Scope of European Competition Law

The substantive range of application of European competition law is the whole of the internal market and all economic sectors, provided that the Treaties do not specify otherwise – for example the effect of normal competition rules on the production and trade of agricultural products is limited pursuant to Articles 38(2) and 42 TFEU.

The territorial range of application of European Competition law is twofold: it includes all undertakings with a seat in the Union's territory, as set out in the Treaties, as well as any undertakings whose behaviour impacts the internal market. In the case of undertakings with a seat in a Member State, Union jurisdiction applies to those undertakings, even if the anti-competitive measure itself was taken outside the geography of the Union (the 'territoriality principle'). Equally, undertakings which have no seat of business in a Member State but whose activities have a substantial effect in the territory of the Union are also subject to Union jurisdiction (the 'effects principle').[708]

2. Relationship with Competition Law in Member States

Articles 101 and 102 TFEU are directly applicable, so they can be applied by national competition authorities and national courts, provided that the anti-competitive activity in question has the potential to affect trade between Member States. European competition law can be applied in parallel to proceedings under national law. Article 3(1) of Regulation 1/2003 provides that when competition authorities or courts in Member States apply na-

---

705 The House of Lords ruled in *Garden Cottage Foods v Milk Marketing Board* that third parties can sue for damages for breach of competition law (1984) 1 AC 130, (1983) 3 CMLR 43.

706 Commission, White Paper on damages actions for breach of the EC antitrust rules, COM(2008) 165 final; Commission, Green Paper on consumer collective redress, COM(2008) 794 final. In February 2011, the Commission launched a public consultation, SEC(2011) 173 final.

707 Cf. European Parliament resolution of 26 March 2009 on the White Paper on damages actions for breach of the EC antitrust rules, TA (2009) 187; Alexander, WRP 2009, 683 et seq.

708 Case T-102/96, *Gencor,* [1999] ECR II-753, para. 90.

tional competition law to behaviour which potentially infringes Article 101 or 102 TFEU, they must apply the European competition provisions in addition to any national laws. However, the application of national competition law relating to infringements pursuant to Article 101 TFEU (insofar as it applies to anti-competitive behaviour which affects trade between Member States) may not lead to stricter competition controls than those provided for by European law. Thus Article 101 TFEU sets a Union-wide standard for the national enforcement of competition law relating to cartels. As regards unilateral conduct by undertakings, Member States are free to apply stricter controls than those set out in European law under Article 102 TFEU (Article 3(2) of Regulation 1/2003). However, in the area of merger control, if the proposed merger has an effect beyond the boundaries of an individual Member State then European, rather than national, law applies.

3. Cooperation between the Commission and National Competition Authorities

The Commission and Member States' national competition authorities cooperate closely in the 'European Competition Network'.[709] Such cooperation is necessary to ensure that whilst Member States can enforce European competition law fully, it is done so in a uniform manner. The Commission focuses on particularly serious anti-competitive offences, and pursuant to Article 16 of Regulation 1/2003, national authorities may not take decisions which would run counter to a decision adopted by the Commission. The allocation of duties within the network of public authorities is set out by the Commission in a notice.[710] It is intended that the network of European competition authorities operates as a forum for discussion and cooperation[711] and is based on the mutual exchange of information.

---

709 See for example Articles 11–14, 16(2), 22 and 35 of Regulation 1/2003.

710 Commission, Notice on cooperation within the Network of Competition Authorities, [2004] OJ C101/43; Commission, Notice on the co-operation between the Commission and the courts of the EU Member States in the application of Articles 81 and 82 EC, [2004] OJ C101/54.

711 De Bronett, Kommentar zum EU-Kartellverfahrensrecht, 2005, preliminary remark ("Vorbemerkung") to Articles 11 to 14, para. 1.

Chapter Seven

MAIN FEATURES OF EUROPEAN MERGER CONTROL

As is the case with other areas of European competition law, EU merger control[712] aims at protecting the internal market from distortions of competition. The focus of the rules on merger control lies in protecting market structures, which in turn enables competitive behaviour resulting in innovation and consumer benefits, and prevents the development of market concentrations which would damage competition and limit the freedom of action of individual market participants. Ultimately, merger control is tasked with ensuring that concentrations (i.e. takeovers or mergers) should not impede competition in the internal market.[713] Thus it may be the case that merger control prevents a planned concentration from occurring and preserves the status quo – not for the sake of the status quo, but rather in order to enable competition in the future.

Merger control shares with the other competition offences set out under Articles 101 and 102 TFEU the aim of preventing distortions of competition in the internal market, however the two aspects of competition law address the matter differently. The prohibitions on abuse of a dominant position and cartels under Articles 101 and 102 TFEU focus on infringements of competition law which have already occurred; they (generally) take a more *ex post* view of infringements and apply appropriate remedies or punishments. In contrast, merger control takes an *ex ante* view and seeks to prevent distortions of competition from occurring in the first place. In this way merger control is necessarily more speculative, as decisions must be taken on the basis of forecast information rather than the evidence of what has already occurred. Merger control also has a more intensive *regulatory impact* with regard to *ex ante* interventions than the prohibitions on abuse of a dominant position and cartels.

European law imposes a strict obligation on undertakings to notify certain proposed concentrations in advance of such mergers going ahead. If a proposed concentration is likely to alter market structure in a disadvantageous way, the rules on merger control allow for the merger to be prohibited or to be allowed to take place only under certain conditions. An *ex ante* consideration must take place, and with it, a forecast of the possible and likely effects of the proposed merger on competition in the internal market.

---

712 A note on terminology: In this chapter we refer to "merger" control as this is the term most frequently applied to this area of law. However, this phrase should be taken as including the control of all "concentrations" (e.g. mergers as well as the acquisition of a controlling interest), as in a number of European jurisdictions (including England and Wales) the concept of a "merger" does not exist.

713 Recital 5 of Council Regulation (EC) No 139/2004 of 20 January 2004 on the control of concentrations between undertakings, [2004] OJ L24/1 (the "Merger Regulation").

I. LEGAL BASES

European Union merger control finds its primary law legal base in Article 103 TFEU as well as the harmonising competence set out in Article 352. The real substance of this area of law is set out in secondary law, however: currently, Council Regulation (EC) No 139/2004 (the "Merger Regulation"). In spite of the differences between the prohibitions on abuse of a dominant position and cartels and merger control, each area of regulation is based on similar principles.

1. Example: "The Old Merger Control" under Articles 101 and 102 TFEU

In the case of *Continental Can*, the Court of Justice had to decide (prior to the existence of the first merger control regulation) whether Article 102 TFEU could be used to prohibit a market-dominant undertaking from acquiring 80 % of the shares in its competitor.[714] The Commission opposed this transaction on the basis that it contravened the prohibition on abuse of a dominant position.[715] The Court held that Article 102 TFEU applied to the behaviour of a dominant undertaking if that undertaking was proposing to strengthen its already dominant position on the market such that competition could not avoid being hindered substantially. Thus Article 102 TFEU (even in the absence of secondary legislation) could prohibit a merger or takeover by a dominant undertaking of its competitor.[716]

In *British American Tobacco*, the Court of Justice explained that a proposed acquisition by a dominant undertaking of a controlling interest in its competitor could be held to be anticompetitive pursuant to Article 101 TFEU even if the acquisition agreement contained no provision for commercial cooperation between the two undertakings.[717] This decision was on the basis that, once a dominant undertaking could exercise legal or *de facto* control of the acquired undertaking, there was nothing to prohibit the possibility that the dominant undertaking could alter its position or decide to exercise control at a later point in time.

Essentially, the protection to consumers offered by Articles 101 and 102 TFEU would be incomplete if the actions of undertakings could be curtailed only after abusive effects were felt, and not prior to an undertaking being placed in a position where it could act abusively in the first place. For this reason, the European Courts have held that Articles 101 and 102 TFEU also form a basis for *ex ante* merger control.

---

714 Case 6/72, *Continental Can*, [1973] ECR-215.

715 Case 6/72, *Continental Can*, [1973] ECR-215, para. 18.

716 Case 6/72, *Continental Can*, [1973] ECR- 215, paras. 25 et seq.

717 Joined Cases 142/84 and 156/84, *British American Tobacco*, [1987] ECR-4487, paras. 37–39.

2. Secondary Legislation

The detailed procedure through which merger control rules are implemented is set out in Commission Regulation (EC) No 802/2004 (the "Implementing Regulation").[718] The Commission has also issued additional guidelines, communications and notices to make clearer its priorities as well as the procedure through which it enforces merger control rules.[719] Key measures include guidelines regarding the assessment of horizontal mergers,[720] non-horizontal mergers[721] and the notice on accepted remedies.[722]

II. ADDRESSEES OF AND LIABILITY UNDER THE MERGER REGULATION

As is the case in the realm of Article 101 TFEU, for the purposes of the Merger Regulation it is important to differentiate between an operating undertaking, i.e. the entity active on a relevant market, and the question of which entity is responsible for said behaviour and therefore is the addressee of any Commission decision. In simple cases, this may be one and the same, but in other circumstances the issue may be more complicated.[723]

As regards the obligation to notify a proposed concentration under Article 4 of the Merger Regulation, that Regulation does not specify on whom the notification burden falls. Case law indicates that this obligation can fall on any number of legal or (in exceptional circumstances) natural persons who are responsible for the commercial decision to enter into the proposed concentration.[724]

---

718 Commission Regulation (EC) No 802/2004 implementing Council Regulation (EC) No 139/2004 on the control of concentrations between undertakings, [2004] OJ L133/1 (the "Implementing Regulation").

719 Such measures are available on the Commission's homepage <http://ec.europa.eu/competition/mergers/legislation/legislation.html> (last accessed on 19 April 2011).

720 Commission, Guidelines on the assessment of horizontal mergers under the Council Regulation on the control of concentrations between undertakings, [2004] OJ C31/5.

721 Commission, Guidelines on the assessment of non-horizontal mergers under the Council Regulation on the control of concentrations between undertakings, [2008] OJ C265/6.

722 Commission, Notice on remedies acceptable under Council Regulation (EC) No 139/2004 and under Commission Regulation (EC) No 802/2004, [2008] OJ C267/1.

723 For further details on this differentiation see Chapter 2, Section III (*Legal Consequences of an Infringement of European Competition Law: Who is the Addressee of a Decision?*).

724 The key factor in the determination is whether a natural person has influenced an undertaking's activities in the market. For further details see Commission, Consolidated Jurisdictional Notice under Council Regulation (EC) No 139/2004 on the control of concentrations between undertakings, [2008] OJ C95/1, para. 12.

III. CONCENTRATIONS WITH AN INTERNAL MARKET DIMENSION

The Merger Regulation applies to "all concentrations with a Community dimension"[725] as defined in Article 3 of that Regulation.[726] A concentration assumes a lasting change of control of the undertaking, resulting in a change in the corporate structure, which in turn has a lasting effect on the structure of competition in the market.[727]

1. Concentrations: Mergers and Acquisitions

The concept of a concentration under the Merger Regulation refers to the change of control on a lasting basis which results from (a) the merger of two or more previously independent undertakings or parts of undertakings or (b) the acquisition, by one or more undertakings,[728] of control of the whole or part of one or more other undertakings (e.g. the acquisition of shares in or the business and assets of an undertaking).[729]

In essence, a concentration arises if:

– two or more independent undertakings amalgamate into a new undertaking and cease to exist as separate legal entities;
– one undertaking is absorbed by another, the latter retaining its legal identity whilst the former ceases to exist as a legal entity;[730] or
– both entities cease to exist in their previous form and now exist as one 'new' legal entity and undertaking.

The reason for this broad description as to how concentrations arise lies in the fact that corporate law is not harmonised in the Union, so individual Member States each retain their own corporate legal structures and procedures. On that basis the wording of the Merger Regulation must be sufficiently broad to catch mergers and acquisitions of undertakings operating under a variety of national legal structures.

The key characteristic of a merger is that after the concentration only one undertaking (the resultant or surviving entity) remains on the market(s). Such a 'legal' concentration requires a change at the ultimate shareholder level; a bare change in a corporate group structure (for example as part of a group reorganisation) is insufficient. An 'economic' concentration can occur without any change in legal ownership – i.e. when the activities of previously independent undertakings results in the creation of a single economic

---

725 Following the Treaty of Lisbon the "European Community" is now termed the "European Union", so a new Merger Regulation would use the term "Union" rather than "Community" dimension. However, as the current Merger Regulation was enacted prior to Lisbon, the term "Community dimension" is still used.

726 The terms "concentration" and "Community dimension" are defined in Articles 1 and 3 of the Merger Regulation.

727 Recital 20 and Article 3(1) of the Merger Regulation.

728 Or by one or more persons already controlling at least one undertaking.

729 Article 3(1) of the Merger Regulation.

730 Cf. Commission, Consolidated Jurisdictional Notice under Council Regulation (EC) No 139/2004 on the control of concentrations between undertakings, [2008] OJ C95/1, para. 9.

unit.[731] Such is the case, for example, when two undertakings retain their legal independence, but enter into common economic management.[732]

2. Change of Control

Article 3(1) of the Merger Regulation refers to concentrations which come into existence upon 'a change of control'. Control, in turn, is described as being "constituted by rights, contracts or any other means which ... confer the possibility of exercising decisive influence on an undertaking".[733]

a) Acquiring of Control

In order for a change of control to occur, a (natural or legal) person[734] must acquire control of an undertaking from another person. Article 3(3) of the Merger Regulation describes two means by which control can be acquired. First, control may be acquired by persons or undertakings which are holders of the rights or entitled to rights under a contract (e.g. an acquisition agreement). Such control is direct, in that the acquirer can exert a decisive influence on an undertaking operating in the market, or that undertaking's parent company.

The second form of change of control addresses a situation where persons or undertakings are not the holders of direct contractual rights but nonetheless have the power to exercise rights deriving from such contracts. Here, a distinction is drawn between the person formally holding a controlling interest and the person who, in fact, has the real power to exercise controlling rights[735] – i.e. a special purpose vehicle may be used to acquire an undertaking, but the real controlling influence may be exercised by the shareholder of that special purpose vehicle. This kind of 'catch-all' is required to prevent a concentration from falling outside of the scope of the Merger Regulation on a pure technicality of ownership. Such indirect control can be indicated by financial or legal ties as well as personal relationships.[736]

Ultimately, both versions of 'change of control' set out in the Merger Regulation aim to catch any form of lasting change of control through which a natural or legal person is able to direct the behaviour of an undertaking.

---

731 Commission, Consolidated Jurisdictional Notice under Council Regulation (EC) No 139/2004 on the control of concentrations between undertakings, [2008] OJ C95/1, para. 10.

732 Commission, Consolidated Jurisdictional Notice under Council Regulation (EC) No 139/2004 on the control of concentrations between undertakings, [2008] OJ C95/1, para. 10.

733 Article 3(2) of the Merger Regulation.

734 For simplicity we refer to control being acquired by a single person, however control may of course also be acquired by two or more persons.

735 Commission, Consolidated Jurisdictional Notice under Council Regulation (EC) No 139/2004 on the control of concentrations between undertakings, [2008] OJ C95/1, para. 13.

736 *KLM/Air UK* (COMP/M.967) Commission Decision, paras. 5 et seq.

b) Means of Control: "Decisive Influence"

Under the Merger Regulation the definition of 'control' set out in Article 3(2) includes the possibility of exercising 'decisive influence' on an undertaking, i.e. the existence of "rights, contracts or any other means which, either separately or in combination … confer the possibility of exercising decisive influence on an undertaking". Such means include, but are not limited to, (a) ownership or the right to use all or part of the assets of an undertaking and (b) rights or contracts which confer decisive influence on the composition, voting or decisions of an undertaking.[737]

> A *decisive influence* requires that the acquirer of control can determine the business strategy of the acquired undertaking in a manner which excludes an autonomous decision-making process on the part of the acquired undertaking.

What is key is that the acquirer of control *can* exert his control over the acquired undertaking, not that he necessarily *does* exert that influence.[738] The *possibility* of such exercise is sufficient to constitute decisive influence for the purposes of the Merger Regulation.[739]

When analysing whether decisive influence exists, the Commission as well as the European Courts will have regard to any considerations of fact or law involved as well. The controlling acquirer does not have to be involved in the day-to-day running of the acquired undertaking – control still exists if his influence is exerted in making strategic decisions or business, financial or investment planning.

aa) Equity Interests

A decisive influence is indicated by the acquisition in law of equity interests in an undertaking[740] (in particular the ability to direct a majority vote of the shareholders in an undertaking)[741] or the ability to influence an undertaking's strategic decision-making.[742] In certain circumstances a minority shareholding can also constitute decisive influence – for example, if the shares grant special or preferential rights (e.g. a power of veto or the right to name more than 50 % of the members of a supervisory board or board of directors). A minority shareholding can also amount to a decisive influence when the remaining shares in an undertaking are spread amongst a large number of other shareholders, such that the large minority shareholder holds a *de facto* ability to veto strategic decisions.[743]

---

737 Article 3(2)(a) of the Merger Regulation.

738 Commission, Consolidated Jurisdictional Notice under Council Regulation (EC) No 139/2004 on the control of concentrations between undertakings, [2008] OJ C95/1, para. 54.

739 Case T-282/02, *Cementbouw trade and industry*, [2006] ECR-II-319, paras. 16 and 58.

740 *SMS/Mannesmann DEMAG* (COMP/M.1450) Commission Decision, [1999] OJ C 176/10, para. 6.

741 *SMS/Mannesmann DEMAG* (COMP/M.1450) Commission Decision, [1999] OJ C 176/10, para. 6.

742 Commission, Consolidated Jurisdictional Notice under Council Regulation (EC) No 139/2004 on the control of concentrations between undertakings, [2008] OJ C95/1, para. 17.

743 Commission, Consolidated Jurisdictional Notice under Council Regulation (EC) No 139/2004 on the control of concentrations between undertakings, [2008] OJ C95/1, paras. 56–58.

bb) Economic/Contractual Basis

In exceptional cases, certain situations of economic dependence can lead to *de facto* control of an undertaking. Such would be the case where, for example, very long term supply or credit agreements confer on the supplier or financier decisive influence. Such an economic situation would have to be coupled with structural links between the supplier or financier and the undertaking in order to be sufficient to lead to a change of control on a lasting basis. Additionally, as mentioned previously, it is not necessary that such control actually be exerted; it is sufficient that the possibility of control being exerted exists.[744]

cc) Veto Power

Veto rights held by e.g. minority shareholders which enable those persons to block essential decisions of an undertaking can constitute decisive influence (and therefore control) over an undertaking.[745]

dd) Internal Restructuring

Internal restructurings and reorganisations of corporate groups are not intended to be caught by the definition of change of control contained in the Merger Regulation. Thus changes of shareholdings in group undertakings or mergers of group undertakings are not considered concentrations, provided that there is no change in the quality of control of an undertaking.[746] Given that such activities are not considered concentrations in the first place, the Merger Regulation does not apply.

c) Kinds of Control

Control of an undertaking can be exercised by one natural or legal person or by multiple natural or legal persons acting together. The simplest form of acquiring control of an undertaking is for one person to acquire all or a majority of the shares or voting rights in an undertaking.[747] When two or more persons exercise control over an undertaking (e.g. two undertakings engaging in a joint venture via a shared subsidiary), decisive influence usually means the ability to block actions which determine the commercial behaviour of an undertaking. In order for two such undertakings to make decisions about an undertaking's operations, they must cooperate with each other.[748]

---

744 Commission, Consolidated Jurisdictional Notice under Council Regulation (EC) No 139/2004 on the control of concentrations between undertakings, [2008] OJ C95/1, paras. 16, 20.

745 Cf. Commission, Consolidated Jurisdictional Notice under Council Regulation (EC) No 139/2004 on the control of concentrations between undertakings, [2008] OJ C95/1, para. 65.

746 Cf. Commission, Consolidated Jurisdictional Notice under Council Regulation (EC) No 139/2004 on the control of concentrations between undertakings, [2008] OJ C95/1, para. 51.

747 Commission, Consolidated Jurisdictional Notice under Council Regulation (EC) No 139/2004 on the control of concentrations between undertakings, [2008] OJ C95/1, para. 56.

748 Commission, Consolidated Jurisdictional Notice under Council Regulation (EC) No 139/2004 on the control of concentrations between undertakings, [2008] OJ C95/1, para. 63.

d) On a Lasting Basis

Article 3(1) of the Merger Regulation specifies that in order to fall within the definition of a concentration, the change of control must be 'on a lasting basis' – i.e. an undertaking must be affected by a lasting structural change. What time frame constitutes 'lasting' depends on the facts of an individual case; the Commission has found that a period of 10 to 15 years was sufficient in the hotel industry, whilst three years was insufficient.[749]

e) Exceptions to the Definition of Concentration

Article 3(5) of the Merger Regulation sets out exceptions to the definition of concentration so that a concentration is not deemed to arise when financial institutions hold shares on a temporary basis or in the administration of an insolvency or winding-up.

f) Example: Engaging in a Joint Venture

As might be expected, the structure of large corporate groups can be highly complex, but the basic elements of change of control are often straightforward, even if the corporate structure itself is not.

In the case of the *Global Transport Solutions* joint venture,[750] an American undertaking called Maersk Data and a German undertaking called Eurogate proposed to engage in a joint venture. Prior to the concentration going ahead, Maersk was the sole shareholder in Global Transport Solutions ("GTS") and it was proposed that Eurogate would acquire 50 % of the shares in and have the right to appoint 50 % of the board of directors of GTS.

The Commission examined the structure of the joint venture, and concluded that the 50 % voting rights and board appointment powers being allotted to Eurogate constituted a change of control – from sole control by MDU to joint control by Maersk and Eurogate. Although Eurogate did not have the sole ability to direct the operations of GTS, any business decisions to be taken required joint agreement between both Maersk and Eurogate, thereby effectively giving Eurogate a veto in the decision-making process.

3. Internal Market Dimension

The Merger Regulation only applies to concentrations with an *internal market dimension* – i.e. those which reach certain turnover thresholds. These thresholds serve to demarcate the boundary between national and EU-level merger control.[751] Article 5 of the Merger Regulation explains in detail the method to be used to calculate turnover.[752]

---

749 *Lehman Brothers/Starwood/Le Meridien* (COMP/M.3858) Commission Decision, para. 8 (3 years) and para. 9 (10–15 years).

750 *Maersk Data/Eurogate IT/ Global Transport Solutions JV* (COMP/M.3097) Commission Decision.

751 See Article 21 of the Merger Regulation.

752 Additional requirements are set out in Commission, Consolidated Jurisdictional Notice under Council Regulation (EC) No 139/2004 on the control of concentrations between undertakings, [2008] OJ C95/1, paras. 169–174.

Article 1(2) of the Merger Regulation sets out the basic turnover test to identify concentrations with a Community dimension: a Community dimension exists where (a) the combined aggregate worldwide turnover of the undertakings concerned is more than EUR 5 billion and (b) the aggregate Community-wide turnover of each of at least two of the undertakings concerned is more than EUR 250 million, unless each of the undertakings concerned achieves more than two-thirds of its aggregate Community-wide turnover within one and the same Member State.

Beyond this basic test, it is possible for a concentration not meeting these thresholds to still have a Community dimension if, *inter alia*, the aggregate turnover of at least two of the undertakings concerned is more than EUR 25 million in each of three Member States (Article 3(3) of the Merger Regulation).

It should be noted that the threshold tests apply to all concentrations of undertakings operating in the European Union, regardless of the country of the undertaking's registration, the nationality of its shareholders, directors or employees or the location of its production plants. The threshold tests are *effects-based*, meaning that as long as the effects of the relevant undertakings' activities are felt in the Union, the proposed concentration is subject to European competition rules (Article 26(2) TFEU).

4. European and National Merger Control

The demarcation between EU- and national-level merger control is set out in Article 21 of the Merger Regulation, which specifies that the Commission shall have sole jurisdiction for concentrations meeting the turnover thresholds. Member States are prohibited from applying their national legislation to concentrations falling within the ambit of the Merger Regulation and may not apply the provisions of the Merger Regulations themselves. However, an exception exists for certain interests (public security, plurality of the media and prudential rules) and Member States can take appropriate measures to protect those interests.[753]

It should also be noted that one or more Member States can effectively refer a case 'upwards', by requesting the Commission to examine a concentration which does not have a Community dimension, but which does affect trade between Member States and threatens to affect significantly competition within the territory of the Member State or States making the request.[754] Equally, the Commission can also refer a notified concentration 'downward' to competition authorities in a Member State if, for example, the concentration affects competition in a market within that Member State, which presents all the characteristics of a distinct market and which does not constitute a substantial part of the internal market.[755]

The intention behind this distribution of responsibilities is that in cases of a concentration which has cross-border effects in the Union, only one competition authority should

---

753 Article 21(4) of the Merger Regulation.
754 Article 22 of the Merger Regulation.
755 Article 9 of the Merger Regulation.

be responsible for applying merger control regulations rather than multiple national authorities (the so-called *'one stop shop'*).[756]

IV. COMPATIBILITY WITH THE INTERNAL MARKET

Effective merger control at the Union level helps to ensure a system of undistorted competition in the internal market. Thus the primary (but not sole) consideration in determining which concentrations are incompatible with the internal market is whether the proposed concentration would create or strengthen a dominant position and thereby impedes effective competition to a substantial degree.[757]

> "A concentration which would significantly impede effective competition, in the common market or in a substantial part of it, in particular as a result of the creation or strengthening of a dominant position, shall be declared incompatible with the common market" (Article 2(3) of the Merger Regulation).

In determining whether a proposed concentration is compatible with the internal market, the Commission takes account of the following:[758]
- the need to maintain and develop effective competition in the internal market;
- the market position, economic and financial power of the undertakings concerned;
- the alternatives available to suppliers and users;
- legal or other barriers to market entry;
- supply and demand trends for the relevant goods and services; and
- the interests of consumers as well as the development of technical and economic progress provided that it is to consumers' advantage and does not form an obstacle to competition.

Prior to 2004, the test as to whether a proposed concentration was incompatible with the internal market was whether it *"create[d] or strengthen[ed] a dominant position* as a result of which effective competition would be significantly impeded in the [internal] market or in a substantial part of it".[759] With the coming into force of the current Merger Regulation, this test has been revised to consider whether the proposed concentration would *"significantly impede effective competition,* in the [internal] market or in a substantial part of it" (the "SIEC test").[760]

Both versions consider the effect of the proposed concentration on competition in the internal market, but the current wording is broader, allowing for a more rounded analysis of the effects of the proposed concentration on competition. Certainly the creation or strengthening of a dominant position which impedes effective competition (as per the previous merger regulation) is still covered by the current wording, but other forms in

---

756   Recitals 8, 12 and 18 of the Merger Regulation.
757   Recital 24 and Article 2 of the Merger Regulation.
758   Article 2(1) of the Merger Regulation.
759   Article 2(3) of the former Merger Regulation No 4064/89.
760   Article 2(3) of the Merger Regulation.

which competition may be impeded are also now caught, so that the test becomes more effects-oriented.

1. Market Definition

The first step in analysing a proposed concentration is the definition of the relevant market.[761] Only if a clearly demarcated market has been identified is it possible to analyse what effect, if any, a proposed concentration will have on competition in that market.

Market definition for the purposes of merger control uses the same criteria as market definition in other areas of competition law, e.g. Articles 101 and 102 TFEU, with some small differences.[762] As might be expected given the future-oriented nature of analysis undertaken in merger control, the existence of demand side substitutability in the past is less important than its existence in future. It stands to reason that any analysis of likely future circumstances will have to rely on existing data and accumulated expectations of future circumstances.

Additionally, the procedural aspects of merger control are quite different to the *ex post* review inherent in the enforcement of Articles 101 and 102 TFEU generally. A proposed concentration must be notified to the Commission, so the relevant parties have a vested interest in providing the Commission with the necessary information to make a determination about the relevant market. This is in contrast to investigations based on Articles 101 and 102 TFEU, where it may not be the case that the relevant parties have an interest in assisting the Commission in its investigation.

Indeed the level of cooperation extended by parties in merger control regulation is quite high. Article 3(1) of Regulation No 802/2004 specifies the documents (including printed forms) which must be used in the notification of a proposed concentration. These forms require detailed information regarding the affected markets, including in particular details of revenues and sales volumes, the market share held by competitors and the supply and demand structure of the market.[763] It should of course be noted, however, that parties seeking clearance of a proposed concentration will present the facts surrounding their case in the most favourable light possible.

2. Market Dominance

The grounds for declaring a proposed concentration compatible or incompatible with the internal market are set out in Articles 2(2) and 2(3) of the Merger Regulation.

> The definition of a dominant position is similar to that used in relation to Article 102 TFEU: the existence of "a situation where one or more undertakings wield economic power which would enable them to prevent effective competition from

---

761 Case T-177/04, *easyJet Airline*, [2006] ECR-II-1931, para. 55.

762 See also Chapter 2, Section V (*Market Definition*) as well as Section 6 (*Market definitions*) of Annex I of the Implementing Regulation.

763 See Sections 6–9 of Annex I of the Implementing Regulation.

being maintained in the relevant market by giving them the opportunity to act to a considerable extent independently of their competitors, their customers and, ultimately, of consumers".[764]

As is the case with abuse of a dominant position, the market share of the relevant undertakings offers a first clue as to dominance in a market for the purposes of merger control – the forecast of a high market share post-merger can form the presumption of dominance.[765]

The Commission often uses a formula called the *Herfindahl Hirschman Index (HHI)* to project the market power of a proposed concentration: $x^2 + y^2 + z^2$ with x, y and z being the market shares of undertakings active in the relevant market. By squaring the input figures, the HHI gives proportionally greater weight to the market shares of larger firms and results in an exponential curve reflecting market power (with a pure monopoly giving an output of 10,000 (100 x 100). The HHI is useful in two particular ways – first in identifying the levels of competition in a market in an absolute sense, and second as a means to visualise the effect of a proposed concentration by calculating the HHI before and after a proposed concentration.[766] Commission practice has developed thresholds which indicate whether doubts about competition exist, e.g. the Commission is unlikely to identify competition concerns where post-merger HHI is less than 1000.[767]

a) Example: Collective Market Dominance – the Airtours Criteria

It is also possible for a collectively dominant position (in contrast to the dominance of a single undertaking) to be held to be incompatible with the internal market.[768] Such a situation exists when market power is concentrated in the hands of only a few market participants (an oligopoly) and evidence indicates tacit coordination of market behaviour by the members of an oligopoly in the long term.[769] European jurisprudence has developed three criteria for determining whether collective market dominance exists.

---

764 Case T-102/96, *Gencor*, [1999] ECR-II-753, para. 200; cf. also Joined Cases C-68/94 and C-30/95, *French republic and Société commerciale of the pot ace et de l'azote (SCPA) and Entreprise minière et chimique (EMC)*, [1998] ECR- I-1375, para. 221. In addition see Chapter 4, Section I (*Dominant Position*).

765 Cf. Commission, Guidelines on the assessment of horizontal mergers under the Council Regulation on the control of concentrations between undertakings, [2004] OJ C31/5, para. 15; additionally see Chapter 4, Section I (*Dominant Position*).

766 Cf. Commission, Guidelines on the assessment of horizontal mergers under the Council Regulation on the control of concentrations between undertakings, [2004] OJ C31/5, para. 16.

767 For further detail see Commission, Guidelines on the assessment of horizontal mergers under the Council Regulation on the control of concentrations between undertakings, [2004] OJ C31/5, paras. 19–21 and Commission, Guidelines on the assessment of non-horizontal mergers under the Council Regulation on the control of concentrations between undertakings, [2008] OJ C265/6, para. 25.

768 Joined Cases C-68/94 and C-30/95, *French Republic and Société commerciale des potasses et de l'azote*, [1998] ECR-I-1375, paras. 165–178.

769 Opinion of Advocate General Kokott, Case C-413/06 P, *Bertelsmann AG and Sony Corporation of America v Impala*, [2008] ECR I-4951, para. 25.

The case of *Airtours* established that collective market dominance exists in the following circumstances:[770]

(1) Market transparency

Each member of the dominant oligopoly must have the ability to know how the other undertakings are behaving in order to monitor whether or not they are adopting the common policy. It is not enough for each undertaking to be aware that interdependent market conduct is profitable for all of them; it is also necessary that each undertaking must have a means of knowing whether the other operators are adopting the same strategy and whether they are maintaining it. Therefore there must be sufficient market transparency for all of the undertakings to be aware of the way in which the others' market conduct is evolving.

(2) Sufficiently long time period

The situation of tacit coordination must be sustainable over time, i.e. there must be an incentive not to depart from the common policy on the market. This is because it is only if all the undertakings involved maintain the parallel conduct that all can benefit. Therefore for a situation of collective dominance to be viable, there must be adequate deterrents to ensure that there is a long-term incentive in not departing from the common policy – i.e. each undertaking must be aware that competitive action on its part designed to increase its market share would provoke identical action by the others, so that it would obtain no benefit from such efforts.

(3) Proof

To prove the existence of a collective dominant position to the requisite legal standard, the Commission must establish that the foreseeable reaction of current and future competitors, as well as of consumers, would not jeopardise the results expected from the common policy.

It is not necessary for all the undertakings involved in collective dominance on a market to engage in active collusion; silent coordination of competitive behaviour and with it the renunciation of active competition is sufficient.[771]

(1) Example: the Recorded Music Market

Was the market for recorded music transparent enough to constitute collective dominance amongst producers?

Bertelsmann Music Group (BMG) and Sony Corporation of America (Sony) planned to form a concentration in the worldwide market for recorded music. It was intended that the joint-venture undertaking would be active in discovering and developing new artists

---

770 Case T-342/99, *Airtours*, [2002] ECR II-2585, para. 62; recently confirmed in Case T-464/04, *Impala*, [2006] ECR II-2289, para. 247 and Case C-413/06 P, *Bertelsmann AG and Sony Corporation of America v Impala*, [2008] ECR I-4951, para. 124.

771 Opinion of Advocate General Kokott, Case C-413/06 P, *Bertelsmann AG and Sony Corporation of America v Impala*, [2008] ECR I-4951, para. 24.

and deal with the marketing and selling of recorded music. Its business activities would not include related activities such as publishing, manufacturing and distribution of recorded music.

A competitor in the recorded industry market alleged that the proposed concentration should be declared incompatible with the internal market on the basis that it amounted to a strengthening of an existing collective market dominance amongst worldwide producers of recorded music. This objection was not based on the specific market dominance of the proposed concentration between BMG and Sony itself, but rather on the fact that such a concentration would reduce the number of major music producers from five to four.

Of particular issue in this case was whether, *inter alia*, according to the *Airtours* criteria, the market for recorded music was transparent enough to allow for tacit coordination amongst top producers (and therefore to constitute collective dominance).[772]

Indicating sufficient market transparency to constitute collective dominance:	Indicating insufficient market transparency and therefore no collective dominance:
A variety of albums were offered at different prices – and normally such variable pricing would indicate a less transparent market. However, as most of the record companies' profits came from only a small number of albums (the top 20 titles each year accounting for between 30 % and 60 % of all sales) it would only be necessary to coordinate a relatively small area of prices to amount to tacit coordination.[773]	Further monitoring beyond the top 20 albums offered by each record company was necessary in order for each record company to offer campaign discounts.[774] Additional transparency came from weekly hit charts which included information on sales levels as well as monitoring of sales at the retail level.[775]

The Commission concluded that there was insufficient evidence to indicate tacit collaboration and therefore collective dominance.[776] The possibility that the top record companies adhered to a 'known set of rules' was insufficient proof of market transparency (the first condition of collective market dominance).[777]

(2) Innocuous Reaction to Market Developments?
As discussed in Chapter 3,[778] it can be difficult to distinguish inappropriate behaviour from innocuous reactions to market developments. As regards merger control, the question is whether collective market dominance can exist in the absence of any provable

---

772 Opinion of Advocate General Kokott, Case C-413/06 P, *Bertelsmann AG and Sony Corporation of America v Impala*, [2008] ECR I-4951, paras. 22, 26.

773 *Sony/BMG* (COMP/M.3333), Commission Decision, para. 111.

774 *Sony/BMG* (COMP/M.3333), Commission Decision, para. 111.

775 *Sony/BMG* (COMP/M.3333), Commission Decision, paras. 112–113.

776 *Sony/BMG* (COMP/M.3333), Commission Decision, para. 113.

777 Cf. Case C-413/06 P, *Bertelsmann AG and Sony Corporation of America v Impala*, [2008] ECR-I-4951, para. 131.

778 See Chapter 3, Section II (*Concerted Practices*).

connection between undertakings,[779] or whether parallel behaviour of undertakings is the result of independent actions taken under competitive conditions.[780]

European jurisprudence has indicated that collective dominance arises where, given the nature and functioning of the relevant market and the changes to the market that would occur if a proposed concentration were to go ahead, the concentration going ahead would make it preferable to adopt a common policy on the market with the aim of selling products above competitive prices.[781] Such behaviour would not have to go so far as entering into an agreement or resorting to concerted practices within the meaning of Article 101 TFEU if the possibility of uniform behaviour can result from a transparent market structure.[782]

b) Example: Market Dominance by a Third Party

In exceptional cases the Merger Regulation can lead to a proposed concentration being declared incompatible with the internal market if it would lead to the strengthening of the dominant position of a third party. This is on the basis that the Merger Regulation provides for structural control relating to a market as a whole, rather than acting as an abuse control system.[783]

In the case of a proposed concentration in the Spanish energy market, the Commission considered whether to declare a proposed concentration incompatible with the internal market on the basis that it would strengthen an existing duopoly on the Spanish wholesale energy market. The Spanish market was dominated by two Spanish suppliers, Endesa and Iberdrola. French EDF was the ultimate owner of an undertaking called EnBW which, together with Grupo Villar Mir, intended to acquire joint control of an undertaking called Hidroeléctrica.[784]

Given the state of the Spanish energy wholesale market, where there was a particularly high degree of concentration and significant isolation of the Spanish market due to a lack of cross-border interconnections with other systems, the Commission was concerned that the proposed concentration would remove the incentive of EDF (the largest non-Spanish supplier on the market) to increase its exports to the Spanish market.

The Commission was of the opinion that the removal of EDF from the Spanish market as a result of the proposed concentration would indeed strengthen the dominant position of the two Spanish suppliers,[785] however, ultimately the concentration was allowed to

---

779 See Joined Cases C-395/96 P and C-396/96 P, *Compagnie maritime belge transport,* [2000] ECR I-1365, para. 45.

780 Cf. Joined Cases C-89/85, C-104/85, C-114/85, C-116/85, C-117/85, C-125/85, C-126/85, C-127/85, C-128/85 and C-129/85, *Ahlström,* [1994] ECR I-99, para. 126.

781 Case T-342/99, *Airtours,* [2002] ECR II-2585, paras. 61 et seq.; Case T-464/04, *Impala,* [2006] ECR II-2289, para. 251.

782 Case C-413/06 P, *Impala,* [2008] ECR-I-4951, paras. 120–123.

783 Cf. *Exxon/Mobile* (COMP/M.1383), Commission Decision, paras. 225–229; *Grupo Villar Mir/EnBW/Hidroeléctrica del Cantábrico* (COMP/M.2432), Commission Decision, para. 71.

784 *Grupo Villar Mir/EnBW/Hidroeléctrica del Cantábrico* (COMP/M.2432), Commission Decision, para. 1.

785 *Grupo Villar Mir/EnBW/Hidroeléctrica del Cantábrico* (COMP/M.2432), Commission Decision, para. 67.

proceed, as EDF had given sufficient commitments for the Commission to judge that the dominant position of Endesa and Iberdrola would not be strengthened.[786]

3. Impediment to Effective Competition

Competition in the internal market can be impeded significantly by the creation or strengthening of a dominant position, but also by other means as well. Articles 2(2) and 2(3) of the Merger Regulation refer "in particular" to the creation or strengthening of a dominant position as impeding effective competition, so the element of a dominant position should be taken as an example only. A concentration can be incompatible with the internal market if it causes a considerable decrease in the competitive pressure on undertakings operating in the market.[787] It may be the case that the proposed concentration, especially in the circumstances of an existing oligopoly, can decrease the competitive pressure of a market simply by removing one competitor from the market. Such an anticompetitive effect is referred to as a "unilateral effect"[788] and includes, for example, the potential ability and incentive of an undertaking post-merger to make the expansion of smaller firms and potential competitors more difficult or otherwise restrict the ability of rival firms to compete.[789]

The consideration as to whether a "significant impediment of effective competition" is possible or likely follows an effects-based approach. As in other areas of EU competition law, the "more economic approach" applies, with the aim of both anticipating any negative effects from the proposed concentration as well considering the value of any efficiency gains. For example, a vertical integration can offer a number of benefits to consumers – e.g. reduced prices or increased production as the merged undertaking will benefit from efficiency gains which lower the costs per unit of production.[790] Concentrations can also contribute to a strengthening of competitiveness in a market and therefore generate efficiency gains for the market as a whole, not just for itself.[791]

Example: T-Mobile Austria and tele.ring

> What are the competition implications of a proposed concentration which does not
> create or strengthen a dominant position, but which removes from the market the
> most active competitor with the most aggressive approach to prices?

---

786   *Grupo Villar Mir/EnBW/Hidroeléctrica del Cantábrico* (COMP/M.2432), Commission Decision, paras. 67, 136–138.

787   Commission, Guidelines on the assessment of horizontal mergers under the Council Regulation on the control of concentrations between undertakings, [2004] OJ C31/5, para. 24.

788   Cf. Recital 25 of the Merger Regulation.

789   Commission, Guidelines on the assessment of horizontal mergers under the Council Regulation on the control of concentrations between undertakings, [2004] OJ C31/5, para. 36.

790   Cf. Commission, Guidelines on the assessment of non-horizontal mergers under the Council Regulation on the control of concentrations between undertakings, [2008] OJ C265/6, paras. 13 et seq.

791   Cf. Commission, Guidelines on the assessment of horizontal mergers under the Council Regulation on the control of concentrations between undertakings, [2004] OJ C31/5, para. 76.

This case centred around T-Mobile Austria's intention to acquire tele.ring, both providers of mobile and fixed telephone services in Austria.[792] Analysis of the pre- and post-merger market shares of T-Mobile Austria and tele.ring indicated that the merger of T-Mobile Austria and tele.ring would lead to a common market share of 30–40 % – i.e. a non-market-dominating share.[793]

However, the Commission nonetheless had doubts as to whether the proposed concentration was compatible with the internal market. The Commission feared that the elimination of tele.ring as an independent network operator would lead to non-coordinated effects on the Austrian telecommunications market. This fear was based on an expected post-merger market structure containing two large network operators of a similar size (one of whom would be T-Mobile Austria), one far smaller operator and one very small operator. Thus even though T-Mobile Austria would not itself be dominant in the retail market, a potential for anticompetitive effects resulting from the proposed concentration still existed.

It was not only the post-merger market structure that gave the Commission cause for concern in this case. The Commission was of the view that tele.ring had played a particularly important role in the retail market, and that the benefits to the market induced by tele.ring's behaviour would disappear if the proposed concentration were to be permitted to go ahead. Tele.ring had been notably active on the retail market, doubling its market share in terms of turnover, and tripling it in terms of number of customers.[794] A large number of tele.ring's new customers had also switched to it from the two largest undertakings acting in the market, T-Mobile Austria and Mobilkom.[795] If tele.ring were to be eliminated from the market, this would lead to an extensive symmetry of the two largest operators in the market with similar market shares, but this time in the absence of an aggressive smaller operator seeking to expand its market share.[796] The Commission did not see it as likely that any of the other, much smaller, operators in the market would compete as aggressively on price as tele.ring had done.[797] Finally, there was no indication of a new operator who intended to enter the Austrian market and who would therefore add to the competitive environment.[798]

Ultimately, the proposed concentration was approved by the Commission, but only as a result of extensive commitments by T-Mobile Austria, including guarantees that one of the smaller remaining operators would be permitted to exert competitive pressure comparable to that previously exerted by tele.ring.[799]

---

792   *T-Mobile Austria/Tele.ring* (COMP/M.3916), Commission Decision.
793   *T-Mobile Austria/Tele.ring* (COMP/M.3916), Commission Decision, paras. 32, 34.
794   *T-Mobile Austria/Tele.ring* (COMP/M.3916), Commission Decision, paras. 41 et seq.
795   *T-Mobile Austria/Tele.ring* (COMP/M.3916), Commission Decision, para. 49.
796   *T-Mobile Austria/Tele.ring* (COMP/M.3916), Commission Decision, paras. 41 et seq.
797   *T-Mobile Austria/Tele.ring* (COMP/M.3916), Commission Decision, para. 55.
798   *T-Mobile Austria/Tele.ring* (COMP/M.3916), Commission Decision, para. 117.
799   *T-Mobile Austria/Tele.ring* (COMP/M.3916), Commission Decision, para. 154.

4. Horizontal versus Vertical Concentrations

European merger control recognises a distinction between horizontal and vertical concentrations.

a) Horizontal Concentrations

A horizontal concentration is indicated by a merger of two undertakings active on the same value added step – i.e. a merger of direct competitors.

Such concentrations can impact effective competition in the internal market, for example, by the removal of important competitive pressure on one or more companies which benefit from increased market power. Alternatively, a change in the structure of competition such that undertakings which had not coordinated their behaviour previously, now decide to do so, would have a negative effect on competition. Such a merger can also make it even easier for undertakings which coordinated their behaviour previously to continue to do so post-merger.[800]

Examples:
– Doubts regarding the effects of a proposed concentration on a market can arise if, for example, concerns exist regarding the ability of customers to change to another supplier post-merger as a result of there being relatively few alternative suppliers. Such was the case in *Boeing/ McDonnell Douglas*, where the Commission prevented the proposed concentration on the basis that alternative suppliers could cover demand for only some, and not all of the products provided in the pre-merger market.[801] A restriction can also be held to exist when changing supplier would result in considerable expense for the customer or be hindered by existing contracts binding a customer to an existing supplier.[802]
– Horizontal concentrations can also raise concerns when the post-merger entity would control the necessary patents or other intellectual property to which a new competitor would require access to (e.g. through licensing,) if it wanted to enter the market. The post-merger entity then has the ability to restrict the entry of new competitors to the market. Additionally, the fact that a proposed concentration would have particular strength from possessing a unique portfolio or brands whereas its competitors possessed only a single brand can have a negative effect on competition.[803]

b) Vertical Concentrations

Vertical concentrations are indicated by the merging of undertakings active at different value added stages. Such situations often give less cause for concern than horizontal

---

800 Commission, Guidelines on the assessment of horizontal mergers under the Council Regulation on the control of concentrations between undertakings, [2004] OJ C31/5, para. 22.
801 Cf. *Boeing/McDonnell Douglas* (COMP/M.877), Commission Decision, para. 70.
802 Cf. *Agfa Gevaert/DuPont* (COMP/M.986), Commission Decision, paras. 63–71.
803 Cf. Case T-114/02, *BaByliss*, [2003] ECR II-1279, para. 344.

mergers, but may still be deemed incompatible with the internal market in certain circumstances.[804]

Competition concerns will be present when non-horizontal mergers give rise to foreclosure – a situation where actual or potential competitors' access to the different value added stages (e.g. supplies or markets) is hampered or eliminated, thereby reducing those undertakings' ability or incentive to compete.[805] Coordinated effects may also be of concern, if the proposed concentration would make it easier for or more likely that firms which were not previously coordinating their behaviour will do so in future.[806]

Examples:
– The proposed merger between an undertaking which produced SIM cards for mobile devices and an undertaking which produced an operating system for such cards' use was objected to by competitors on the ground that such a merger would allow one entity to hinder substantially the activities of its competitors. The fear was that the proposed concentration would be able to introduce e.g. certain compatibility standards which would restrict the development of alternative products.[807]
– Vertical concentrations may also create a situation in which a concentration could use offers of bundled products to edge non-vertically integrated competitors out of the market. In the case of *Honeywell* objections were raised as the proposed concentration would result in one undertaking producing both marine gas turbines as well as the controls and other components used in those turbines.[808]

5. Burden of Proof

It is incumbent on the Commission to prove that a proposed concentration is incompatible with the internal market.[809] The Merger Regulation does not contain a presumption of compatibility or incompatibility, so it falls to the Commission to make an assertion of incompatibility when preventing a proposed merger from going ahead or permitting it to do so only under certain conditions.[810]

---

804 Commission, Guidelines on the assessment of non-horizontal mergers under the Council Regulation on the control of concentrations between undertakings, [2008] OJ C265/6, para. 11.

805 Commission, Guidelines on the assessment of non-horizontal mergers under the Council Regulation on the control of concentrations between undertakings, [2008] OJ C265/6, para. 18.

806 Commission, Guidelines on the assessment of non-horizontal mergers under the Council Regulation on the control of concentrations between undertakings, [2008] OJ C265/6, para. 19.

807 Cf. *Axalto/Gemplus* (COMP/M.3998), Commission Decision, para. 75.

808 Case T-209/01, *Honeywell Internationally*, [2005] ECR II-5527, paras. 88, 92.

809 Case T-342/99, *Airtours*, [2002] ECR II-2585, para. 63; Case T-5/02, *Tetra Laval*, [2002] ECR II-4381, para. 155 (upheld in Case C-12/03 P, *Tetra Laval*, [2005] ECR I-987, paras. 37–51, 44); Case T-210/01, *General Electric Company*, [2005] ECR II-5575, paras. 60–64.

810 Case T-210/01, *General Electric Company*, [2005] ECR II-5575, para. 61.

V. MERGER CONTROL PROCEDURE

Proposed concentrations which fall within the ambit of the Merger Regulation must be notified to the Commission (Article 4 of the Merger Regulation) – a system of preventative control. A notified proposed concentration is prohibited from going ahead by Article 7 of the Merger Regulation, until the Commission has issued a decision on compatibility with the internal market or has not issued a decision within a set period of time. The Commission either makes a decision itself or refers the case to the relevant national competition authorities (Article 6 and 9 of the Merger Regulation). If the Commission does not delegate the case to national authorities, Member State merger control rules do not apply to the proposed concentration (Article 21 of the Merger Regulation). However, if the Merger Regulation does not apply to the proposed concentration, then the case will be within the competence of the relevant national competition authorities and national law will apply.

1. Mandatory Notification

Proposed concentrations with an internal market dimension must be notified to the Commission prior to their implementation and following the conclusion of the agreement, the announcement of the public bid, or the acquisition of a controlling interest.[811] Article 4(1) of the Merger Regulation also allows for notification to be made where the undertakings concerned demonstrate to the Commission a good faith intention to conclude an agreement or, in the case of a public bid, where they have publicly announced an intention to make such a bid, provided that the intended agreement or bid would result in a concentration with a Community dimension.

Once a notification has been made, the Commission must make a decision within a relatively short period of time (see Article 10 of the Merger Regulation for details). If the Commission fails to issue a decision within the specified time limits, the proposed concentration is deemed to have been declared compatible with the internal market.

The advantage of this system from the point of view of undertakings is that, if the proposed concentration falls within the range of application of the Merger Regulation, no further notifications to national competition authorities are necessary (the *'one stop shop'*[812] mentioned above).

The Merger Regulation also addresses the steps to be taken when it may be less clear whether a proposed concentration should be examined at EU or national level. Article 4 of the Merger Regulation provides for the circumstance where the relevant undertakings believe the proposed concentration may significantly affect competition in one Member State which presents the characteristics of a distinct market and therefore should be examined by that particular Member State. Article 5 of the Merger Regulation explains how proposed concentrations which do not meet the definition of a Community dimension can nonetheless be examined by the Commission, provided that the relevant national competition authorities raise no objection.

---

811 For simplification we use the general term "merger agreement".

812 See Chapter 7, Section III(4) (*European and National Merger Control*).

2. Procedure

EU merger control operates on a set maximum timetable and ends with a decision by the Commission. The procedure consists of two phases.

a) The First Phase

The first phase consists of the Commission – usually within 25 working days of notification – examining the notification and confirming whether the proposed concentration falls within the ambit of the Merger Regulation.[813] If the Merger Regulation does not apply to the proposed concentration, this is confirmed by the Commission in a decision. If the Commission determines that the Merger Regulation does apply, but that the concentration would not significantly impede effective competition in the internal market, then the concentration shall be declared compatible with the internal market (Article 2(2) of the Merger Regulation). Should serious doubts regarding competition in the internal market exist, then the Commission will initiate formal proceedings.[814]

b) The Second Phase

The second phase usually does not extend beyond 90 days from the date of notification and in this time the Commission must issue a decision declaring the proposed concentration either compatible or incompatible with the internal market. A decision in favour of compatibility may include certain conditions or commitments from the undertakings involved.[815]

Where the undertakings involved have provided commitments to the Commission or the Commission has imposed conditions on its approval of the proposed concentration, the Commission's approval is deemed to be subject to those conditions and obligations being adhered to or implemented.[816]

---

813 Article 6(1)(a) and (b) in conjunction with Article 10(1) of the Merger Regulation.
814 Article 6(1)(c) of the Merger Regulation.
815 Article 6(1)(c) in conjunction with Article 10(3), Article 8 of the Merger Regulation.
816 Article 6(2) of the Merger Regulation.

Chapter Eight

EUROPEAN UNION STATE AID LAW

Article 107
"1. Save as otherwise provided in the Treaties, any aid granted by a Member State
or through State resources in any form whatsoever which distorts or threatens
to distort competition by favouring certain undertakings or the production of
certain goods shall, in so far as it affects trade between Member States, be incompatible with the internal market.

2. The following shall be compatible with the internal market:
   (a) aid having a social character, granted to individual consumers, provided
       that such aid is granted without discrimination related to the origin of the
       products concerned;
   (b) aid to make good the damage caused by natural disasters or exceptional oc-
       currences;
   (c) aid granted to the economy of certain areas of the Federal Republic of Ger-
       many affected by the division of Germany, in so far as such aid is required
       in order to compensate for the economic disadvantages caused by that divi-
       sion. Five years after the entry into force of the Treaty of Lisbon, the Coun-
       cil, acting on a proposal from the Commission, may adopt a decision repeal-
       ing this point.

3. The following may be considered to be compatible with the internal market:
   (a) aid to promote the economic development of areas where the standard of
       living is abnormally low or where there is serious underemployment, and of
       the regions referred to in Article 349, in view of their structural, economic
       and social situation;
   (b) aid to promote the execution of an important project of common European
       interest or to remedy a serious disturbance in the economy of a Member
       State;
   (c) aid to facilitate the development of certain economic activities or of certain
       economic areas, where such aid does not adversely affect trading conditions
       to an extent contrary to the common interest;
   (d) aid to promote culture and heritage conservation where such aid does not
       affect trading conditions and competition in the Union to an extent that is
       contrary to the common interest;
   (e) such other categories of aid as may be specified by decision of the Council
       on a proposal from the Commission."

A key component of EU competition law is the regulation of State aid pursuant to Articles 107–109 TFEU, which seek to protect the internal market from distortions of competition resulting from certain actions by Member States. State aid can affect competitive equality between undertakings by granting financial advantages to individual undertakings. Thus competition in the internal market can be distorted by State actions which favour inefficient undertakings and thereby keep them in business artificially due to State support.

The protection of the internal market (which is characterised by open borders and the freedoms of goods, services and capital) would be jeopardised if States were allowed to show a preference for undertakings within their own borders or operate policies benefiting certain undertakings over others.

However, State aid also plays an important role in national policy-making (e.g. policies relating to industrial and regional development as well as cultural and environmental aims) as is an important instrument of public regulation in Member States. For example, financial support by the State has (to a certain extent) counteracted the negative effects of the financial crisis in recent years, acting to prevent mass job losses and the insolvency of vulnerable undertakings (in particular financial institutions). Notably, the EU itself supports similar aims through a variety of financing instruments – and when such instruments are used at Union level, they are not subject to the rules on State aid set out in Articles 107–109 TFEU. Direct support at Union level (which will have been decided upon by the Member States, and whether delivered directly by the Union or via Member States) must be distinguished from aid granted by Member States of their own volition. Only the latter is subject to the EU State aid regime.

With the progressive integration of trade in the internal market as well as the liberalisation of formerly monopolistic industries (e.g. postal services, telecommunications, energy), the value of State aid as a mechanism to control the development of competitive conditions in the internal market has increased. The current structure of State aid regulation in the EU is the product of many years' development. In earlier years of the EU, State aid was generally regarded as a matter for individual Member States, but over time the Commission began to exert its influence in this area comparable to its regulation of cartels and abuse of a dominant position. Today, State aid control is part of the broad network of cooperation between Member States, the Commission and national and European courts which focuses on regulation in the context of the actual economic circumstances (the "more economic approach").[817]

I. SYSTEM AND STRUCTURE OF EU STATE AID REGULATION

European law does not contain an absolute prohibition on the granting of aid by Member States, but rather a qualified prohibition which incorporates a number of exemptions. Pursuant to Article 108(3) TFEU, those exemptions are supervised by the Commission.

---

817 Details of the implementation of the "more economic approach" as set out in the State Aid Action Plan can be found on the Commission's website at <http://ec.europa.eu/competition/state_aid/reform/reform.html> (last accessed on 20 April 2011).

Article 107(1) TFEU sets out the general concept of State aid which, in principle, is not considered to be compatible with the internal market; Article 107(2) and (3) specify what aid is, or may be, considered to be compatible with the internal market.

Assessing the compatibility of State aid with the internal market involves a four-step analysis:

(1) Does the support given by the Member State constitute "aid" under Article 107(1) TFEU?

(2) Is the aid compatible with the internal market pursuant to Article 107(2) TFEU?

(3) If the aid is not deemed compatible with the internal market pursuant to Article 107(2) TFEU, can it fall within the conditions of Article 107(3) TFEU to be classified as compatible with the internal market?

(4) If the aid in question cannot benefit from the exemptions in either Article 107(2) or (3) TFEU, can it nonetheless be considered compatible with the internal market pursuant to Article 106(2) TFEU (undertakings entrusted with the operation of services of general economic interest)?

II. LEGAL ASPECTS OF EU STATE AID REGULATION

The primary law basis for EU State aid regulation is contained in Articles 107–109 TFEU. These provisions are supplemented heavily by measures issued by the Commission,[818] relating both to the scope of application of the State aid rules as well as the related procedural mechanisms.

1. Applicability of State Aid Rules

On basis of Article 109 TFEU and Council Regulation (EC) No 994/98/EC the Commission is authorised to adopt regulations declaring that certain categories of State aid are compatible with the internal market and shall not be subject to the notification requirements contained in Article 108(3) TFEU.[819] This provision is used in particular in cases where the value of the aid granted is low[820] (*'de minimis'* aid) and certain kinds of aid which benefit from block exemption regulations.[821] In addition, the Commission has developed guidelines relating to certain sectors (e.g. public broadcasting), purposes (e.g. regional

---

818 State aid rules currently in force can be found on the Internet at <http://ec.europa.eu/competition/state_aid/legislation/compilation/index_en.html> (last accessed on 20 April 2011).

819 Article 1 of Council Regulation (EC) No 994/98 of 7 May 1998 on the application of Articles 92 and 93 of the Treaty establishing the European Community to certain categories of horizontal State aid, [1998] OJ L142/1.

820 Cf. Chapter 8, Section III(1)(c) (*De minimis Aid*).

821 Commission Regulation (EC) No 800/2008 of 6 August 2008 declaring certain categories of aid compatible with the common market in application of Articles 87 and 88 of the Treaty, [2008] OJ L214/3 (the "General Block Exemption Regulation"); for further details see Chapter 8, Section IV(2)(b) (*General Block Exemption Regulation*).

aid) and kinds of aid instruments (e.g. guarantees). Secondary legal instruments used by the Commission in this area include communications, which tend to refer to the basic provisions of the prohibition contained in Article 107(1) TFEU, and guidelines and frameworks, which tend to refer to the potential exceptions contained in Article 107(3) TFEU.

Secondary law instruments issued by the Commission are numerous and varied in subject matter, meaning that the structuring and development of this area of law can be challenging. Measures can be categorised under the following broad headings.

a) Purposes of the Aid

A variety of instruments address the provision of horizontal aid. "Horizontal" aid describes aid which aims to achieve a certain goal whilst not being limited to a certain sector of the economy. Such aid includes, for example, aid for education, employment, research, development and innovation as well as the rescue and restructuring of undertakings in difficulties.[822] As a result of the economic and financial crisis, in 2009 the Commission instituted a set of temporary rules to simplify the granting of aid and support by States to financial institutions (including recapitalisations).[823]

b) Aid Instruments

The Commission has also formulated specific rules relating to different kinds of aid instruments.[824] These include in particular the "guarantee communication"[825] and the "property communication"[826] which offer State-aid guidance relating to the use of such measures.[827]

---

822   In particular for aid for education, [2009] OJ C188/1; for the employment of disadvantaged and disabled workers, [2009] OJ C188/6; for regional aid, [2006] OJ C54/13; for regional aid to large investment projects, [2009] OJ C223/3; for research, development and innovation, [2006] OJ C323/1; for aid for environmental protection, [2008] OJ C82/1; for venture capital investments in small and middle-size enterprises, [2006] OJ C194/2; for the rescue and restructuring of undertakings in difficulties, [2004] OJ C244/2 and [2009] OJ C156/3 (corrigendum of the communication, [2009] OJ C174/17). A compilation of such measures is available on the Internet at <http://ec.europa.eu/competition/state_aid/legislation/compilation/index_en.html> (last accessed on 20 April 2011).

823   In particular the Temporary Community framework for State aid measures to support access to finance in the current financial and economic crisis, [2009] OJ C83/1; the Communications from the Commission amending the Temporary Community Framework [2009] OJ C261/2 and [2009] OJ C303/6; on the application of State aid rules to measures taken in relation to financial institutions in the context of the current global financial crisis, [2008] OJ C270/8; on limitation of aid to the minimum necessary, [2009] OJ C10/2; on the treatment of impaired assets, [2009] OJ C72/1; on the return to viability and the assessment of restructuring measures, [2009] OJ C195/9. A compilation of such measures is available on the Internet at <http://ec.europa.eu/competition/state_aid/legislation/compilation/index_en.html> (last accessed on 20 April 2011).

824   E.g. to short-term export credit insurance, [1997] OJ C281/4; [2009] OJ C217/2; [2004] OJ C307/12 and [2005] OJ C325/22 and to measures relating to direct business taxation, [1998] OJ C384/3. A compilation of such measures is available on the Internet at <http://ec.europa.eu/competition/state_aid/legislation/compilation/index_en.html> (last accessed on 20 April 2011).

825   Commission, Notice on the application of Articles 87 and 88 of the EC Treaty to State aid in the form of guarantees, [2008] OJ C155/10.

826   Commission, State aid elements in sales of land and buildings by public authorities, [1997] OJ C209/3.

827   As regards the legal effect of communications see Chapter 8, Section IV(2)(a) (*Commission Analysis*).

c) Services of General Economic Interest

The package of Commission rules relating to services of general economic interest is particularly important. These rules expand upon the Article 106(2) TFEU exemption and make clear the basis on which the Commission will treat aid which is granted in relation to the carrying out of services of general economic interest.[828]

d) Sector-Specific Regulation

The Commission has published guidelines relating to a number of individual sectors, including broadcasting, postal services and shipbuilding.[829]

Much attention has been given recently to the Commission's guidelines for the application of State aid rules in relation to the rapid deployment of broadband networks.[830] These guidelines aim to promote the development of broadband infrastructure (in particular in rural and economically underperforming areas) and set out the rules for Member States in granting State aid for this purpose.[831]

2. Procedural Rules

Article 108 TFEU sets out the basic functioning of State aid regulation in the EU but it is essential that these provisions are supplemented by measures from the Council and the

---

828 In particular Commission Decision 2005/842/EC of 28 November 2005 on the application of Article 86(2) of the EC Treaty to State aid in the form of public service compensation granted to certain undertakings entrusted with the operation of services of general economic interest (notified under document number C(2005) 2673), [2005] OJ L312/67 (as the "Exemption Decision") and the Community framework for State aid in the form of public service compensation, [2005] OJ C297/4 (the "Community Framework for State Aid").

829 In particular guidelines relating to cinematographic and other audiovisual works, [2002] OJ C43/6, [2007] OJ C134/5, [2009] OJ C31/1; to public service broadcasting, [2009] OJ C257/1; to the postal sector, [1998] OJ C39/2; to shipbuilding, [2003] OJ C317/11, [2003] OJ C263/2, [2006] OJ C260/7 and [2008] OJ C173/3; to the steel industry, [2002] OJ C70/21; to large investment projects, [2002] OJ C70/8. A compilation of such measures is available on the Internet at <http://ec.europa.eu/competition/state_aid/legislation/compilation/index_en.html> (last accessed on 20 April 2011).

830 Commission, Community Guidelines for the application of State aid rules in relation to rapid deployment of broadband networks, [2009] OJ C235/7.

831 However, the asymmetric approach taken in this communication is questionable as such an approach is not inherent in EU competition law, cf. Koenig/Fechtner, EStAL 2009, 463 et seq. Such an asymmetric approach is characterised by the rules being applicable depending on the addressee's nature, while the competition rules set out in primary law (which of course constitute the legal basis upon which the Commission's communication is based) follow a symmetric approach: they equally apply to all addressees and relate to the addressee's behaviour rather than identity. For further information on this distinction cf. Schreiber, Das Zusammenspiel der Regulierungsinstrumente in den Netzwirtschaften Telekommunikation, Energie und Eisenbahn, 2009, p. 100.

Commission.[832] Secondary legal instruments address key factors such as the Commission's procedural approach to cases of State aid,[833] the repayment of unlawful aid[834] and the cooperation between the Commission and the national courts.[835]

III. THE PROHIBITION SET OUT IN ARTICLE 107(1) TFEU

In order for EU rules on State aid to apply, "aid" must have been granted. Article 107(1) TFEU specifies five factors in determining whether aid has been granted.

State aid has been granted when:
(1) an undertaking has benefited from a selective advantage;
(2) the aid was granted by a Member State or through State resources;
(3) the aid was granted to certain undertakings or to a certain sector;
(4) the aid distorts or threatens to distort competition; and
(5) trade between Member States is affected.

1. Selective Advantage

European jurisprudence has established that in order to constitute State aid the measure must grant an advantage to certain undertakings *selectively* over others.[836]

Under Article 107(1) TFEU a selective advantage exists if an undertaking receives a benefit without providing adequate (i.e. market-standard) compensation (a *quid pro quo*) in return.

a) Benefit

For the purposes of the above definition an undertaking receives a benefit when it receives something of value in money's worth for which it has not provided adequate compensation in return.[837] Such a benefit can result from positive actions in the form of e.g.

---

832 Council Regulation (EC) No 659/1999 of 22 March 1999 laying down detailed rules for the application of Article 93 of the EC Treaty, [1999] OJ L83/1 (the "State Aid Implementing Regulation"); Commission Regulation (EC) No 794/2004 of 21 April 2004 implementing Council Regulation (EC) No 659/1999 laying down detailed rules for the application of Article 93 of the EC Treaty, [2004] OJ L140/1, last amended by Commission Regulation (EC) No 1125/2009 of 23 November 2009 amending Regulation (EC) No 794/2004 implementing Council Regulation (EC) No 659/1999 laying down detailed rules for the application of Article 93 of the EC Treaty, as regards Part III.2, Part III.3 and Part III.7 of its Annex I, [2009] OJ L308/5 (the "Regulation 1125/2009").

833 Code of Best Practice for the conduct of State aid control procedures, [2009] OJ C136/13.

834 Commission, Towards an effective implementation of Commission decisions ordering Member States to recover unlawful and incompatible State aid, [2007] OJ C272/4.

835 Commission, Notice on the enforcement of State aid law by national courts, [2009] OJ C85/1.

836 Cf. Case 30/59, *Steenkolenmijnen*, [1961] ECR 1.

837 As to the issue of a mere indirect economic advantage see Heidenhain, EuZW 2007, 623.

classical financial subsidies granted by the State or through measures which reduce the liabilities of an undertaking (e.g. the writing off of an outstanding debt).[838]

Examples:
- A selective advantage can be constituted by e.g. a waiver from paying certain taxes or other social costs, special rates such as tax and sales relief, investment allowances or the granting of subsidies or loans on non-market standard terms. Selective advantage also occurs when an existing demand is not pursued in the usual manner, e.g. purchase of a quantity of goods in excess of actual requirements.
- The motivation behind the granting of the aid is unimportant at the initial stage of determining whether a selective advantage exists – only the economic effects of the measure are relevant (however, the political motivation behind the granting of the aid is indeed examined when considering whether the aid was justified (Articles 106(2) and 107(2) and (3) TFEU).[839] The advantageous effect of aid can exist in the reduced costs to or increased profits of the relevant undertaking, without these effects having been "earned" in the marketplace or "paid for" on the basis of adequate compensation. State financial support of certain products or services (e.g. the encouraging of customers) can also constitute a selective advantage.

b) Insufficient Compensation

A selective advantage can exist if an undertaking does not have to pay market standard compensation. Such is the case when the compensation paid by an undertaking to the State does not correspond to the value received by the undertaking.[840] The whole of the exchange between the undertaking and the State is considered against the backdrop of "normal trading conditions". Determining whether an undertaking has received a benefit via the State is straightforward when a clear market price is determinable according to an existing market – e.g. the basic purchase or sale of a limited stock of items. For other exchanges not so easily quantified by market prices, the Commission and European courts have developed a number of methods and criteria to assess whether adequate performance and adequate compensation exist.

aa) The "Private Investor" Test

A key standard of comparison used by the Commission and the European courts to assess the standard of performance and *quid pro quo* between an undertaking and the State is the "private investor" (or "market economy investor") test.[841]

---

838 Case C-387/92, *Banco Exterior de España*, [1994] ECR I-877, paras. 13 et seq.; Case C-256/97, *DM Transport,* [1999] ECR I-3913, para. 19; Case C-295/97, *Piaggio,* [1999] ECR I-3735, para. 34; Case T-157/01, *Danske Busvognmænd,* [2004] ECR II-917.

839 Case 173/73, *Italy v Commission*, [1974] ECR 709, para. 26; Case 310/85, *Deufil,* [1987] ECR 901, para. 8.

840 Cf. e.g. Case T-14/96, *BAI,* [1999] ECR II-139, paras. 71 et seq.

841 Case C-305/89, *Alfa Romeo,* [1991] ECR I-1603, paras. 19 et seq.; Case C-303/88, *ENI-Lanerossi,* [1991] ECR I-1433, paras. 20 et seq.; Joined Cases C-328/99 and C-399/00, *Seleco,* [2003] ECR I-4035; Joined Cases T-129/95, T-2/96 and T-97/96, *Neue Maxhütte Stahlwerke,* [1999] ECR II-17, paras. 104 et seq.; *Alitalia,* Commission Decision, [2001] OJ L66/36, para. 21.

The "private investor" and "market economy investor" tests consider whether the investment made by the State was done under conditions which would be satisfactory to a comparative hypothetical private investor (for example a bank) under normal free-enterprise conditions.

The analysis considers the moment in time that the investment decisions was made and also allows for a hypothetical "long-term investor", i.e. long-term investment strategies.[842] The principle of the market economy or private investor test is applied within the scope of considering whether the compensation paid by an undertaking to the State is sufficient.[843] The market economy or private investor test has been adapted to include a hypothetical "private vendor" or "private purchaser" test when analysing whether *sale or purchase activities by public authorities* are on market terms.[844] Key is whether the public authorities have behaved as a free-enterprise acting seller or buyer in the same situation would do as regards any sales terms or conditions of purchase.[845]

The so-called "private creditor" test is applicable when determining if the terms of repayment or writing off a debt constitute State aid. The writing off of a debt is not usually characteristic of an investment on market terms, though it is the case that e.g. the financial difficulties of a debtor are to be taken into account. In assessing the terms and structure of payment the test is whether a hypothetical private investor, aware of the financial difficulties of the debtor, would have considered the payment structure agreed by the State to be appropriate.[846] Therefore, an extension of payment or a reduction in the amount to be repaid may be justified to avoid the debtor's insolvency and for the creditor to recoup a portion of the outstanding funds. In addition, the interest or penalties resulting from the delay in repayment must be taken into account.[847]

The Commission's guarantee communication[848] makes clear that individual guarantees do not constitute a benefit when the applicant for the credit is not in financial difficulties, the extent of the guarantee at the time of it being put in placed can be determined, the guarantee covers at most 80 % of the outstanding financial liabilities and market-standard remuneration is paid for the guarantee.

---

842   Case C-305/89, *Alfa Romeo*, [1991] ECR I-1603, para. 20; Joined Cases C-328/99 and C-399/00, *Seleco*, [2003] ECR I-4035; Joined Cases T-129/95, T-2/96 and T-97/96, *Neue Maxhütte Stahlwerke*, [1999] ECR II-17, para. 109; Case T-296/97, *Alitalia*, [2000] ECR II-3871, paras. 81 et seq.

843   For further detail see Heidenhain, Handbuch des Europäischen Beihilfenrechts, 2003, § 4, para. 2 et seq.

844   *BAI*, Commission Decision, [2002] OJ L12/33.

845   *Privatisation of Bank Burgenland* (Case State aid C 56/06 (ex NN 77/06)), Commission Decision 2008/719/EC (notified under document number C(2008) 1625), [2008] OJ L239/32, para. 118.

846   Cf. Case C-342/96, *Tubacex*, [1999] ECR I-2459, para. 46; Case C-276/02, *GEA*, [2004] ECR I-8091; Case T-152/99, *HAMSA*, [2002] ECR II-3049, para. 166; Case T-36/99, *Lenzing*, [2004] ECR II-3597; Opinion of Advocate General Jacobs, Case C-256/97, *DM Transport*, [1999] ECR I-3913, paras. 34–36; cf. also Soltész/Makowski, EuZW 2003, 73.

847   Cf. Case C-256/97, *DM Transport*, [1999] ECR I-3913, paras. 24, 21.

848   Commission, Notice on the application of Articles 87 and 88 of the EC Treaty to State aid in the form of guarantees, [2008] OJ C155/10, para. 3.1.

bb) Method of Analysis

(1) Benefit: does the undertaking receive a financial advantage?
    If no, then no selective advantage exists.
    If yes, then:

(2) Market-standard *quid pro quo* (determined by analysing e.g. a certification of value or a competitive invitation of tenders)?
    If yes, then no selective advantage exists.

If no, then:

(3) "Private investor" test: Would a hypothetical private investor/ creditor/ purchaser have acted in the same manner (and why)?
    If yes, then no selective advantage has been granted.
    If no, then a selective advantage has been granted.

Example:
– Adequate consideration exists in the case of a sale where only one bidder remains at the final stage of the tender process if, in the full course of the bidding process, all potential participants had access to the same information.[849]
– No adequate consideration exists when the State, as a vendor, imposes conditions on the buyer which potentially lower the sale price and thus means the State forgoes additional revenue. Such conditions interfere with the competitive nature of the sales procedure, so that even the highest bid submitted does not represent the actual current value of the asset being sold.[850] The sale can nonetheless be held to be on market-standard terms (notwithstanding the imposition of price-diminishing conditions) if a hypothetical private seller may also have imposed such conditions. This would be the case, for example, if the conditions in question related to securing the earning power of the asset being sold – such as e.g. an objectively necessary condition to maintain bilateral transport rights as regards the sale of an airline.[851]

Example: Bank Burgenland

If an independent valuation justifies the sale of an undertaking to a person other than the highest bidder, is it possible for advantageous treatment as per Article 107(1) TFEU not to exist?[852]

The case of *Bank Burgenland*[853] related to the decision by the Austrian federal state of Burgenland to privatise Bank Burgenland. The public authorities initiated a tender proce-

---

849   For an example of a satisfactory tender procedure see *SMC,* Commission Decision, [1999] OJ L198/1, para. 5.2.1; in contrast an unsatisfactory tender procedure can be found in *Georgsmarienhütte,* Commission Decision, [2002] OJ L105/33, paras. 35 et seq.

850   *Austrian Airlines,* Commission Decision, [2010] OJ L59/1, paras. 183–185.

851   *Austrian Airlines,* Commission Decision, [2010] OJ L59/1, in particular para. 225.

852   *Privatisation of Bank Burgenland* (Case State aid C 56/06 (ex NN 77/06)), Commission Decision 2008/719/EC (notified under document number C(2008) 1625), [2008] OJ L239/32, paras. 108 et seq.

853   *Privatisation of Bank Burgenland* (Case State aid C 56/06 (ex NN 77/06)), Commission Decision 2008/719/EC (notified under document number C(2008) 1625), [2008] OJ L239/32.

dure which narrowed the field of potential purchasers down to two. There was a significant difference in the prices being offered by the bidders: one was more than 50 % higher than the other (ca. EUR 150 million versus ca. EUR 100 million). Nonetheless, the public authority accepted the lower bid.

The first point at issue in this case related to the role to be played in the sales process by an independent valuation of an asset. The independent valuation established a market value below both prices being offered by the bidders. Given that a valuation is based on a hypothetical assessment, whereas the invitation for tenders procedure leads to an actual market-based offer,[854] the tender procedure offers a better approximate value for the current value of the property in question. Even a highly thorough valuation estimate cannot determine exactly the market value of an asset, especially in cases of undertakings which present practical difficulties for accurate valuation. Thus Bank Burgenland was sold below the market value and therefore a selective advantage existed.

In a reversed scenario, when a property is sold to the party who offers the highest bid, no selective advantage has been granted, even if an (hypothetical) independent valuation indicates a higher (hypothetical) market value.[855]

The second issue in this case concerned the extent to which the public authority was bound by the private investor/ seller test – would the circumstances surrounding the privatisation of the Bank have prompted a private seller to accept a lower bid as well? Here, the Austrian government had issued a guarantee covering Bank Burgenland's liabilities of EUR 3.1 billion at the time of sale (and the guarantee would remain in place post-sale). Austria indicted that the sale of Bank Burgenland to the lower bidder was justified on the grounds that that bidder was less likely to trigger the government's guarantee obligation – thus representing the best offer all around.[856] However, the Commission argued that a public authority seller must make a distinction between its role as the seller of an asset on the open market and its role as a public authority which has granted State aid in the form of a guarantee. It is unlikely a private seller would have taken account of the guarantee obligations when choosing a seller; more likely is that he would have accepted the highest absolute bid.[857] Therefore, as the sale of Bank Burgenland was done at a price lower than that which would have been achieved by a private seller, a selective advantage existed.

c) De minimis Aid

Small amounts of aid (EUR 200,000 over the course of three tax years) are excluded from the range of application of Article 107(1) TFEU.[858] Such *de minimis aid* is calculated on the

---

854 *Privatisation of Bank Burgenland* (Case State aid C 56/06 (ex NN 77/06)), Commission Decision 2008/719/EC (notified under document number C(2008) 1625), [2008] OJ L239/32, para. 112.

855 *Georgsmarienhütte*, Commission Decision, [2002] OJ L105/33, paras. 37, 48.

856 *Privatisation of Bank Burgenland* (Case State aid C 56/06 (ex NN 77/06)), Commission Decision 2008/719/EC (notified under document number C(2008) 1625), [2008] OJ L239/32, para. 120.

857 *Privatisation of Bank Burgenland* (Case State aid C 56/06 (ex NN 77/06)), Commission Decision 2008/719/EC (notified under document number C(2008) 1625), [2008] OJ L239/32, para. 118.

858 Article 2 of Commission Regulation (EC) No 1998/2006 of 15 December 2006 on the application of Articles 87 and 88 of the Treaty to de minimis aid, [2006] OJ L379/5 deems that such aid shall be considered as not meeting all the criteria of Article 107(1) TFEU.

basis of the difference between the amount paid in consideration for the relevant goods or services and the actual market value of those goods or services ("aid equivalent").[859]

Actual current market value of the performance – consideration = aid equivalent.

2. By a Member State or through State Resources

Article 107(1) TFEU specifies that the aid must be granted "by a Member State or through State resources in any form". This is found to be the case when the selective advantage granted by the State is imputable to or performed via public resources.

a) Accountability to the State

The granting of a selective advantage is imputable to the State if it originates directly or indirectly from an organ of the State. It is irrelevant which part of the State grants the benefit to the undertaking – it can be national, state or local government or other public bodies such as public banks, institutions or foundations.[860] However, regardless of which entity of the State grants the aid, in terms of State aid supervision the Member State itself remains liable for any breaches of State aid rules.

The phrasing of "by a Member State" and "through State resources" makes clear that Article 107(1) TFEU catches "both advantages which are granted directly by the State and those granted by a public or private body designated or established by the State".[861] The granting of an advantage in an indirect fashion is nonetheless imputable to the State as otherwise Member States could remove their activities from the realm of Article 107(1) TFEU simply by devising creative structures through which to grant aid. Determining State accountability for aid granted assumes that the State (in whatever form) has had an influence on the granting of aid on the facts of the particular case at hand. The bare supposition that the State exercises a controlling influence over certain public undertakings is not enough.[862] However, equally, "the imputability to the State of an aid measure taken by a public undertaking may be inferred from a set of indicators arising from the circumstances of the case and the context in which that measure was taken".[863]

European jurisprudence has considered whether an undertaking governed by private law, but which was created by the State to perform certain tasks, is capable of granting an advantage.[864] The fact that the State set up the undertaking and uses it for certain purposes is not sufficient; nor is it relevant whether the undertaking is legally independent of State authority. Rather, the key consideration in determining whether the State granted

---

859 Case T-16/96, *Cityflyer Express,* [1998] ECR II-757, paras. 52 et seq.

860 Case 248/84, *Germany v Commission,* [1987] ECR 4013, para. 17.

861 Cf. Joined Cases C-52/97, C-53/97 and C-54/97, *Viscido,* [1998] ECR I-2629, para. 13.

862 Case C-482/99, *Stardust Marine,* [2002] ECR I-4397, para. 52.

863 Case C-482/99, *Stardust Marine,* [2002] ECR I-4397, para. 55.

864 Case T-358/94, *Air France,* [1996] ECR II-2109, paras. 55 et seq.

aid indirectly is whether the means by which the aid was granted "constantly remain under public control, and therefore available to the competent national authorities".[865]

Example: Independence of the Public Body

The case of *Stardust Marine*[866] considered the extent to which a public company's actions spoke for itself or represented the actions of the State. The Court of Justice held that "[a] public undertaking may act with more or less independence, according to the degree of autonomy left to it by the State... Therefore, the mere fact that a public undertaking is under State control is not sufficient for measures taken by that undertaking, such as the financial support measures in question here, to be imputed to the State. It is also necessary to examine whether the public authorities must be regarded as having been involved, in one way or another, in the adoption of those measures".[867]

b) State Involvement in the Indirect Granting of Aid

The European courts have considered a number of cases relating to the indirect granting of State aid and a large body of jurisprudence exists on this point. In the case of *Pearle*[868] the Court of Justice confirmed that the conditions set out in Article 107(1) TFEU are cumulative and that there is no need to draw any distinction between aid granted directly by the State or by public or private bodies established or appointed by the State.[869]

Two cases involving electricity suppliers (*PreussenElektra*[870] and *Wienstrom*[871]) highlight the conditions for the indirect granting of State aid regarding parafiscal charges.

In the case of *PreussenElektra*, a German law required electricity suppliers to purchase electricity from renewable energy sources at minimum prices higher than the real economic value of that type of electricity. The Court of Justice found that the degree of Member State involvement in the measure was insufficient to constitute State aid, as the cash-flow budget of the Member State was not diminished. Private undertakings alone had to pay the special charge for electricity from renewable energy sources.

In contrast, in the case of *Wienstrom* the Court of Justice held that payment of additional costs by consumers can constitute State aid, even if the cash-flow budget of the Member State is unaffected. This can be the case if (i) all electricity users have to pay the special charge, whether they use the aided product or not and (ii) a public body collects the payment in a first step and transfers it to the aided undertakings in a second step afterwards. If these conditions are fulfilled, the nature of the payment changes at the moment the public body collects it: from that moment on, the aid is considered to be "State aid" pursuant to Article 107(1) TFEU.[872]

---

865 Case C-482/99, *Stardust Marine*, [2002] ECR I-4397, para. 37; cf. Heidenhain, Handbuch des Europäischen Beihilfenrechts, 2003, § 4, para. 20.

866 Case C-482/99, *Stardust Marine*, [2002] ECR I-4397.

867 Case C-482/99, *Stardust Marine*, [2002] ECR I-4397, para. 52.

868 Case C-345/02, *Pearle*, [2004] ECR I-7139.

869 Case C-345/02, *Pearle*, [2004] ECR I-7139, para. 34.

870 Case C-379/98, *PreussenElektra*, [2001] ECR I-2099.

871 Case C-384/07, *Wienstrom*, [2008] ECR I-10393.

872 *Wienstrom* (Case N317A/2006), Commission Decision, [2006] OJ C221/6, paras. 46–60.

To summarise, a parafiscal charge qualifies as State aid pursuant to Article 107(1) TFEU if national law constitutes a compellable link between the charge all users have to pay and the use of this charge for a particular aid. In cases where such a link exists, the parafiscal charge directly impacts the amount of the aid.[873]

3. Certain Undertakings or the Production of Certain Goods

Article 107(1) TFEU specifies that the aid must favour certain undertakings or the production of certain goods.

a) Requirement of Selectivity

Only elements of an advantage favouring certain undertakings or industries are considered incompatible with the internal market.

As is the case in relation to Articles 101 and 102 TFEU, the concept of an "undertaking" for the purposes of EU State aid rules is an autonomous, Union-level concept.[874] Additionally, Article 107(1) TFEU catches aid granted to an entire industry (e.g. the textile or film industry).

The criterion of selectivity is the determining constituent fact which moves a State measure from the realm of indiscriminate support of the whole economy to a measure subject to controls on State aid. In order for aid to be selective, it has to place one or more undertakings in a position which is not comparable to that held by other undertakings generally.[875]

Thus selectivity is also indicated when a State measure could be applicable to the economy as a whole, but is used in such a way as to benefit a certain undertaking or industry.[876] It is sufficient if the possibility exists that certain undertakings or industries receive an advantage.

b) Example: Preference Pursuant to Tax Law

In the area of direct company taxation the Commission has issued a communication[877] to assist in differentiating between general economic measures and those which favour certain undertakings. The first consideration is whether the tax measure in question

---

873   Joined Cases C-128/03 and 129/03, *AEM*, [2005] ECR I-2861, para. 46 referring to Case C-174/02, *Streekgewest Westelijk Noord-Brabant*, [2005] ECR I-85, para. 26; Case C-175/02, *Pape*, [2005] ECR I-127, para. 15.

874   For details see Chapter 2, Section II(1) (*Undertakings*).

875   *Commission v Denmark*, Commission Decision, [2009] OJ L345/18, paras. 36 et seq.

876   Case C-241/94, *Kimberly Clark*, [1996] ECR I-4551, paras. 22 et seq.; see also *Technolease*, Commission Decision, [2000] OJ L297/13, paras. 26 et seq.; regarding the exercise of discretion in a tender procedure see *Regional Venture Capital Funds*, Commission Decision 2001/712/EC, [2001] OJ L263/28, para. 51. The absence of a precise and generally accepted definition can also constitute discretionary powers; see Commission Decision, [2003] OJ L17/1, para. 69.

877   Commission, Notice on the application of the State aid rules to measures relating to direct business taxation, [1998] OJ C384/3, paras. 14 to 16.

diverges from the application of the general system of taxation; the second step involves analysing whether the measure is justified by the nature or structure of the general tax law system.[878]

The General Court has contributed to the list of criteria to be used when analysing tax cases. It has stated that the starting point for determining whether a tax measure is selective is first to analyse the common or 'normal' tax system applicable[879] and then to consider whether any advantage granted by the tax measure in question is selective. If it is selective, it is for the Member State to prove that it is justified by the nature and general scheme of its tax system.[880]

The elements of advantage and selectivity are closely related to each other and, in practice, the Commission does not always differentiate between them clearly. However, the separation of the two topics is important as regards burden of proof: the burden of proving the existence of selectivity rests with the Commission, whilst it falls to the Member State to prove the absence of a selective advantage.

c) Example: Measures Supporting Infrastructure

Measures to support public infrastructure are not considered to be selective if they are for the general public good. Although such measures (if limited to the area of a Member State) affect infrastructure competition between the Member States, they are not considered to be selective if they refrain from advantaging certain undertakings or sectors.[881] *General infrastructure measures* are available to all undertakings without discrimination and are subject to equivalent conditions. The Commission has held that a variety of measures such as urban traffic infrastructure, tourism-related infrastructure (e.g. a cable railway, nature protection areas) and town development (e.g. protected environmental areas, education-related infrastructure) are not considered to be selective and therefore do not infringe rules on State aid.[882]

In contrast, certain forms of publicly-supported infrastructure are considered to grant an advantage to certain specific undertakings. This can occur first in the form of an advantage to one or more undertakings involved in the construction or development project, e.g. in cases of so-called "public private partnership", where an advantage may

---

878   Cf. para. 16 of Commission, Notice on the application of the State aid rules to measures relating to direct business taxation, [1998] OJ C384/3; Opinion of Advocate General *Darmon,* Joined Cases C-72/91 and C-73/91, *Sloman Neptun,* [1993] ECR I-887, para. 58; Case C-75/97, *Maribel,* [1999] ECR I-3671, paras. 32 et seq.; Opinion of Advocate General Mischo, Case C-143/99, *Adria-Wien Pipeline,* [2001] ECR I-8365, paras. 35 et seq.; Case C-351/98, *Spain v Commission,* [2002] ECR I-8031; Case C-308/01, *GIL Insurance,* [2004] ECR I-4777, para. 61; Case C-159/01, *Netherlands v Commission,* [2004] ECR I-4461, para. 42; Case T-55/99, *CETM,* [2000] ECR II-3207.

879   Joined Cases T-211/04 and T-215/04, *Gibraltar v Commission,* [2008] ECR II-3745, para. 143.

880   Joined Cases T-211/04 and T-215/04, *Gibraltar v Commission,* [2008] ECR II-3745, para. 144.

881   Case C-75/97, *Maribel,* [1999] ECR I-3671, paras. 32 et seq.; *Broadband infrastructure development in Germany* (Case N 238/2008), Commission Decision C(2009)1339, in contrast see para. 27.

882   *Support for nature experience areas in Schleswig-Holstein* (Case N 86/2000), Commission Decision, [2000] OJ C127/11; Commission communication to the Member States and other interested parties concerning State aid N 376/01 – Aid scheme for cableways – Authorisation of State aid under Articles 87 and 88 of the EC Treaty (Proposal to which the Commission has no objection), [2002] OJ C172/2, para. 13 et seq.; *Measures to promote village and city development* (Case N 392/1999), Commission Decision, [2000] OJ C110/41.

be granted to the private investors involved with the project. Additionally, certain (usually large-scale) projects such as a sports stadium can be found to advantage one or more undertakings over others (e.g. the undertakings using the stadium, the owners of those undertakings and/or the operators of the stadium).

At all levels of the relevant upstream (construction) and downstream (maintenance, operation) infrastructure markets it must be ensured that public funds are not dedicated to the production of infrastructure for the benefit of certain undertakings who act on the market in a commercial role. The granting of such an advantage largely can be avoided through the use of a non-discriminatory tender procedure or an independent expert valuation. Additionally, if any undertaking is involved in the development of the project and will also benefit from the completed project going forward, it is important that the infrastructure or equipment being provided is adequately remunerated so that that undertaking is not selectively favoured.

d) Example: Sectors of Industry

> Is a State programme for employers intended to reduce the social security contributions which must be made in relation to certain workers considered to be 'selective'?

Belgium introduced the "Maribel" scheme under which employers in Belgium who employed manual workers were granted a reduction in social security contributions for each such worker.[883] In the years following the introduction of the scheme, it evolved such that the reductions in contributions varied depending on the number of persons employed by an undertaking and the sector in which the undertaking operated.[884]

The Commission was of the view that the Maribel scheme infringed Article 107(1) TFEU and was incompatible with the internal market.[885] The Court of Justice agreed with the Commission, holding that the different benefits which applied to different sectors of industry made the measure selective, such that it constituted State aid.[886]

4. Distortion of Competition

Under Article 107(1) TFEU State aid is incompatible with the internal market if it "distorts or threatens to distort competition". The concept of distorting competition is interpreted widely; the Commission applies a low threshold to this criterion.

> A distortion of competition exists if the aid affects, or has the potential to affect, competition between undertakings or sectors and thereby alters the structure of competition.

---

883 Case C-75/97, *Maribel*, [1999] ECR I-3671, para. 2.

884 Case C-75/97, *Maribel*, [1999] ECR I-3671, paras. 3 et seq.

885 Case C-75/97, *Maribel*, [1999] ECR I-3671, para. 12.

886 Case C-75/97, *Maribel*, [1999] ECR I-3671, para. 31.

Key is that undertakings or sectors of industry receive an economic advantage under conditions which do not comply with normal market functioning and which therefore altered the trading conditions for their competitors.[887] Thus the standard for comparison is the hypothetical competitive environment without the State intervention and the actual competitive environment following the State intervention. It is also necessary that the amount of aid involved in the distortion of competition exceeds the *de minimis* limits in place at the time the aid is granted (at the moment EUR 200,000).[888]

In previous years the Commission found that a distortion of competition existed without undertaking a particularly close analysis. However, following the publication of the State aid action plan[889] as part of the strengthening of the more economic approach to State aid within the EU, the Commission announced that in future it would undertake a full analysis of any distortions of competition in the context of the relevant market.[890]

Examples:
– A relatively small amount of aid can distort competition if the beneficiary of the aid acts in a market filled with lively competition. This is because if a market is characterised by intense competition amongst a large number of small undertakings, even a small financial advantage may strengthen an undertaking over its competitors.[891]
– The effect of granting an advantage to one undertaking is that market forces are prevented from having their normal effects – which of course affects competition. In this way, the granting of reduced costs to an undertaking effectively lowers the amount an undertaking would ordinarily have had to pay for modernisation, which has a direct competitive effect on its costs and thereby competition in the market generally.[892]
– The elimination of the operating expenses an undertaking would normally have to bear constitutes a distortion of competition.[893]

5. Effect on Trade between Member States

Article 107(1) TFEU requires that the aid in question distorts competition such that it affects trade between Member States. Thus State aid which has only local, regional or national effects, and no-cross border effects, is not caught.

---

887 Case 730/79, *Philip Morris*, [1980] ECR 2671, para. 11; Case T-369/06, *Holland Malt*, [2009] ECR II-3313, paras. 53–56.

888 Commission Regulation (EC) No 1998/2006 of 15 December 2006 on the application of Articles 87 and 88 of the Treaty to de minimis aid, [2006] OJ L379/5; see also Case T-55/99, *CETM*, [2000] ECR II-3207.

889 Commission, State aid action plan – Less and better targeted state aid: a roadmap for state aid reform 2005–2009, COM(2005) 107 final, available on the Internet at <http://eur-lex.europa.eu/LexUriServ/ LexUriServ.do?uri=COM:2005:0107:FIN:EN:PDF> (last accessed on 20 April 2011).

890 Cf. Röller, WZB-Mitteilungen March, 2006, 27, available on the Internet at <http://ec.europa.eu/ dgs/competition/economist/we.pdf> (last accessed on 20 April 2011).

891 Cf. Case T-288/97, *Friuli Venezia Giulia*, [2001] ECR II-1169, paras. 43-47.

892 Case C-301/87, *France v Commission*, [1990] ECR I-307, paras. 41, 44.

893 Case C-156/98, *Germany v Commission*, [2000] ECR I-6857, para. 30.

Cross-border trade is affected if the aid granted has, or may have in future, an effect on cross-border trade.[894]

The Commission does not have to prove that the aid does now or will have in future an actual effect on trade between Member States.[895] A presumption of an effect on trade between Member States is valid when it can be shown that the aid will strengthen the financial power of the beneficiary undertaking.[896] Additionally, the criterion of an effect on cross-border trade is satisfied when the market position of an undertaking is improved not just in a national context (e.g. an improvement as compared to domestic competitors) but also compared to competitors in other Member States.

It is debatable (as in the case of other areas of competition law relating to distortions of competition) what degree of distortion must exist in order to satisfy the requirements of Article 107(1) TFEU – i.e. must the distortion be appreciable. On the one hand, a number of factors argue against the imposition of an appreciability qualification: the importance of the concept of a genuine internal market, the difficulties in defining the necessary degree of distortion and the danger of Member States trying to avoid the rules prohibiting distortions of competition in the internal market. On the other hand, the ongoing extension of the scope of the EU primary law may account for the requirement of an appreciable distortion in order for EU rules to apply.

a) Examples: An Improved Market Position

European jurisprudence has indicated that trade between Member States is affected in the following circumstances:
– The Netherlands released an undertaking from a EUR 45 million rescue aid liability, thereby strengthening that undertaking's position in the Dutch market. The criterion of an effect on cross-border trade was satisfied as the undertaking operated in a market in which international undertakings were also active.[897]
– The Netherlands granted aid to an undertaking which exported almost exclusively to non-EU countries. In this case, the effect on cross-border trade was satisfied as (a) even a small effect on sales within the internal market is sufficient to meet the threshold and (b) the beneficiary undertaking was placed in a more competitive position *vis-à-vis* other undertakings operating in the internal market and exporting to non-EU countries.[898]

---

894 Case 730/79, *Philip Morris*, [1980] ECR 2671, para. 11; Case T-217/02, *Ter Lembeek*, [2006] ECR II-4483, para. 181.

895 Joined Cases T-298/97, T-312/97, T-313/97, T-315/97, T-600/97 to 607/97, T-1/98, T-3/98 to T-6/98 and T-23/98, *Alzetta Mauro*, [2000] ECR II-2319, paras. 76 et seq.; Case T-189/03, *ASM*, [2009] ECR II-1831, para. 66.

896 Case 730/79, *Philip Morris*, [1980] ECR 2671, para. 11.

897 Joined Cases T-81/07, T-82/07 and T-83/07, *Jan Rudolf Maas*, [2009] ECR II-2411, para. 77.

898 Case T-369/06, *Holland Malt BV*, [2009] ECR II-3313, paras. 45, 47–50.

b) Examples: Regional Activity

An effect on cross-border trade can be ruled out if the aid in question relates to purely local economic activities:

- German aid to the operator of a swimming pool complex did not have an effect on cross-border trade as its services were purely local – a limited geographic catchment area and there existed no cross-border competition amongst suppliers.[899]
- In contrast, the Court of Justice held in *Altmark Trans* that a selective advantage granted to one undertaking only operating on a regional/local market can have a cross-border effect by virtue of the fact that it can reduce the chance of potential competitors from other Member States gaining access to the regional/local market. Neither the local or regional character nor the amount of the aid can rule out an effect on cross-border trade if the aid nonetheless has the effect of actively excluding competitors from the market.[900]

6. The Altmark Conditions Rendering Article 107(1) TFEU Inapplicable

Aid granted in relation to services of general economic interest is usually assessed in the context of Article 106(2) TFEU.[901]

In the case of *Altmark Trans*,[902] the Court of Justice identified a different structure of analysis of selective advantage relating to State aid when the aid is granted in relation to certain activities of public benefit.[903]

> State aid will fall outside the scope of Article 107(1) TFEU if the following conditions are met (known as the *Altmark* conditions):
>
> (1) The undertaking receiving compensation constituting a selective advantage must be entrusted with public service obligations. The form of the obligations can vary from Member State to Member State, as long as the following aspects are clearly defined:
>   (a) nature and duration of the obligations;
>   (b) undertaking appointed to carry out the obligations;
>   (c) geographic area to which the obligations relate;
>   (d) nature and duration of the exclusive rights or special obligations granted to the undertaking (if necessary); and
>   (e) the basis on which compensation for carrying out the obligations is calculated.

---

899 *Freizeitbad Dorsten* (Case N 258/00), Commission Decision.

900 Case C-280/00, *Altmark Trans*, [2003] ECR I-7747, para. 77; see also Case C-75/97, *Maribel*, [1999] ECR I-3671, para. 49; Case T-55/99, *CETM*, [2000] ECR II-3207, para. 86.

901 For general information regarding the scope of application of Article 106(2) TFEU see Chapter 5 (*The Article 106(2) TFEU Exemption*).

902 Case C-280/00, *Altmark Trans*, [2003] ECR I-7747, paras. 83 et seq.

903 The applicability of these conditions has recently been confirmed by the Union courts; see Case T-266/02, *Deutsche Post*, [2008] ECR II-1233, para. 91; also Opinion of Advocate General Jääskinen, Case C-399/08 P, *Commission v Deutsche Post*, paras. 78, 125.

(2) The parameters on the basis of which the compensation is calculated must be established in advance in an objective and transparent manner.

(3) The compensation cannot exceed what is necessary to cover all or part of the costs incurred in discharging the public service obligations.

The costs considered 'necessary' in discharging the public service obligations are those which relate to the discharge of the public service obligations after having deducted any income received and allowing for an adequate profit. A return on investment capital in the form of interest may also be permitted. Such costs are considered 'additional' to those the undertaking would incur if it did not carry out those obligations.

The calculation of the net additional costs relating to the discharge of public service obligations must include only the costs incurred by the undertaking which are not compensated (or which are compensated only in part) by amounts received by the undertaking from users of the service.

(4) If the undertaking which is to discharge the public service obligations has been chosen other than pursuant to a public procurement procedure[904] (which would allow for the selection of the undertaking capable of providing those services at the least cost to the community), the level of compensation to be paid to the undertaking must be determined on the basis of an analysis of the costs which a typical undertaking, well run and adequately provided with means so as to be able to meet the necessary public service requirements, would have incurred in discharging those obligations, taking into account the relevant receipts and a reasonable profit for discharging the obligations (the 'benchmark procedure').

If any of the *Altmark* conditions are not fulfilled, then the compensation paid to an undertaking for carrying out public service obligations will be subject to the rules on State aid set out in Article 107(1) TFEU.[905] However, the *Atlmark* conditions have not rendered Article 106(2) TFEU itself obsolete. Rather, the *Altmark* conditions relate to the classification of a particular measure as State aid (or not) and specifically relate to determining whether an undertaking has received a selective advantage (i.e. does State aid exist); this is separate from the test set out in Article 106(2) TFEU, which is used to determine whether a measure constituting State aid may be regarded as compatible with the internal market.[906]

Examples:
– The first *Altmark* condition, requiring an undertaking to be entrusted with public service obligations, is not satisfied if a legal measure envisages merely the possibility that a government authority will establish undertakings of different legal forms to undertake

---

904 Public procurement law is the subject of Chapter 9.

905 Case T-354/05, *Télévision française 1 SA (TF1)*, [2009] ECR II-471, para. 135; see also the Commission's practice as set out in its decision of 15 October 2003, *RAI SpA*, C(2003) 3528, [2004] OJ L119/1, paras. 99 et seq; *BBC* (Case N 37/2003), Commission Decision C(2003) 3371, [2003] OJ C271/47; for details see Chapter 8, Section IV(3) (*Article 106(2) TFEU in the Context of State Aid*).

906 Case T-354/05, *Télévision française 1 SA (TF1)*, [2009] ECR II-471, summary point 6.

the delivery of non-profit services. In such circumstances, the nature of the public service obligations has not been defined sufficiently clearly.[907]
- The *Altmark* conditions were fulfilled in a case relating to tax advice centres in Italy which were granted an exclusive right to pursue certain tax advice and assistance services. Such services could indeed be classified as public service obligations, and the compensation level per tax declaration completed and filed with the authorities had been established in a sufficiently clear manner in advance.[908]

IV. EXCEPTIONS TO THE PROHIBITION ON STATE AID

Once it has been established that State aid exists, the next step is to consider whether that aid is compatible with the internal market.

1. Legal Exceptions – Article 107(2) TFEU

The legal exceptions set out in Article 107(2) TFEU are, in the view of the Commission, of limited application. They describe a number of very specific circumstances in which the disadvantages of State aid for the internal market are outweighed by the benefits of that aid. Article 107(2) TFEU refers to the following: (a) aid having a social character, granted to individual consumers, (b) aid to make good damage caused by natural disasters of exceptional occurrences and (c) aid granted to the economy of certain areas of Germany affected by the division of Germany. Aid falling under these headings is deemed to be compatible with the internal market *per se*, with no further analysis required (e.g. as to the purpose, quantity or distortive or commercial effects of the aid).

Examples:
- Aid having a social character which is granted to individual consumers is deemed to be compatible with the internal market, as long as the aid is granted without discrimination regarding the origins of the products concerned. This kind of aid includes measures such as financial allowances to pay for clothing, food or heating expenses and, following the recent financial crisis, has included aid granted to e.g. home owners to enable them to pay their mortgages and avoid their homes being repossessed.[909]
- Aid relating to natural disasters was used when large parts of European airspace were closed down due to the effects of an ash cloud following the eruption of an Icelandic volcano in 2010.[910]
- As regards the exception relating to the effects of the division of Germany, such aid may only be used to compensate for the disadvantages to some regions caused by the physical division of Germany (primarily relating to infrastructure); aid may not be

---

907   Case T-189/03, *ASM*, [2009] ECR II-1831, para. 129.

908   Case C-451/03, *Servizi Ausiliari Dottori Commercialisti Srl*, [2006] ECR I-2941, paras. 60–72.

909   Commission, IP/09/602 of 20 April 2009 and IP/09/1123 of 13 July 2009.

910   Commission, MEMO/10/152 of 27 April 2010.

used to remedy damage caused by the different political systems in place whilst Germany was divided.[911]

2. Potential Exceptions – Article 107(3) TFEU

In contrast to the exceptions set out in Article 107(2) TFEU, those set out in Article 107(3) grant the Commission a discretion in determining whether or not the aid in question is compatible with the internal market.

a) Commission Analysis

The European courts have confirmed that the Commission's discretion regarding Article 107(3) TFEU is wide.[912] In the course of the more economic approach to competition law in the EU, the Commission has indicated that its analysis will relate primarily to economic considerations of (a) the negative effects of the distortion of competition in the internal market as compared to (b) the positive effects of remedies against the negative effects of market failures.[913]

Article 107(3) TFEU mentions the following types of aid: (a) aid to under-developed areas and regions, (b) aid to promote projects of common European interest or to remedy a serious disturbance in the economy of a Member State, (c) aid to facilitate the development of certain economic activities or areas (e.g. certain sectors of industry) and (d) aid to promote culture and heritage.

In order to provide a degree of certainty and transparency (notwithstanding its discretion) the Commission has issued a number of frameworks, communications and guidelines indicating how it will approach the exceptions listed in Article 107(3) TFEU.[914] Where the Commission has adopted such measures designed to specify the criteria which it intends to apply in the exercise of its discretion, it does to a certain extent limit its discretion in that it must comply with the indicative rules which it has imposed upon itself.[915] In this way, such measures do provide an element of legal certainty. However, it should also be noted that although the Commission is bound by the measures it issues, this is only to the extent that those texts do not depart from the proper application of the rules on State aid as set out in the Treaties[916] and therefore circumstances may

---

911 Case C-156/98, *Germany v Commission,* [2000] ECR I-6857, paras. 46 et seq.; Joined Cases T-132/96 and T-143/96, *VW Sachsen,* [1999] ECR II-3663, paras. 129 et seq.

912 Case C-301/87, *Boussac,* [1990] ECR I-307, para. 49; Case C-303/88, *Lanerossi,* [1991] ECR I-1433, para. 34; Case C-355/95 P, *Textilwerke Deggendorf,* [1997] ECR I-2549, para. 26; Case T-109/01, *Fleuren Compost,* [2004] ECR II-127, para. 90.

913 Commission, State aid action plan – Less and better targeted state aid : a roadmap for state aid reform 2005–2009, COM(2005) 107 final, available on the Internet at <http://eur-lex.europa.eu/LexUriServ/LexUriServ.do?uri=COM:2005:0107:FIN:EN:PDF> (last accessed on 20 April 2011).

914 A compilation of State aid rules is available on the Internet at <http://ec.europa.eu/competition/state_aid/legislation/compilation/index_en.html> (last accessed on 20 April 2011).

915 Case T-254/00, *Hôtel Cipriani,* [2001] ECR I-7567, para. 293.

916 Cf. Joined Cases C-75/05 P and C-80/05 P, *Glunz/Kronofrance,* [2008] ECR I-6619, para. 65.

arise where, in the exercise of its role under primary law, the Commission may make a determination at odds with its issued guidance measures.

b) General Block Exemption Regulation

The Commission has issued Commission Regulation (EC) No 800/2008[917] declaring certain categories of aid compatible with the internal market (the "General Block Exemption Regulation"). These include aid in relation to (*inter alia*): small and medium size enterprises ("SMEs"), research, development and innovation, venture capital, environmental protection, the support of employers and start-up undertakings.

The General Block Exemption Regulation provides that aid meeting the conditions set out therein is considered to be compatible with the internal market and is therefore exempt from the requirement under Article 108(3) TFEU that it be notified to the Commission. Thus the regulatory burden on Member States, undertakings who receive aid and the Commission is reduced considerably. Article 288 TFEU ensures that the General Block Exemption Regulation is directly binding on Member States.

aa) General Requirements

Articles 9–11 of the General Block Exemption Regulation require that Member States communicate to the Commission a summary of the details relating to aid granted pursuant to the General Block Exemption Regulation, cooperate with the Commission's monitoring procedures and deliver an annual report to the Commission on the application of the General Block Exemption Regulation. Chapter II of that Regulation sets out specific provisions for different categories of aid.

bb) Exemption Conditions

Key aspects of the exemption conditions under the General Block Exemption Regulation include:
– Article 5 of the General Block Exemption Regulation sets out certain transparency requirements as a basic condition for aid to be exempted under the Regulation. The transparency requirements are inseparable from the general methodology used in the Regulation, according to which the intensity of every aid measure must be calculated (Article 4 of the Regulation) and then notified if it meets certain thresholds (Article 6 of the Regulation). Such thresholds are either an absolute limit (e.g. EUR 7.5 million per undertaking per investment project in cases of SME investment and employment aid) or relate to proportional limits as set out in Chapter II of the Regulation. The aim of the transparency requirement is to eliminate the need for a complicated consideration and assessment of business risks in each individual case of aid. Broadly, aid in the form of subsidies and interest subsidies is transparent, whilst aid in the form of start-up and venture capital (which requires an element of

---

917   Commission Regulation (EC) No 800/2008 of 6 August 2008 declaring certain categories of aid compatible with the common market in application of Articles 87 and 88 of the Treaty, [2008] OJ L214/3.

risk, and is subject to certain exceptions) does not fulfil the transparency requirements of Article 5 of the Regulation.

- Chapter II of the General Block Exemption Regulation sets out the detailed limits
on certain categories of aid in order for that aid to benefit from the exemption contained in the Regulation. Each category of aid is subject to rules relating to what
kind of aid and expenses should be included in the calculation of overall limits.
For example, in the case of aid for newly created small enterprises, Article 14(5) of
the Regulation specifies a variety of legal, advisory, consultancy and administrative
costs directly related to the creation of the enterprise which are designated as "eligible
costs" (i.e. those costs to be used in calculating aid intensity).

- Article 7 of the Block Exemption Regulation sets out rules for determining the cu-
mulation of aid – effectively the adding together of public support measures from
different sources (e.g. local, regional or Union level measures) when calculating the
threshold limits for aid under the Regulation.

- The role of the Union's more economic approach is clear from the way that the
Regulation deals with aid possessing an "incentive effect" and the procedure to be
followed when a beneficiary of aid receives 'windfall profits'. Article 8(2)-(6) and
recitals 28-32 specify the applicable rules in individual cases. In the case of SMEs,
aid is considered to have an incentive effect if, before work on the project or activity
has started, the beneficiary has submitted an application for the aid to the Member
State concerned. In contrast, aid granted to large enterprises is considered to have an
incentive effect only if, in addition to the timing requirement which applies to SMEs,
the beneficiary of the aid can prove that the aid will result in a material increase in e.g.
the size, scope or speed of completion of the project or activity.

3. Article 106(2) TFEU in the Context of State Aid

The exception relating to undertakings entrusted with the operation of services of
general economic interest set out in Article 106(2) TFEU plays a significant role in the
realm of State aid regulation.[918] The Commission has formalised a number of elements
of Article 106(2) TFEU which relate to the realm of State aid, i.e. the requirement for
an entrustment, the obstruction of performance and proportionality, in a package of
secondary law measures (known as the "SGEI package" or "Monti package").[919]

The three relevant measures are:

- Commission Decision on the application of Article 106(2) TFEU to State aid granted to
undertakings entrusted with the operation of services of general economic interest (the
"Exemption Decision");[920]

---

918   For further discussion of Article 106(2) TFEU see Chapter 5 (*The Article 106(2) TFEU Exemption*).

919   The Commission launched a public consultation on the application of this package in June 2010, cf.
IP/10/715 of 10 June 2010.

920   Commission Decision 2005/842/EC of 28 November 2005 on the application of Article 86(2) of the
EC Treaty to State aid in the form of public service compensation granted to certain undertakings en-
trusted with the operation of services of general economic interest (notified under document number
C(2005) 2673), [2005] OJ L312/ 67.

- Commission Directive on the transparency of financial relations between Member States and public undertakings (the "Transparency Directive");[921] and
- Community framework for State aid in the form of public service compensation.[922]

a) Entrustment of an Undertaking

The case of *Altmark Trans*[923] established a list of formal criteria to be applied in determining whether the conditions set out in Article 107(1) TFEU were met.[924] The first criterion, that the undertaking receiving aid be required to discharge public service obligations, relates directly to Article 106(2) TFEU.[925]

The SGEI package, as part of an attempt to revise the European rules relating to the financing of services of general economic interest and improve the Commission's regulation in this area, expands upon the requirements relating to the entrustment of an undertaking with public service obligations as originally set out in *Altmark*.

> The Article 106(2) TFEU exemption may apply to a State aid measure when:
> (1) the recipient undertaking is required to discharge public service obligations and those obligations have been clearly defined – i.e. it has been entrusted with the operation of services of general economic interest;
> (2) a legally binding obligation exists regarding the obligations and the compensation has been calculated accordingly; and
> (3) the amount of the compensation does not exceed that which is necessary for the carrying out of the service.

In contrast to the *Altmark* judgement, the SGEI package does not include the fourth *Altmark* condition relating to the calculation of compensation. Thus a degree of convergence between the *Altmark* criteria and the rules relating to Article 106(2) TFEU is achieved.

b) Obligation to Notify

State aid which fulfils the first three *Altmark* criteria and the following conditions is exempt from the notification obligation contained in Article 108(3) TFEU. Aid granted to:

---

921   Commission Directive 2006/111/EC of 16 November 2006 on the transparency of financial relations between Member States and public undertakings as well as on financial transparency within certain undertakings (Codified version), [2006] OJ L318/17 (the "Transparency Directive").

922   Community framework for State aid in the form of public service compensation, [2005] OJ C297/4.

923   Case C-280/00, *Altmark Trans*, [2003] ECR I-7747, para. 95.

924   See Chapter 8, Section III(6) (*The Altmark Conditions Rendering Article 107(1) TFEU Inapplicable*).

925   Case C-280/00, *Altmark Trans*, [2003] ECR I-7747: (1) The obligations entrusted to the undertaking must be clearly defined; (2) the basis on which the compensation is calculated must be established in advance in an objective and transparent manner; (3) the compensation cannot exceed what is necessary to cover all or part of the costs incurred in discharging the public service obligations; and (4) the amount of compensation must have been determined on the basis of an objective cost analysis. For details see Chapter 8, Section III(6) (*The Altmark Conditions Rendering Article 107(1) TFEU Inapplicable*).

- an undertaking:
  - which, in the year when it is entrusted with the public service obligation, has an annual turnover of less than EUR 100 million;
  - receives a yearly compensation of less than EUR 30 million in exchange for provision of the relevant service;[926]
- notwithstanding the above mentioned thresholds: undertakings such as hospitals and social housing undertakings entrusted with public service obligations;[927]
- air or maritime links to islands on which annual traffic does not exceed 300,000 passengers;[928]
- airports and ports for which annual traffic does not exceed 1,000,000 passengers for airports or 300,000 passengers for ports.[929]

c) Transparency

The Commission made use of its competence relating to Article 106(3) TFEU to issue the Transparency Directive.[930] The Transparency Directive deals with the disclosure of financial links between public authorities and public undertakings[931] and requires that accounting methods be used which clearly indicate the costs and revenues associated with different activities and the means by which these are assigned or allocated.[932] Such rules aim to limit cross-subsidisation amongst undertakings entrusted with the operation of services of general economic interest.

The Transparency Directive effectively addresses the fourth *Altmark* condition relating to transparency regarding the method by which compensation for the performance of public service obligations is calculated.[933] The Transparency Directive defines "undertakings required to maintain separate accounts"[934] which ensures that undertakings entrusted with the operation of services of general economic interest must maintain separate accounts. In this way, no hidden cross-subsidisation amongst such undertakings can take place.

---

926 Article 2(1)(a) of the Exemption Decision.

927 Article 2(1)(b) of the Exemption Decision.

928 Article 2(1)(c) of the Exemption Decision.

929 Article 2(1)(d) of the Exemption Decision.

930 The Transparency Directive 2006/111/EC is currently in force. Previously the relevant directive was Commission Directive 80/723/EEC of 25 June 1980 on the transparency of financial relations between Member States and public undertakings, [1980] OJ L195/35, last amended by Commission Directive 2005/81/EC of 28 November 2005, [2005] OJ L312/42; confirmed in Joined Cases 188 to 190/80, *France and others v Commission*, [1982] ECR 2545, para. 875.

931 Article 1(1) of the Transparency Directive.

932 Article 1(2) of the Transparency Directive.

933 See in addition see Chapter 8, Section III(6) (*The Altmark Conditions Rendering Article 107(1) TFEU Inapplicable*).

934 Article 2(1)(d) of the Transparency Directive.

V. PROCEDURAL ASPECTS OF STATE AID REGULATION

Article 108(3) TFEU requires Member States to notify the Commission of any plans to grant or alter State aid. Further details of the State aid regulatory procedure are contained in the remainder of Article 108 TFEU, Council Regulation (EC) No 659/1999[935] (the "State Aid Implementing Regulation") and Commission Regulation (EC) No 794/2004.[936] The State Aid Implementing Regulation in particular sets out the practical steps involved in the Commission's supervision of State aid and provides for a degree of transparency and legal certainty regarding State aid regulation in the EU.

Within the context of the 'State aid action plan' and associated reforms, the EU State aid regulatory procedure has been revised in recent years and remains an object of ongoing discussion (in particular as regards possible improvements to protect the rights of third parties who have been affected by illegally granted aid).

The burden of State aid supervision rests upon the Commission, with the only exception being pursuant to Article 108(2) TFEU, which allows for the Council, in unusual circumstances, to exempt a measure of State aid from the rules usually applicable or to declare such aid to be compatible with the internal market.

1. The Notification Procedure

The procedure relating to State aid control is bilateral: it exists only between the Member State and the Commission and decisions by the Commission are always addressed to the Member State.

Article 108 TFEU makes a distinction between the ongoing review of existing aid (Article 108(1)) and the notification of new aid (Article 108(3)). The State Aid Implementing Regulation addresses the issue of 'unlawful' aid, i.e. aid which was granted without having been notified or approved and aid which has been 'misused' i.e. granted prior to being approved but which was nonetheless later authorised by the Commission.

a) Existing Aid

The Commission is obliged under Article 108(1) TFEU to keep existing aid under "constant review", which it does in the context of Articles 17–19 of the State Aid Implementing Regulation and Article 4 of Commission Regulation (EC) No 794/2004 (which allow for a simplified notification procedure for certain alterations to existing aid).[937]

---

935   Council Regulation (EC) No 659/1999 of 22 March 1999 laying down detailed rules for the application of Article 93 of the EC Treaty, [1999] OJ L83/1.

936   Commission Regulation (EC) No 794/2004 of 21 April 2004 implementing Council Regulation (EC) No 659/1999 laying down detailed rules for the application of Article 93 of the EC Treaty, [2004] OJ L140/1, last amended by Commission Regulation (EC) No 1125/2009 of 23 November 2009, [2009] OJ L308/5.

937   Cf. Articles 1(b), 4(6) and 15 of Regulation 1125/2009.

b) New Aid

Article 1(c) of the State Aid Implementing Regulation defines "new aid" as "all aid ... which is not existing aid, including alterations to existing aid". New aid must be notified to the Commission pursuant to Article 108(3) TFEU and is subject to a 'standstill period' during which the aid may not be implemented until the Commission has granted its approval.

2. Preliminary Examination

Once the Commission has been notified of proposed State aid, it undertakes a preliminary examination as to whether the proposed aid is likely to be compatible with the internal market. There are three possible outcomes to this investigation: (i) that the measure in question does not constitute aid, (ii) that it constitutes aid but is compatible with the internal market, or (iii) that it constitutes aid and doubts exist as to whether it is compatible with the internal market. In the cases of (i) and (ii), the Commission must record its views in a decision and no further investigation is required. In the case of (iii), the Commission will then commence the formal investigation procedure.

The Commission has two months following the date of notification[938] to issue either a decision indicating that the notified measure does not constitute aid, or a decision that it constitutes aid and is compatible with the internal market.[939] If the Commission does not respond in this timeframe, the measure is deemed to have been authorised by the Commission.[940] Notably, however, such deemed authorisation does not mean that the measure in question cannot later be challenged as "unlawful aid" and be subject to a decision by the Commission requiring the Member State to recover such unlawful aid pursuant to Article 11(2) of the State Aid Implementing Regulation.[941]

3. Formal Investigation Procedure

If, in the course of the preliminary examination procedure the Commission finds reason to doubt whether the proposed measure is compatible with the internal market, the Commission must, under Article 108(2) TFEU, initiate a formal investigation. This involves the Member State and the undertaking(s) concerned receiving a summary of the Commission's initial assessment of the aid character of the proposed measure and being invited to submit comments within a prescribed period (usually one month).

The formal investigation procedure can lead to one of two outcomes.

---

938 Supplementary information sheets used when notifying concentrations are annexed to Regulation 1125/2009.

939 Article 4(2)–(3) of Regulation 1125/2009.

940 Article 4(6) of Regulation 1125/2009.

941 Article 13(2) of Regulation 1125/2009.

a) Positive Decision

If the Commission determines that the notified measure does not constitute aid, or that it constitutes aid but that the aid is compatible with the internal market (pursuant to Article 107(2) or (3) or Article 106(2) TFEU), it shall issue a decision to that effect (Articles 7(2) and (3) of the State Aid Implementing Regulation). A positive decision issued by the Commission may be conditional and can lay down obligations with which the Member State or undertaking(s) involved must comply (Article 7(4) of the State Aid Implementing Regulation).

b) Negative Decision

In the event that the Commission concludes that the proposed aid measure is incompatible with the internal market, the Commission will issue a negative decision pursuant to Article 7(4) of the State Aid Implementing Regulation confirming that the aid must not be put into effect, or if it has already been put into effect, requiring that the relevant aid be recovered.

Insofar as possible the Commission shall take a positive or negative decision within 18 months from the date of opening the formal investigation procedure (subject to extension upon the common agreement of the Commission and the Member State). Once the period of 18 months has passed, the Member State can require the Commission to take a decision on the basis of the information available to it; however, where the information provided is not sufficient to establish compatibility, the Commission will take a negative decision (Article 7(7) of the State Aid Implementing Regulation).

It should again be noted that the time periods applicable to the formal investigation procedure do not alter the fact that aid can be challenged in future on the grounds of being unlawful.

4. Infringements of the State Aid Regime

Articles 107–109 TFEU can be infringed in a number of different ways. A "misuse of aid"[942] occurs if a beneficiary uses aid in contravention of the approval procedure set out in the State Aid Implementing Regulation – i.e. if the aid was put into effect prior to a compatibility decision being issued in the course of a preliminary examination, prior to the issuing of a positive decision in the course of the formal investigation procedure, or in contravention of any conditions or obligations imposed by the Commission pursuant to Article 7(4) of the State Aid Implementing Regulation.[943] State aid is considered "unlawful aid"[944] if it was put into effect in contravention of Article 108(3) TFEU or if a beneficiary uses the aid in spite of the Commission issuing a negative decision in the course of the formal investigation procedure.

---

942 Article 1(f) of Regulation 1125/2009.
943 Articles 4(3) and 7(3) and (4) of Regulation 1125/2009.
944 Article 1 of Regulation 1125/2009.

a) Commission Competence

Articles 10–15 of the State Aid Implementing Regulation govern the procedure to be followed regarding unlawful aid. In particular, these provisions grant the Commission certain rights to examine cases of alleged unlawful aid, request further information from a Member State or issue a decision requiring certain information to be provided (called an "information injunction").[945] The Commission can also issue a decision obliging Member States to recover unlawful aid from the beneficiary, including interest on the amount of the aid.[946]

b) Repayment of Aid later notified to the Commission

The repayment of unlawful aid (i.e. aid granted in contravention of Article 108(3) TFEU or in disregard of a negative decision by the Commission) is straightforward: the beneficiary of the aid must repay the amount of the aid plus interest to the Member State. However, the concept of repaying unlawful aid becomes more complicated where the aid was granted prior to the Commission's approval of the aid measure, but where such approval was indeed granted at a later point in time. In such cases it is appropriate for the beneficiary to pay interest on the amount of the aid granted for the time period between which it made use of the aid and the Commission granting its approval of the measure.

In cases relating to an infringement of the standstill period imposed by Article 108(3) TFEU, the issue arises as to whether the beneficiary must repay aid in question in full. The answer to this question depends on whether the aid infringed only a procedural step (i.e. it infringed only the standstill obligation) or whether it also infringed substantive legal rules as well. In cases where the infringement was substantive, it is clear that the aid in question must be repaid in full.[947] If the aid in question was granted legally save only for the procedural infringement of Article 108(3) TFEU, it *may* need to be repaid.

European jurisprudence does not require the full recovery of aid granted in circumstances amounting to an infringement of procedural rules.[948] Rather, the Court of Justice has left it to the national courts to decide whether such aid must be repaid in part or in whole according to national law.[949] The result of this approach is the unusual situation that aid granted in contravention of procedural rules may or may not need to be repaid, depending on the approach of different courts in different Member States.[950]

Even though the question of full recovery of aid granted in contravention of procedural rules is governed by national law, a national court must still bear in mind the overriding aims of the EU State aid regime when making its determination. Although the standstill provision in Article 108(3) TFEU is intended to ensure that "incompat-

---

945 Article 10 of the State Aid Implementing Regulation.
946 Article 14 of the State Aid Implementing Regulation.
947 Recital 13 and Article 14 of the State Aid Implementing Regulation.
948 Case C-199/06, *CELF I*, [2008] ECR I-469, paras. 46, 53, 55.
949 Case C-1/09, *CELF II*, para. 26.
950 Case C-199/06, *CELF I*, [2008] ECR I-469, para. 53.

ible aid will never be implemented",[951] the Court of Justice has held that this principle is not contradicted by aid which was granted in contravention of procedural rules but which is later approved by the Commission.[952]

However, given that a positive decision by the Commission does not regularise or retrospectively remedy the original infringement of the standstill obligation,[953] the State aid in question must not "remain at the free disposal of the recipient during the period remaining until the Commission makes its decision".[954] Moreover, the recipient of the State Aid must at least pay interest in respect of the period of unlawfulness, i.e. for the period between its first use of the aid and the date of the Commission's final positive decision or the aid having been placed in a blocked account.[955]

c) Repayment of Unlawful Aid

Any decision by the Commission or the European Courts that aid was granted unlawfully will mean that the aid in question must be repaid by the beneficiary to the Member State.[956] It does not matter if the effect of such decision is that the contract pursuant to which the aid was granted is rendered void or to what extent it is rendered void.

The Commission's ability to order a Member State to recover aid from a beneficiary (a "recovery order") is set out in Article 14 of the State Aid Implementing Regulation; the specific means by which this is achieved is left to the discretion of the Member State.

aa) Recovery of Unlawful Aid – Identity of the Debtor

Article 14 of the State Aid Implementing Regulation indicates that aid shall be recovered from the original "beneficiary" of the aid,[957] however difficulties can arise in ascertaining the exact nature of the party from whom the aid is to be recovered if the original beneficiary no longer exists or if its legal form has changed.[958]

Analysis in each case will depend on the exact legal nature of the beneficiary and the structure of the applicable national law, but a broad distinction can be drawn between share acquisitions and business or asset acquisitions. When one undertaking

---

951   Case C-199/06, *CELF I*, [2008] ECR I-469, para. 47; Case C-1/09, *CELF II*, para. 29.

952   Case C-199/06, *CELF I*, [2008] ECR I-469, para. 49.

953   Case C-354/90, *FNCE*, [1991] ECR I-5505, para. 16; Case C-199/06, *CELF I*, [2008] ECR I-469, para. 40: "Any other interpretation would have the effect of according a favourable outcome to the non-observance by the Member State concerned of the last sentence of Article [108(3)] and would deprive it of its effectiveness."

954   Case C-1/09, *CELF II*, para. 30; to satisfy this requirement "the national court may order either the repayment of the aid with interest or, for example, the placement of the funds on a blocked account" (para. 37).

955   Case C-199/06, *CELF I*, [2008] ECR I-469, paras. 51, 52, 54.

956   See e.g. Case C-75/97, *Maribel*, [1999] ECR I-3671, para. 44.

957   Case law has established that the beneficiary of State aid is the person who has taken advantage of the aid, cf. Case C-277/00, *SMI*, [2004] ECR I-3925, para. 86.

958   Cf. Case C-305/89, *Alfa Romeo*, [1991] ECR I-1603; Case C-390/98, *Banks*, [2001] ECR I-6117; more recently Joined Cases C-328/99 and C-399/00, *Seleco*, [2003] ECR I-4035; Case C-277/00, *SMI*, [2004] ECR I-3925, para. 87.

acquires the entire share capital in a second undertaking which was the beneficiary of unlawful State aid, the acquiring undertaking becomes liable for the acquired undertaking's legal obligations, including e.g. an obligation to repay unlawful State aid.

In contrast, when one undertaking has acquired only the business and assets of a second undertaking which was the beneficiary of unlawful State aid (rather than assumed legal ownership of the second undertaking as a whole), it is unlikely that the acquiring undertaking can be held to be responsible for the acquired undertaking's obligation to repay unlawful State aid. The Court of Justice has confirmed this position in *Seleco* and *SMI*, though it should be noted that the Court did not specifically exclude the possibility that a third party could be liable for the repayment of unlawful State aid. The position may well be different if a business acquisition took place on non-market terms or if the transaction was undertaken with a specific intention to avoid the obligation to repay the unlawful aid.[959] The burden of proving the existence of such circumstances rests on the Commission.

It should also be noted that the Court of Justice's recent decision in *AkzoNobel*[960] relating to third party (corporate group) liability for infringements of Article 101 TFEU may indicate that the European Courts will be more open to holding that third-party undertakings should be held responsible for the repayment of unlawful State aid as well.

bb) Legal Confidence and Legal Certainty

Of particular issue in the realm of State aid is the extent to which a beneficiary of aid is liable to repay aid monies granted unlawfully, when that beneficiary acted in good faith and in reliance upon a Member State. State aid regulation in the EU is characterised by a bilateral, direct and exclusive relationship between the Commission and the Member State as regards the legality of a State aid measure, yet in the event that a measure is found to be unlawful, the burden of repayment will fall on the beneficiary of the unlawful aid (who itself is not a party in the regulatory relationship). This somewhat unusual structure can lead to concerns relating to legal confidence and legal certainty.

However, the beneficiary usually cannot rely on legal confidence to argue that, as he was not aware of the unlawfulness of the aid, he should not have to repay the monies granted unlawfully. The obligation to ascertain that State aid is lawful rests upon the beneficiary of the aid, before he accepts the aid.

(1) Example: Kahla

The case of *Kahla*[961] related to a Commission decision requiring the German government to recover aid it had granted to Kahla over a course of five years on the grounds that that aid had been granted unlawfully. The Commission had approved an aid scheme for the region of Thuringia on the basis of Article 107(3)(a) TFEU (aid to promote

---

959   Joined Cases C-328/99 and C-399/00, *Seleco*, [2003] ECR I-4035; Case C-277/00, *SMI*, [2004] ECR I-3925, para. 86.

960   For details see Chapter 2, Section III (*Legal Consequences of an Infringement of European Competition Law: Who is the Addressee of a Decision?*).

961   Case C-537/08 P, *Kahla*.

economically-deprived regions), however such approval was conditional upon the aid in question not being granted, in one case, to companies in difficulty, and in a second case, to private undertakings.[962] Upon becoming aware of the unlawful aid, the Commission required the German government to recover it from Kahla.

Kahla opposed the order to repay the relevant aid, arguing that it had not been, nor could it reasonably have been expected to be, aware of the restrictions affecting the State aid scheme in question, as they were set out in correspondence between the Commission and the German government, to which Kahla was not privy. Kahla was therefore of the view that an order by the Commission which would have the effect of requiring repayment of the aid by Kahla infringed the principles of the protection of legitimate expectations and legal certainty.

The Commission pointed out that its authorisation of the aid schemes in question was addressed directly and exclusively to the German government (not to Kahla); as Kahla was not the addressee of any binding Commission decision, Kahla could not allege before the European courts that the Commission had infringed the principle of legal certainty. Additionally, the Commission pointed out that its approval of the relevant State aid schemes had related to the schemes in general and the burden of determining the individual and specific allocation of aid monies under an authorised State aid scheme rested solely with the Member State.[963]

The Court of Justice noted that European jurisprudence confirmed that the scope of the Commission's approval of an aid scheme was determined not only by reference to the actual wording of that decision, but also by taking account of the aid scheme notified by the Member State concerned.[964] In this case, that included correspondence between the Commission and the German government clarifying the scope of the aid schemes. The fact that Kahla was not aware of the conditions imposed by the Commission on the aid schemes in question did not render them legally uncertain. As regards the principle of the protection of legitimate expectations, the Court of Justice confirmed that this principle only applies "to any individual in a situation in which an institution of the European Union, by giving that person precise assurances, has led him to entertain well-founded expectations"[965] and that such was not the case here, as the Commission's decision authorising the aid applied to a class of undertakings which did not include Kahla.[966]

(2) Example: ROM-projecten

The case of *ROM-projecten*[967] concerned State aid granted by the Dutch government to small and medium size enterprises. The conditions relating to the grant of that aid were set out in the Commission decision authorising the aid, but the Dutch government neither published nor made the beneficiary of the aid aware of those conditions. When the Commission indicated that the aid granted by the Dutch government to ROM-projecten was unlawful and issued a decision requiring the Dutch government to recover those aid

---

962   Case C-537/08 P, *Kahla*, para. 5.

963   Case C-537/08 P, *Kahla*, para. 35.

964   Case C-537/08 P, *Kahla*, para. 44.

965   Case C-537/08 P, *Kahla*, para. 63.

966   Case C-537/08 P, *Kahla*, para. 65.

967   Case C-158/06, *ROM-projecten*, [2007] ECR I-5103.

monies, ROM-projecten appealed that decision on the grounds that it had been unable to ascertain unequivocally what its rights and obligations under European law were.

The Court of Justice held that the principle of legal certainty could be applied so that a beneficiary of unlawful aid (provided that it was acting in good faith) did not have to repay the aid it had unlawfully received. Additionally, in such a situation it may be appropriate for the Member State concerned to be held financially liable for the amounts not recovered from the beneficiary in order to give effect to the Community's right to obtain repayment of the amount of the unlawful aid.[968]

---

968 Case C-158/06, *ROM-projecten*, [2007] ECR I-5103, para. 34.

Chapter Nine

EUROPEAN PUBLIC PROCUREMENT LAW

The field of public procurement law includes the rules and regulations which describe how the State and its various bodies may enter into contracts relating to the purchase of goods and services. In the course of the development of the 'four freedoms' of the Union and the removal of barriers to the internal market, European law has established directives to maintain competition in the internal market and standardise national procedures relating to public procurement. European public procurement law aims to ensure that activities of the State in this realm adhere to economic principles and do not distort competition: Member States may not discriminate against any economic actor and must ensure the allocation or bidding process is transparent.

The current "Public Sector Directive"[969] sets out the procedures applicable to the awarding of public works contracts, supply contracts and service contracts. The "Utilities Directive"[970] deals with the public procurement procedures relating to the water, energy, transport and postal services sectors. Both Directives, which must be implemented in national law,[971] set out the rules relating to the award of public contracts, in particular the requirements relating to the aim of European-wide standardisation of tenders whilst maintaining the Union's 'four freedoms', avoiding discrimination (e.g. on a national basis) and encouraging transparency.

I. THE RANGE OF APPLICATION OF PUBLIC PROCUREMENT LAW

Public procurement law applies when:

(1) the appointing contracting partner acts in a public capacity (is a "contracting authority");

(2) the contract is a public works, services or supplies contract;

---

969 Directive 2004/18/EC of the European Parliament and of the Council of 31 March 2004 on the coordination of procedures for the award of public works contracts, public supply contracts and public service contracts, [2004] OJ L134/114; last amended by Commission Regulation (EC) No 1177/2009 of 30 November 2009 amending Directives 2004/17/EC, 2004/18/EC and 2009/81/EC of the European Parliament and of the Council in respect of their application thresholds for the procedures for the award of contracts, [2009] OJ L314/64 (the "Public Sector Directive").

970 Directive 2004/17/EC of the European Parliament and of the Council of 31 March 2004 coordinating the procurement procedures of entities operating in the water, energy, transport and postal services sectors [2004] OJ L134/1; last amended by Commission Regulation (EC) No 1177/2009 of 30 November 2009 amending Directives 2004/17/EC, 2004/18/EC and 2009/81/EC of the European Parliament and of the Council in respect of their application thresholds for the procedures for the award of contracts, [2009] OJ L314/64 (the "Utilities Directive").

971 In England and Wales, the Public Sector Directive has been implemented via the Public Contracts Regulations 2006 and the Utilities Directive via the Utilities Contracts Regulations 2006.

(3) the estimated value of the contract reaches specified *threshold levels;* and

(4) no exception to the applicability of public procurement rules applies.

1. "Contracting Authority"

In order for the European rules on public procurement to apply, the body appointing or tendering the relevant work must be a 'contracting authority'.[972]

> *Contracting authorities* are the State and its related bodies, including national, re-
> gional or local authorities as well as public bodies. A public body is one:[973]
> (1) established for the specific purpose of meeting needs in the general interest,
>   not having an industrial or commercial character;
> (2) having legal personality; and
> (3) financed, for the most part, by the State or its related bodies or managed or
>   governed according to public law.[974]

Whether these conditions are fulfilled is analysed in the context of the body's actual functioning,[975] rather than its stated rules and operations. If a definition of a 'contracting authority' were not considered in light of the actual role played by a body (i.e. a functional assessment), then the entire purpose of public procurement law would be jeopardised, as a public works contract could be removed from the ambit of that area of law solely because it was not part of the formal State administration. It must, instead, be the case that a body which carries out tasks entrusted to it by legislation is subject to public procurement law, whether formally part of the State or not.[976] Additionally, public procurement law applies if a body's status changes over time – e.g. if it was previously a private body but then becomes a 'contracting authority', existing contracts become subject to public procurement rules from the date the body's status changes.[977]

Annex III to the Public Sector Directive sets out a non-exhaustive list of bodies and categories of bodies which meet the definition of 'bodies governed by public law'. In the event that it is unclear to a national court whether a body falls within this definition, it falls to the European courts (upon a request for a preliminary ruling) to ascertain whether the facts indicate that the relevant body is indeed a body governed by public law for the purposes of the Public Sector Directive.[978] Thus the list of bodies set out in Annex III to the Public Sector Directive is indicative, rather than definitive and, of

---

972   Article 1(9) of the Public Sector Directive; Article 2 of the Utilities Directive.

973   Article 1(9) of the Public Sector Directive.

974   Cf. the legal definition in Article 1(9) of the Public Sector Directive.

975   Cf. Case 31/87, *Beentjes,* [1988] ECR 4635; Case C-360/96, *Gemeente Arnhem v BFI Holding,* [1998] ECR I-6821; Case C-44/96, *Mannesmann,* [1998] ECR I-73, para. 3; Case C-470/99, *Universale-Bau AG,* [2002] ECR I-11617, para. 53.

976   Case 31/87, *Beentjes,* [1988] ECR 4635, para. 11.

977   Case C-470/99, *Universale Bau AG,* [2002] ECR I-11617, paras. 56–63.

978   Case C-300/07, *Hans & Christophorus Oymanns,* [2009] ECR I-4779, para. 45: This procedure "is a requirement of legal certainty, which is a general principle of [European Union] law".

course, bodies not listed or described in Annex III can nonetheless be considered bodies governed by public law, depending on the facts of each case.

a) In the General Interest

The concept of a 'public contract' is determined at Union rather than national level and so is subject to an autonomous and uniform interpretation according to Union law.[979]

> European case law has established that "needs in the general interest, not having an industrial or commercial character ... are generally needs which are satisfied otherwise than by the supply of goods and services in the marketplace and which, for reasons associated with the general interest, the State chooses to provide itself or over which it wishes to retain a decisive influence".[980]

The concept of public contracts includes those which aim to satisfy the interests of the public as a whole, rather than those of a limited group of individuals only. Activities in the general interest can include such diverse areas as e.g. ensuring water supply and waste disposal[981] or the financial support of exhibitions and trade shows.[982]

When determining whether a need in the general interest not having an industrial or commercial character exists, it is necessary to consider all the relevant legal and factual circumstances of the case, "such as those prevailing when the body concerned was formed and the conditions in which it carries on its activity, including, *inter alia*, lack of competition on the market, the fact that its primary aim is not the making of profits, the fact that it does not bear the risks associated with the activity, and any public financing of the activity in question".[983]

aa) Example: A Centre for Technological Development

> Does the establishment of a technology centre by a limited company owned and managed by a public body meet a need in the general interest?

The Finnish town of Varkus owned a limited company called Taitotalo whose purpose was to deal in property and to organise property maintenance services. The town of Varkus decided to create on its territory a technological development centre with Taitotalo involved in the building of the centre and aiming, after completion of the centre, to purchase the land on which the centre was built and to lease the buildings on the land to firms in the technology sector.

At issue in this case was whether Taitotalo, which did not itself aim to make a profit but which intended to create favourable conditions for the pursuit of commercial or in-

---

979 Case C-373/00, *Adolf Truley*, [2003] ECR I-1931, paras. 35 et seq., 40, 45; Case C-283/00, *Commission v Spain*, [2003] ECR I-11697, para. 79.

980 Case C-283/00, *Commission v Spain*, [2003] ECR I-11697, para. 80.

981 Case C-360/96, *BFI Holding*, [1998] ECR I-6821.

982 Joined Cases C-223/99 and C-260/99, *Agorà*, [2001] ECR I-3605.

983 Case C-283/00, *Commission v Spain*, [2003] ECR I-11697, paras. 81 et seq.

dustrial activities on the territory of a local authority, was undertaking activities aimed at meeting a need in the general interest. The Court of Justice held that yes, this type of activity was aiming to meet a need in the general interest, as the purpose of the technology centre was to develop trade for the community generally. The centre would be in the interests of not only the companies immediately affected by the project, but also the town and community generally.[984]

bb) Example: Acquisition of Property for the Purpose of Building Prisons

Is the acquisition of property, inter alia for the purpose of building prisons, a private or public aim?

SIEPSA was a commercial public limited company created and operated by the Spanish State whose purpose was to engage in property acquisition, management and works projects, including in relation to prison facilities. SIEPSA published a tender notice which drew the attention of the Commission, as it did not comply with the requirements of Directive 93/37/EEC (the public procurement directive then in effect).

Spain argued that SIEPSA was not a contracting authority, as its activities were of a commercial rather than non-commercial character – it carried out its activities in the same manner as other bodies governed by private law and acted with an intention to make profit. Spain also separated the building of prisons from the concept of enforcing penal policy.

The Court of Justice sided with the Commission and held that as SIEPSA had been established for the specific purpose of putting into effect certain programmes to implement the Spanish State's prison policy, it was engaged in meeting a public order need which clearly fell within the realm of meeting a need in the common interest. The Court also held that, although SIEPSA's activities did generate profits, it was inconceivable that such profit itself should be the company's chief aim. Thus SIEPSA constituted a contracting authority for the purposes of European public procurement law and as such its tender procedure should have complied with public procurement rules.[985]

b) Legal Personality

A body must have legal personality in order to constitute a body governed by public law – i.e. it must be able to possess rights and bear duties. This question is again one of Union rather than national law.

c) Body Governed by Public Law

The definitive analysis as to whether a State body, e.g. a national or local authority, constitutes a body of the State must include a consideration of all relevant facts relating to the

---

984 Case C-18/01, *Korhonen*, [2003] ECR I-5321.

985 Cf. to the pros and cons Case C-283/00, *Commission v Spain*, [2003] ECR I-11697, paras. 78–94; Opinion of Advocate General Alber, Case C-283/00, *Commission v Spain*, [2003] ECR I-11697, paras. 30–68; cf. Case C-470/99, *Universale Bau AG*, [2002] ECR I-11617, paras. 47–63 and the Opinion of Advocate General Alber, Case C-470/99, *Universale Bau AG*, [2003] ECR I-11617, paras. 27–50.

case. State influence can be indicated by e.g. financing predominantly by the Sate, State supervision of the operations of a body or the right of the State to name management or other key figures in the body.

aa) Predominantly Public Financing

A body is financed predominantly by public sources if the State contributes more than 50 % of its financing in a financial year (either directly or indirectly).[986] Payments relating to a specific *quid pro quo* for contractual performance, e.g. within the scope of scientific certifications, seminars or conferences, are not included in the financing calculation as they do not relate directly to State support of the body, but rather correspond to a normal exchange in a business relationship.[987]

Example: Public Broadcasters – Contracts Unrelated to Broadcasting Functions

> To what extent do public broadcasters have to comply with EU public procurement law?

A dispute existed as to whether German public broadcasting bodies constituted contracting authorities for the purposes of Directive 92/50 (the legislation relating to public procurement in force at the time).[988] Article 1(a)(iv) of Directive 92/50 provided that "contracts for the acquisition, development, production or co-production of programme material by broadcasters and contracts for broadcasting time" were excluded from the rules set out in that Directive.

This case centred around the issue as to whether a body established by German public broadcasters for administration and fee collection purposes (the "GEZ") was obliged to adhere to European public procurement rules when tendering for services unrelated to broadcasting services – i.e. did the 'public broadcasting' exclusion contained in Article 1(a)(iv) of Directive 92/50 extend to all activities of public broadcasters, or only to those activities directly related to their public broadcasting purpose.

The GEZ had sent a written invitation to a number of cleaning businesses asking for tenders for the provision of cleaning services for its premises; it did not put in place a formal procedure for the awarding of public contracts compatible with Union rules for public procurement. One undertaking which was not awarded the contract objected that the correct rules relating to public procurement had not been followed, infringing German and Union law. As the GEZ did not have legal personality itself, the broadcasters which controlled it responded themselves. They argued that they were not contracting authorities, as the public broadcasting service is financed for the most part by the fees paid by the television viewers so there is no public funding or public control of that service. They also highlighted Article 1(a)(iv) of Directive 92/50 which provided that that legislation did

---

986 Case C-380/98, *University of Cambridge,* [2000] ECR I-8035, paras. 30–33; Case C-337/06, *Bayerischer Rundfunk,* [2007] ECR I-11173, para. 33.

987 Case C-380/98, *University of Cambridge,* [2000] ECR I-8035, paras. 23–26.

988 Case C-337/06, *Bayerischer Rundfunk,* [2007] ECR I-11173.

not apply to public contracts for services which fell within the essential function of public broadcasting bodies (i.e. the creation and production of programme material).

The Court of Justice noted that the origin of the public broadcasters' fees was in State legislation, as such fees were not fixed on commercial terms.[989] National law required television viewers to pay the fees. On a functional interpretation, the Court concluded that financing which "is brought into being by a measure of the State, is guaranteed by the State and is secured by methods of charging and collection which fall within public authority powers" satisfies the condition of "financing ... by the State" for the purposes European public procurement law.[990]

As regarded the exemption for public broadcasting services contained in Article 1(a)(iv) of Directive 92/50, the Court of Justice held that this exemption served the purpose of guaranteeing freedom of the press[991] and that it should be construed restrictively: only those public contracts which relate to the services specified in that provision are excluded from the scope of that Directive.[992] Therefore public contracts which did not relate to essential broadcast activities, i.e. cleaning services, were subject to the full measure of European public procurement law.

bb) State Supervision

'State supervision' of a body's activities exists for the purposes of public procurement law if the supervision is such that the decisions of the body (as relate to public contracts) are influenced by the State.[993] Simple managerial supervision is not sufficient, as such supervision does not enable the public authorities to influence the decisions of the body in question in relation to public contracts.[994]

In Case C-237/99 *Commission v France* the Court of Justice held that, in order to constitute "State supervision", such supervision must "give rise to dependence on the public authorities equivalent to that which exists where one of the other alternative criteria is fulfilled, namely where the body in question is financed, for the most part, by the public authorities or where the latter appoint more than half of the members of its managerial organs".[995] On the facts of the case, the Court held that, *inter alia*, although the French Minister for Housing's ability to step in to control the body in question would only be exercised in exceptional circumstances, such a provision in French law nonetheless implied permanent supervision and was sufficient to constitute State supervision.[996]

---

989 Case C-337/06, *Bayerischer Rundfunk*, [2007] ECR I-11173, paras. 41–41.

990 Case C-337/06, *Bayerischer Rundfunk*, [2007] ECR I-11173, para. 48.

991 Case C-337/06, *Bayerischer Rundfunk*, [2007] ECR I-11173, para. 63.

992 Case C-337/06, *Bayerischer Rundfunk*, [2007] ECR I-11173, para. 67.

993 Case C-237/99, *Commission v France*, [2001] ECR I-939, para. 48.

994 Case C-373/00, *Adolf Truley*, [2003] ECR I-1931, paras. 70 et seq.

995 Case C-237/99, *Commission v France*, [2001] ECR I-939, para. 49.

996 Case C-237/99, *Commission v France*, [2001] ECR I-939, para. 56.

d) Specific Features of the Utilities Directive

As regards determining which contracts are subject to the rules contained in the Utilities Directive, the key factor is not the nature of the body awarding the contract (as is the case under the Public Sector Directive), but instead the nature of the activity to be performed: e.g. water supply, energy supply, transportation and postal services are all covered.[997] Previously the telecommunications sector was also included, but it has subsequently been removed following the general liberalisation of this sector in the Union.

The Utilities Directive applies to the State and its related bodies, but also to undertakings to whom special or exclusive rights have been granted in sectors where limited or no competition exists due to the granting of the special or exclusive rights. In such circumstances, European public procurement rules ensure that the undertaking to whom rights have been granted does not discriminate against any economic actors and that the allocation or bidding process is transparent.[998]

A clear boundary exists between the application of the Public Services Directive and the Utilities Directive. Article 20(1) of the Utilities Directive provides that that Directive applies only to contracts which the contracting entities award for purposes described in Articles 3 to 7 of that Directive. The corresponding provision in the Public Services Directive is Article 12, which makes clear that that Directive does not apply to public contracts which are covered by the Utilities Directive.[999]

2. What Constitutes Public Procurement?

Public procurement in the EU describes a wide range of contracts entered into by State bodies.

> 'Public contracts' are contracts for pecuniary interest concluded between one or more economic operators and one or more contracting authorities which have as their object the execution of works, the supply of products or the provision of services.[1000]

A key characteristic of such contracts is that they include consideration – in exchange for the economic operator's performance of his contractual obligations he receives money or money's worth. In this context consideration is construed widely and interpreted functionally and is not limited to a *quid pro quo*.

If a contract contains elements of different kinds of public contracts (execution of works, supply of products or provision of services), the European courts will look to the

---

997   Cf. Articles 3–6 of the Utilities Directive.

998   Cf. recitals 2 and 3 of the Utilities Directive; Case C-393/06, *Ing. Aigner v Fernwärme Wien*, [2008] ECR I-2339, paras. 25, 26, 37.

999   Case C-393/06, *Ing. Aigner v Fernwärme Wien*, [2008] ECR I-2339, para. 59.

1000   Cf. Article 1(2) of the Public Sector Directive; Article 1(2) of the Utilities Directive.

main purpose of the contract to determine which public procurement rules apply.[1001] It should be noted that, in order for public procurement rules to apply, it is necessary that a valid contract exists between the State body and its contractual counterparty. Such contract may exist under public or private law, depending on the law of the Member State. This point is distinct from the question of whether a contract to which a State body is party is subject to EU public procurement rules.[1002]

a) Contracts for the Execution of Works, the Supply of Products or the Provision of Services

In order to fall within the rules on public procurement, a contract must have as its object the execution of works, the supply of products or the provision of services, e.g. the purchase of office equipment by a local authority or the building of premises for a new police station.

b) Framework Agreements

EU public procurement rules cover a variety of types of agreements, including *framework agreements*.[1003]

> "Framework agreements" establish the basic terms (e.g. price or quantity) which will govern all contracts entered into by a contracting authority and an economic operator over the course of a specified period of time and are followed by individual contracts which set out additional details (e.g. timing of delivery).

Framework agreements involve an agreement between the parties to a contract of the basic terms which will apply to future contracts for a set period of time. They streamline the negotiating process, as certain basic terms and conditions have already been agreed, and a more limited number of details need to be negotiated in future.

Framework agreements fall within the realm of public procurement if they agree the identity of the parties to the contract, the subject matter of the contract (e.g. the products or services to be provided) and the principles of consideration to apply to future contracts. It is not necessary to agree specific quantities of the subject matter of the contract (e.g. the number of units of a product or the duration of services to be provided), and various other terms can also be left up to future negotiation. Only the 'basic conditions' have to be agreed in advance, but equally, once such conditions have been agreed, future contracts may not deviate from them.

Provided that a framework agreement complies with EU public procurement rules, it removes the need for an economic operator to submit tenders repeatedly for individual contracts. In practice, this makes framework agreements more efficient than repeated contractual negotiations, as it is only necessary to invite tenders once, and subsequent

---

1001 Case C-220/05, *Auroux*, [2007] ECR I-385, para. 37; Case C-536/07, *Koelnmesse*, [2009] ECR I-10355, para. 57.

1002 Case C-399/98, *Ordine degli Architetti di Milano et Lodi*, [2001] ECR I-5409, paras. 73 et seq.

1003 Article 1(5) of the Public Sector Directive; Article 1(4) of the Utilities Directive.

single contracts will be concluded on the basis of the terms of the framework agreement (and be subject to less strict procedural guidelines).[1004]

Example: Framework Agreements including Third Parties

European jurisprudence has held that a framework agreement exists even when orders are placed via a third party, rather than by the contracting authority directly. In the case of *Hans & Christophorus Oymann,* a German statutory sickness insurance fund invited orthopaedic footwear makers to submit tenders for the manufacture and supply of footwear. The quantity of shoes to be supplied was not fixed, as it depended upon the number of patients who would require the prescribed footwear. Upon being prescribed the relevant footwear by a doctor, patients would contact the manufacturer for measuring, fitting, etc. It would be the patients, rather than the contracting authority, who were the manufacturer's customers (with payment being made by both patient contributions as well as the statutory sickness insurance fund).

The Court of Justice held that a framework agreement existed between the statutory sickness insurance fund and the manufacturer, as the key aspects of the contract – duration and price – had been agreed and, importantly, the manufacturer benefited from a limited exclusivity of supply. The fact that some contractual details would only be finalised once a patient contacted the manufacturer to order his or her specific items of footwear, was consistent with the concept of a framework agreement where some element of uncertainty exists beyond the core terms agreed in the framework agreement.[1005]

c) Concessions

In contrast to a more straightforward type of contract where an economic actor agrees to provide certain goods or services in exchange for payment (a simple *quid pro quo*), a 'concession' is a type of contract based on an economic actor's right to benefit from the work it has undertaken. Put simply, instead of an economic actor receiving payment in e.g. money for carrying out certain works, he is granted a right to exploit the work he has undertaken, or to exploit that work and also charge an additional fee to other users.

> A concession exists when a contracting authority grants to a concessionaire the special or exclusive right to operate a particular service, and the latter enjoys a certain economic freedom to determine the conditions under which that right is exercised. Inherent in such a situation is that a concessionaire is, to a large extent, exposed to the risks involved in financing the operation of the service by prices for the service products being related to the demand from final consumers (and often subject to retail price (cap) regulation (e.g. in the public transportation sector)). Contracts concluded by a concessionaire during a given period must comply with the conditions laid down in the concession agreement.[1006]

1004 Cf. Article 32(3) and (4) of the Public Sector Directive.

1005 Case C-300/07, *Hans & Christophorus Oymanns,* [2009] ECR I-04779, paras. 74–76.

1006 Case C-300/07, *Hans & Christophorus Oymanns,* [2009] ECR I-04779, paras. 71 et seq.

aa) Works Concessions

Public procurement law applies to *works concessions*.[1007] Works concessions differ from 'normal' contracts for work in that, instead of being remunerated by money, a concessionaire receives the right to use the works for himself, or to charge third parties for doing so.

Example: Construction Concession or Town Planning Activity?

> Does a public body selling land grant a concession if, in making its decision to whom to sell, it takes account of which prospective purchaser is most likely to use the property in a way that benefits the public?

In *Helmut Müller* the Court of Justice had to consider whether certain town planning activities constituted the grant of a concession. The case concerned a parcel of land owned by the Bundesanstalt für Immobilienaufgaben (the German federal agency responsible for managing property). The Bundesanstalt wished to sell the property and the local town council where the property was situated indicated its desire that the land be used in a manner beneficial for town planning and development (and the Bundesanstalt agreed to respect the town council's opinion on such). As a result the property was sold to the prospective purchaser who had presented the planning concept most favourable to local authorities. The sale contract was entered into between the Bundesanstalt and a company known as GSSI and was a simple contract for sale – it contained no terms or conditions relating to the future use of the property.[1008]

Helmut Müller, a prospective purchaser who lost out to GSSI, brought an action in the German courts alleging that the sale of the property should have been undertaken in accordance with public procurement rules (and that as it had not complied with those rules, the sale contract between the Bundesanstalt and GSSI was void).[1009] The Court of Justice considered whether or not the sale of the property constituted a works concession under EU public procurement law.

Indicating the existence of a concession:	Indicating no existence of a concession:
A key characteristic of a concession is that the concessionaire bears the economic risk of the activity. Here, GSSI had been awarded the contract on the basis of its intended use of the land in future.[1010]	GSSI had not assumed any legally binding obligations regarding the use of the land which it had purchased, so although it had expressed certain intentions regarding the use of the property, it was in no way obliged to proceed in such a manner. Therefore it was not possible for a contract for works to be held to exist.[1011]

1007   Article 1(3) of the Public Sector Directive; Article 1(3)(a) of the Utilities Directive.

1008   Cf. Case C-451/08, *Helmut Müller*, paras. 8 et seq.; Opinion of Advocate General Mengozzi, Case C-451/08, *Helmut Müller*, paras. 5–13.

1009   Summing up the arguments: Vetter/Bergmann, NVwZ 2010, pp. 299, 301 et seq.

1010   Opinion of Advocate General Mengozzi, Case C-451/08, *Helmut Müller*, para. 85.

1011   Opinion of Advocate General Mengozzi, Case C-451/08, *Helmut Müller*, para. 78.

Indicating the existence of a concession:	Indicating no existence of a concession:
The wording of the Public Sector Directive does not require a public authority to procure anything from any other person in order for a public works contract to exist.[1012]	The bare sale of a property by a public authority does not constitute a public works contract within the meaning of the Public Sector Directive.[1013]
The sale of the property by one public authority and the intention of a second public authority to award a works contract in respect of that land are linked and should be considered as one transaction for the purposes of public procurement law.[1014]	The Court of Justice did not rule out the possibility that a two-phase award procedure for the sale of land which will subsequently form the subject of a works contract could exist and that those two transactions should be considered in unity. However, such was not the case here, as neither GSSI nor the town planning authority had assumed any legally binding obligations, nor did the sale contract indicate in any way that the award of a public works contract was imminent.[1015]

The Court of Justice held that no works concession existed in this case. The Bundesanstalt had simply sold a parcel of land, without any associated suggestion of a works concession (either by it or in conjunction with the town authorities) and GSSI was free to use the land it had purchased in any way it wished.

bb) Service Concessions

In contrast to works concessions, *service concessions* are expressly excluded from the realm of EU public procurement law.[1016]

> Service concessions are contracts in which the remunerative *quid pro quo* exists not in the form of a pre-agreed price, but instead in the right to market the relevant service independently.

It is necessary that the concessionaire bears at least the predominant share of the financial risk of operating the services in question on the market[1017] and that the provision of the relevant service lies in the public interest.

In such cases the public body is not forced to adhere to public procurement rules. However, a public body nonetheless must act in conformity with certain principles enshrined

---

1012 Opinion of Advocate General Mengozzi, Case C-451/08, *Helmut Müller*, para. 44.

1013 Cf. Article 16(a) of the Public Sector Directive; Case C-451/08, *Helmut Müller*, paras. 41, 43. However, an exception exists when abusive avoidance of EU public procurement law is intended; cf. Opinion of Advocate General Mengozzi, Case C-451/08, *Helmut Müller*, paras. 30, 106 et seq.

1014 Case C-451/08, *Helmut Müller*, para. 81.

1015 Case C-451/08, *Helmut Müller*, paras. 81–89.

1016 Article 17 of the Public Sector Directive; Case C-324/98, *Telaustria*, [2000] ECR I-10745, para. 62; Case C-358/00, *Buchhändlervereinigung v Deutsche Bibliothek*, [2002] ECR I-4685, para. 30.

1017 Cf. Case C-206/08, *Eurawasser*, [2009] ECR I-8377, paras. 59 et seq.

in primary European law, as set out by the Court of Justice in the case of *Telaustria* – including *non-discrimination, transparency* and *competitive openness*.[1018] In practice it is advisable to adhere to the formalised rules regarding public procurement, including, for example allocation via an invitation of tenders (which provides at least a significant degree of protection regarding the *Teleaustria* principles).[1019]

(1) Example: Gambling Licenses

A public service concession granting the right to deal in horse race betting must adhere to the fundamental principles of non-discrimination, transparency and competitive openness.[1020] In Case C-260/04 *Commission v Italy*, existing licenses were renewed without inviting tenders and the public procurement procedure was therefore non-transparent. Whilst exceptions to the requirement to invite tenders can exist when there are compelling reasons of national interest (as per Article 51 TFEU *et seq.*),[1021] such exceptions only apply insofar as any restriction of fundamental rights is proportionate.[1022]

(2) Example: Water Supply

In the case of *Acoset*, the Court of Justice reiterated that, although public service concessions are excluded from the scope of EU public procurement law, such contracts must nonetheless comply with the fundamental principles of the Treaty in general and with the principle of non-discrimination on the ground of nationality in particular.[1023] Here, a contract regarding water supply was clearly a concession, as its payment of water fees to the economic operator was identified in the invitation for tenders as compensation for the operator.[1024] Although the contract contained a small element of public works, it could not be considered a public works concession (which would then fall under the EU public procurement rules) as the vast majority of the contract related to the provision of water services.[1025]

d) "In House" Procurement

It may be the case that one public body wishes to enter into a contract for goods or services with another public body, rather than with an economic operator; such 'in house' agreements (so termed as they are 'internal' between public bodies) are not subject to public procurement rules if they fulfil specific in house conditions. This is because the essence of EU public procurement law relates to the preservation of competition in the

---

1018   Case C-324/98, *Telaustria*, [2000] ECR I-10745, paras. 39, 62; confirmed in Case C-458/05, *Parking Brixen*, [2005] ECR I-8612; Case C-410/04, *ANAV*, [2006] ECR I-3303; Case C-220/06, *Asociación Profesional de Empresas de Reparto y Manipulado de Correspondencia*, [2007] ECR I-12175, paras. 71 et seq.; Case C-196/08, *Acoset*, [2009] ECR I-9913, para. 46; Case C-324/07, *Coditel Brabant*, [2008] ECR I-8457, para. 25.

1019   Cf. Case C-203/08, *Sporting Exchange*, paras. 39, 41.

1020   Case C-260/04, *Commission v Italy*, [2007] ECR I-7083, paras. 22–24, 38.

1021   Case C-260/04, *Commission v Italy*, [2007] ECR I-7083, para. 26.

1022   Case C-260/04, *Commission v Italy*, [2007] ECR I-7083, para. 28.

1023   Case C-196/08, *Acoset*, [2009] ECR I-9913, para. 46.

1024   Case C-196/08, *Acoset*, [2009] ECR I-9913, para. 41.

1025   Case C-196/08, *Acoset*, [2009] ECR I-9913, paras. 19 et seq.

internal market which involves economic actors, i.e. undertakings which operate under market conditions: Article 2 of the Public Sector Directive refers specifically to "economic operators" being treated equally and non-discriminatorily. This aim of protecting competition in the market does not apply when the relevant contractor does not exist as an economic participant in the market in the first place.[1026]

It is clear that a public body is at liberty to perform the tasks conferred on it by using its own resources without calling on any other undertaking.[1027] More complicated is a situation where one public body enters into a contract with another public body which has separate legal personality to the first.

> In order for the rules of public procurement not to apply to a contract on the grounds of that contract being 'in house', two conditions must be met:
> (1) the contracting authority must exercise over the supplying entity a control which is similar to that which it exercises over its own departments; and
> (2) the supplying entity must carry out the essential part of its activities with the local authority or authorities which control it.[1028]

aa) Control Similar to that it Exercises over its own Departments

The standard needed to demonstrate control in this context is more stringent than in other areas of competition law (e.g. Articles 101 and 102 TFEU or the Merger Regulation).[1029] In other areas of competition law, control may be indicated by e.g. a majority shareholding or a right to appoint a majority of directors or members of a supervisory board; however, such elements are insufficient to indicate a level of control "similar to that which [a contracting authority] exercises over its own departments" – such a level of control is more extensive than 'normal' control in competition law.[1030]

> The test used to determine if the control exercised by a contracting authority is similar to that which it exercises over its own departments requires effective and direct access to the decision-making of the supplying entity. The contracting authority must be able to influence the decisions of the second entity in the same way internal decisions are taken.

(1) No Involvement of a Private Entity

Even a small degree of involvement by a private entity in a contractor establishes that the contracting authority cannot exercise the degree of control necessary to fall within the

---

1026 Cf. Case C-340/04, *Carbotermo*, [2006] ECR I-4137, para. 60.

1027 Cf. Opinion of Advocate General Kokott, Case C-458/03, *Parking Brixen*, [2005] ECR I-8612, para. 42.

1028 Case C-337/05, *Commission v Italy*, [2008] ECR I-2173, para. 36; see also Case C-107/98, *Teckal*, [1999] ECR I-8121, para. 50; Case C-26/03, *Stadt Halle*, [2005] ECR I-1, para. 49; Case C-84/03, *Commission v Spain*, [2005] ECR I-139, para. 38; Case C-29/04, *Commission v Austria*, [2005] ECR I-9705, para. 34; Case C-340/04, *Carbotermo*, [2006] I-4137, para. 33; Case C-295/05, *Asemfo*, [2007] ECR I-2999, para. 55.

1029 Cf. Chapter 7, Section III(2) (*Change of control*).

1030 Opinion of Advocate General Kokott, Case C-458/03, *Parking Brixen*, [2005] ECR I-8612, para. 52.

exception to public procurement rules.[1031] The involvement of a private entity indicates the existence of a mixed public and private contractor, and the applicability of public procurement rules in such cases is clear. This is the case even if the private element of the contractor is not participating in the undertaking at the time of the award of the contract; it is sufficient that the private element might become active at a later point in time,[1032] or if a private entity holds any (even a small minority) of shares in the contractor.[1033]

The legal form taken by the contractor is unimportant – whether a contractor is organised as a private company or in the form of a public body, the test as to the contracting authority's control is one of effect and substance, rather than form.[1034]

(2) Activity Undertaken by the Contractor

The kinds of activities undertaken by the contractor must be quite limited: it must operate as an extension of the contracting authority and be steered directly by the management of the contracting authority, with its activities limited to the geographic and substantive competence of the contracting authority.[1035] Again, this issue is considered in light of the substance of the relationship between the two bodies, rather than the form of that relationship. The contractor must not act independently of the contracting authority.

> Where a contractor possesses even a small degree of *operational independence*, the rules of public procurement law apply.

Example: Cable Television Network Provider

In the case of *Coditel Brabant* the Court of Justice found that municipal authorities exercised sufficient control over a cable television network provider so that public procurement rules did not apply. The contractor in question was owned and governed by a number of municipalities, all themselves public bodies. Those municipalities controlled the decision-making bodies of the contractor and thus determined its strategic aims and decisions.[1036] Finally, the contractor was entirely non-commercial in nature and exercised no private activities.[1037]

1031   Opinion of Advocate General Colomer, Case C-196/08, *Acoset*, [2009] ECR I-9913, para. 99; Case C-26/03, *Stadt Halle*, [2005] ECR I-1, para. 49. See also Case C-337/05, *Commission v Italy*, [2008] ECR I-2173, para. 38; Case C-324/07, *Coditel Brabant*, [2008] ECR I-8457, para. 30; Case C-573/07, *Sea Srl*, [2009] ECR I-8127, para. 46.

1032   Case C-410/04, *ANAV*, [2006] ECR I-3303, paras. 30–32; Case C-29/04, *Gemeinde Mödling*, [2005] ECR I-9705, in particular para. 41; Case C-573/07, *Sea Srl*, [2009] ECR I-8127, paras. 50, 49.

1033   Case C-573/07, *Sea Srl*, [2009] ECR I-8127, para. 53.

1034   Case C-480/06, *Commission v Germany*, [2009] ECR I-4747, para. 47; Case C-573/07, *Sea Srl*, [2009] ECR I-8127, para. 41.

1035   Case C-458/05, *Parking Brixen*, [2005] ECR I-8612; see also Case C-340/04, *Carbotermo*, [2006] ECR I-4137; Case C-324/07, *Coditel Brabant*, [2008] ECR I-8457, para. 28.

1036   Case C-324/07, *Coditel Brabant*, [2008] ECR I-8457, para. 34.

1037   Case C-324/07, *Coditel Brabant*, [2008] ECR I-8457, paras. 37, 38, 41.

bb) Contractor Must Carry out its Activities with the Contracting Authority

In addition to establishing that the contracting authority exercises sufficient control over the contractor, the contractor must also carry out the essential part of its activities with the contracting authority.[1038] Only if such is the case (i.e. the contractor does not act in competition with other entities in the market) can the rules relating to public procurement be avoided, as those rules have as their aim the protection of competition.

> A contractor can be viewed as carrying out the essential part of its activities with the controlling authority only if that undertaking's activities are devoted principally to that authority and any other activities are only of marginal significance.[1039]

Notably, a contractor does not have to act exclusively for the contracting authority.[1040] For sector specific procurements, Article 23 of the Utilities Regulation specifies a threshold of 80 %. However, it should be noted that each case is assessed on its facts, and the 80 %-threshold is indicative only, rather than definitive. In each case a comprehensive assessment should be undertaken with the help of qualitative and quantitative criteria, including i.e. a consideration of what proportion of the contracting authority's turnover is generated by the contractor.[1041]

cc) Example: Obligation to Invite Tenders for Gaming Licenses

> Is a Member State obliged to invite tenders for monopolistic gaming licenses?

Dutch gambling law is structured as a system of exclusive licences under which (i) only licensed entities may organise or promote games of chance and (ii) only one licence is granted by the national authorities in respect of each of the games of chance authorised. At the time of the *Sporting Exchange* case, one undertaking, a non-profit foundation governed by private law, had held the licence for all sports-related prize competitions, the lottery and numbers games since 1961. A separate undertaking held a licence for horse race betting. In both cases, the licenses had been extended previously for terms of five years without open invitations for tenders. The Dutch government justified such restrictions on the gambling industry on public safety grounds – e.g. protecting the public from the dangers of gambling addiction and fraud.

Betfair, operating from the UK, wished to offer its services on the Netherlands market, and applied to the Dutch government for a gaming licence. When the Dutch government refused Betfair's request, Betfair challenged that refusal to a grant of a licence as well as the extensions of the licenses the Dutch government had granted to other providers of gambling services in the Netherlands.

1038   Case C-340/04, *Carbotermo*, [2006] ECR I-4137, paras. 59–62; Case C-220/06, *Correos*, [2007] ECR I-12175, paras. 61 et seq.

1039   Case C-340/04, *Carbotermo*, [2006] ECR I-4137, paras. 63, 70 et seq.

1040   Case C-573/07, *Sea Srl*, [2009] ECR I-8127, paras. 79, 80.

1041   Case C-340/04, *Carbotermo*, [2006] ECR I-4137, paras. 58–72.

(1) Invitation of Tenders Duty for Monopoly Concessions?
In *Sporting Exchange*, the Court of Justice had to determine whether the extension of the licences granted to monopoly concession holders without an invitation of tenders was permitted under EU law. Specifically, did not inviting tenders in such a situation infringe the primary law principles of equal treatment and transparency?

Indicating an obligation to invite tenders:	Indicating no obligation to invite tenders:
The principle of ensuring transparency in the realm of public procurement exists to protect fundamental freedoms in the Union, regardless of the legal basis or form taken by a public body's actions.[1042] The potential discriminatory effects on other gambling operators exist whether the public body acts via an administrative authorisation or pursuant to a contract.[1043]	The Dutch government argued that the principle of transparency (and the associated obligation to invite tenders) did not apply here as the licensing procedure was an instance of administrative authorisation and not a contract entered into between a public body and an economic operator.[1044]
Any public policy concerns held by the Dutch government could be addressed by imposing conditions on the terms of a licence granted. A call for tenders at the stage of selecting a single operator for an area of gambling would not necessarily compromise the government's ability to impose the restrictions it considered necessary to protect the public.[1045]	The Dutch government argued that putting the licensing procedure out to tender would have the same detrimental effects as allowing full competition in the gambling sector, as if the licence were temporary, the gambling service provider would be tempted to make the maximum profit during the term of the license.[1046] Thus, in order to protect the public from dangers such as gambling addiction and fraud, the licensing system should not be open to tenders.

Although the European Courts have consistently held that Member States may restrict the organisation and exploitation of gaming in their territory in order to protect consumers from excessive expenditure on gaming and to preserve public order by reason of the risk of fraud created by the considerable amounts yielded by gaming,[1047] and to limit supply of such services to one provider only per category of games,[1048] the principles of non-discrimination and transparency still apply to the process used to select that single provider. It is permissible to limit the operation of the gambling market in this way, but a minimum of competition in the internal market must be allowed to determine which operators are allowed to operate in the monopoly role ("competition *for* the market, instead of competition *in* the market").

1042   Opinion of Advocate General Bot, Case C-203/08, *Sporting Exchange*, para. 153.

1043   Case C-203/08, *Sporting Exchange*, para. 47; Opinion of Advocate General Bot, Case C-203/08, *Sporting Exchange*, paras. 155 et seq.

1044   Opinion of Advocate General Bot, Case C-203/08, *Sporting Exchange*, para. 149.

1045   Opinion of Advocate General Bot, Case C-203/08, *Sporting Exchange*, paras. 162 et seq., 187.

1046   Opinion of Advocate General Bot, Case C-203/08, *Sporting Exchange*, para. 149.

1047   Cf. also Case C-42/07, *Liga Portuguesa*, [2009] ECR I-7633; Case C-203/08, *Sporting Exchange*, paras. 26–28, 30; Koenig/Ciszewski, ZfWG 2009, pp. 330 et seq.

1048   Case C-203/08, *Sporting Exchange*, para. 37; Opinion of Advocate General Bot, Case C-203/08, *Sporting Exchange*, paras. 53, 55.

(2) An "In House" exemption?

Sporting Exchange also touched upon the question of whether one of the undertakings granted a license to operate gaming services by the Dutch government could benefit from 'in house' status and therefore be exempt from public procurement rules on that basis. As noted above,[1049] two criteria must be fulfilled for a contractor to be considered 'in house': (i) sufficient control of the contractor by the contracting authority, and (ii) the contractor must carry out a sufficient degree of its operations with the contracting authority. Here, although the gambling licensee operated under the supervision of the Dutch government (e.g. using its receipts for the purposes specified by the government) it nonetheless operated as a subsidiary of an American company which itself operated with an intention to make profit. Thus it could not benefit from the 'in house' exemption from public procurement rules.[1050]

In general, it remains unclear whether the 'in house' criteria also apply in the case of service concessions to which the Public Sector Directive does not apply. The Court of Justice has commented on the point on several occasions, referring to restrictions on fundamental freedoms being justified where a contractor's management is "subject to direct State supervision" or a private operator's activities are "subject to strict control by the public authority".[1051] Two particular cases of note are *Läärä*[1052] and *Liga Portuguesa*,[1053] though neither sets out a complete set of criteria. In *Läärä*, the contractor licensed to operate gambling services was a public-law association whose activities were carried out under the control of the State and which was required to pay over to the State the net distributable proceeds it received from the licensed activity.[1054] In *Liga Portuguesa*, the licensee was a 'legal person in the public interest' which operated for the public's benefit rather than with an intention to make profit.[1055]

e) Public-Private Partnerships

Closely related to the discussion about the "in house" exemption from public procurement rules is the area of *public-private partnerships (PPP)*. These partnerships exist between public bodies and private undertakings and as such do not meet the criteria necessary to benefit from in house status in the area of public procurement law. However, it is sufficient if public procurement rules are adhered to at the first stage of the partnership – i.e. the determination of the identity of the private partner in the first place. The second stage where a project is actually undertaken can then carry on without an additional invitation for tenders.[1056]

1049   See Chapter 9, Section I(2)(d) *("In House" Procurement)*.

1050   Case C-208/03, *Sporting Exchange*, para. 62; Opinion of Advocate General Bot, Case C-203/08, *Sporting Exchange*, paras. 171, 173.

1051   Case C-203/08, *Sporting Exchange*, para. 59.

1052   Case C-124/97, *Läärä*, [1999] ECR I-6067.

1053   Case C-42/07, *Liga Portuguesa*, [2009] ECR I-7633.

1054   Case C-124/97, *Läärä*, [1999] ECR I-6067, in particular para. 40.

1055   Case C-42/07, *Liga Portuguesa*, [2009] ECR I-7633, as to the organisation of Santa Casa in particular paras. 12–19.

1056   Case C-196/08, *Acoset*, [2009] ECR I-9913, paras. 59–62.

3. Threshold Values

The Public Sector Directive and Utilities Directive specify that the rules contained therein only apply to public contracts above a certain value. In order for these threshold figures to remain up-to-date, the Commission issues a regulation approximately every two years specifying the applicable values. Currently, the threshold for works contracts is EUR 4,845,000 and for other supply and service contracts EUR 193,000.[1057]

Below these threshold values, national legislation governs governmental budgetary rules, though the principles of non-discrimination and transparency stemming from the fundamental freedoms must nonetheless be incorporated in the issue of public contracts.

a) Total Value of the Contract

Article 9 of the Public Sector Directive and Article 17 of the Utilities Directive set out in detail the methods to be used in calculating the estimated value of contracts, framework agreements and dynamic purchasing systems.[1058] The total value of each contract must be assessed – no contract should be subdivided in order to prevent it from falling within public procurement rules (see e.g. Article 9(3) of the Public Sector Directive). Thus, when in doubt, a higher figure is assumed to be correct so as to fall within the scope of the Directives.[1059]

The starting point for calculating the value of a contract is the total amount payable, net of any value added tax, as estimated by the contracting authority. This calculation will include the total compensation (*quid pro quo*) of all elements of the contract for the entire duration of the contact including any form of option and any renewals of the contract (Article 9(1) Public Sector Directive). Additionally, any payments to be made to the contractor by third parties should also be included when assessing the total value of the contract.[1060] This is because the total value of the project or contract to the contractor includes not only sums paid by the contracting authority, but also any amounts it will receive from third parties.[1061]

b) Leasing, Hire, Rental or Hire-Purchase Contracts

Article 9(6) of the Public Sector Directive specifies that the value of leasing, hire, rental or hire-purchase contracts with fixed terms shall be calculated as the value of the contract over its full term. For such contracts where the terms of the contract are unlimited, how-

---

1057   Commission Regulation (EC) No 1177/2009 of 30 November 2009 amending Directives 2004/17/EC, 2004/18/EC and 2009/81/EC of the European Parliament and of the Council in respect of their application thresholds for the procedures for the award of contracts, [2009] OJ L314/64.

1058   For simplicity we refer to "contracts" in short. For details see Article 9 of the Public Sector Directive; Article 17 of the Utilities Directive.

1059   For a detailed discussion of the calculation of the estimated value of supply and public service contracts see Koenig/Schreiber, WuW 2009, pp. 1118 et seq.

1060   Case C-220/05, *Auroux,* [2007] ECR I-385, para. 53.

1061   Case C-220/05, *Auroux,* [2007] ECR I-385, paras. 53, 57.

ever, the value of the contract shall be calculated by the monthly value of the contract multiplied by 48 (i.e. the value of the contract for a four year term).

c) Standing Orders or Renewable Contracts

Article 9(6) of the Public Sector Directive specifies that the value of contracts which are regular in nature or which are intended to be renewed within a given period shall be calculated as either (a) the total actual value of the successive contracts of the same type awarded during the preceding 12 months (adjusted to take account of any changes in quantity or value which would occur in the course of the 12 months following the initial contract) or (b) the total estimated value of the successive contracts awarded during the 12 months following the first delivery.

d) Framework Agreements and Contracts Awarded in Lots

The value of a framework agreement is the maximum estimated value (net of value added tax) of all the contracts envisaged for the total term of the framework agreement (Article 9(9) of the Public Sector Directive). As regards contracts awarded in lots, i.e. multiple separate contracts awarded at the same time in separate groups, the overall value of all the lots awarded should be considered. When the aggregate value of all the lots meets the current thresholds laid down by the Commission, then public procurement rules shall apply to each lot. An exception to this rule exists if certain additional limits are met and the contracting authority waives the applicability of public procurement rules.[1062]

4. Exemptions to Public Procurement Rules

Articles 12–18 of the Public Sector Directive and 19–23 of the Utilities Directive identify a range of exemptions which exclude certain sectors and activities from the ambit of those Directives. These exemptions are construed restrictively.[1063] As noted above,[1064] in the case of German public broadcasters, exemption from public procurement rules on the basis of Article 16 of the Public Sector Directive was held to apply only to activities directly related to the nature of the exemption; unrelated activities, such as cleaning services, were subject to the full ambit of public procurement law.

As regards contracts requiring special security measures (e.g. in the field of defence and security), such contracts are excluded from public procurement rules only if an actual security concern exists which affects the fundamental interests of the State. However, the exclusion of such contracts from public procurement law must be proportionate

---

1062 Lots can be excluded if their estimated value is less than EUR 80,000 net as regards services and less than EUR 1,000,000 net as regards construction works, provided that the total value of these lots does not amount to more than 20 % of the total value of all lots – i.e. the other lots must add up to at least 80 % of the total value of all lots; see Articles 9(5)(a)(2) and (3) of the Public Sector Directive.

1063 Case C-337/06, *Bayerischer Rundfunk*, [2007] ECR I-11173, para. 64.

1064 See Chapter 9, Section I(1)(c)(aa) (*Predominantly Public Financing*).

– i.e. there must be no less severe way of managing the security concern, such as imposing confidentiality restrictions.[1065]

Additionally, it should be noted that, even if an exemption to public procurement rules applies, the fundamental freedoms set out in the Treaties must still be respected, including in particular the principles of non-discrimination and transparency.[1066]

II. AWARD PROCEDURES

If the EU rules on public procurement apply to a contract, there are four kinds of procedures available through which contracts may be awarded: open, restricted and negotiated procedures and competitive dialogue. The basic characteristics of each procedural method are set out below.

	Open procedure	Restricted procedure	Competitive dialogue[1067]	Negotiated procedure
When should each procedure be used?[1068]	Should be used generally.	Should be used generally.	Should be used only in cases of particularly complex contracts.[1069]	Should be used only if the other procedures are impractical.[1070] However, note that under the Utilities Directive the open, restricted and negotiated procedures rank equally.[1071]
Who may tender?	Unrestricted (everybody)	Restricted after previous selection.	Restricted after previous selection.	Restricted after previous selection.

1065   Case C-337/05, *Commission v Italy*, [2008] ECR I-2173, para. 53; Case C-157/06, *Commission v Italy*, [2008] ECR I-7313, para. 31.

1066   See also Chapter 9, Section I(2)(c)(bb) (*Service Concessions*) regarding service concessions.

1067   Only provided for in the Public Sector Directive, not the Utilities Directive.

1068   Article 28 of the Public Sector Directive.

1069   Article 29(1) of the Public Sector Directive; recital 31.

1070   Articles 30 and 31 of the Public Sector Directive: complete and conclusive catalogues that need to be handled restrictively because of their exceptional nature.

1071   Article 40(2) of the Utilities Directive; note that even fully private undertakings are bound by the Utilities Directive.

1072   Articles 45–52 of the Public Sector Directive.

1073   Article 53 of the Public Sector Directive.

1074   Articles 45–52 of the Public Sector Directive.

1075   Article 53 of the Public Sector Directive.

1076   Article 29(1)(2) of the Public Sector Directive.

	Open procedure	Restricted procedure	Competitive dialogue	Negotiated procedure
Award criteria	Suitability test[1072] and pre-determined contract award criteria linked to the subject-matter of the public contract in question.[1073]	Suitability test[1074] and pre-determined award criteria.[1075]	The tender most economically advantageous from the point of view of the contracting authority.[1076]	Suitability test[1077] and pre-determined contract award criteria.[1078]
Procedure to be followed	Publication of a contract notice in the Supplement of the Official Journal including an invitation to submit a tender.[1079]	Publication in the Supplement of the Official Journal including an invitation to submit a request to participate.[1080]	Publication of the intent to contract in the Supplement of the Official Journal.[1081]	As a general rule, a notice of the intent to contract including an invitation to submit a request to participate needs to be published in the Supplement of the Official Journal.[1082]
	Receipt of tenders within a certain time limit.[1083]	Receipt of requests to participate and – in a second step[1084] after a non-discriminating selection of candidates – receipt of tenders[1085] of the selected[1086] candidates within a certain time limit (shorter time limits permissible).[1087]	Receipt of requests to participate (shorter time limits permissible)[1088] and suitability test.[1089]	Receipt of requests to participate (shorter time limits permissible).[1090]

1077 Articles 45–52 of the Public Sector Directive.

1078 Article 53 of the Public Sector Directive.

1079 Articles 35–37 of the Public Sector Directive.

1080 Articles 35–37 of the Public Sector Directive.

1081 Articles 29(2) and 35(2) of the Public Sector Directive.

1082 Articles 30(1) and 35(2) of the Public Sector Directive (exception as per Article 31); Article 40(2) of the Utilities Directive (exception as per Article 40(3)).

1083 Article 38 of the Public Sector Directive; Article 45 of the Utilities Directive.

1084 After examination of the requests to participate, selected candidates are invited to submit tenders: Article 40 of the Public Sector Directive; Article 47 of the Utilities Directive.

1085 Article 40 of the Public Sector Directive.

1086 As to the selection criteria cf. Article 44 of the Public Sector Directive.

1087 Article 38 of the Public Sector Directive; Article 45 of the Utilities Directive.

1088 Article 38 of the Public Sector Directive.

1089 Article 44 of the Public Sector Directive.

1090 Article 38 of the Public Sector Directive.

	Open procedure	Restricted procedure	Competitive dialogue	Negotiated procedure
Proce-dure to be followed	Dialogue prohibited.	Dialogue prohibited.	(Non-discriminating) dialogue with the se-lected[1091] and admit-ted candidates.[1092]	(Non-discriminat-ing) negotiation about the tenders submit-ted by the selected candidates.[1093]
			May be conducted in successive stages of discussion.[1094]	May be conducted in successive stages of negotiation.[1095]
	Decision[1096] and information of the candidates and ten-derers[1097] – may be preceded by an electronic auction (automatic evalua-tion).[1098]	Decision[1099] and information of the candidates and tenderers[1100] – may be preceded by an electronic auction (automatic evalua-tion).[1101]	After completion of the dialogue phase: decision[1102] between the final tenders[1103] by means of an elec-tronic auction (auto-matic evaluation)[1104] and information of the candidates and tenderers.[1105]	Decision[1106] and information of the candidates and tenderers[1107] – may be preceded by an electronic auction (automatic evalua-tion).[1108]
Addition-al points to note	Dynamic pur-chasing system:[1109] all-electronic pro-cedure for the pur-chase of customary services.[1110]			

1091   Cf. to the selection criteria Article 44 of the Public Sector Directive.

1092   Articles 29(3) and (5) of the Public Sector Directive; Article 40 of the Public Sector Directive.

1093   Articles 30(2)–(3) and 40 of the Public Sector Directive.

1094   Article 29(3)–(5) of the Public Sector Directive.

1095   Article 30(4) of the Public Sector Directive.

1096   The decision is based on an examination of the tenders submitted which must comply with Article 44 of the Public Sector Directive.

1097   Article 41 of the Public Sector Directive.

1098   Cf. the legal definition in Article 1(7) of the Public Sector Directive; Article 1(6) of the Utilities Direc-tive.

1099   As to the criteria cf. Article 44 of the Public Sector Directive.

1100   Article 41 of the Public Sector Directive.

1101   Cf. the legal definition in Article 1(7) of the Public Sector Directive; Article 1(6) of the Utilities Direc-tive.

1102   Cf. to the criteria Article 44 of the Public Sector Directive.

1103   Article 29(6)–(7) of the Public Sector Directive.

1104   Cf. the legal definition in Article 1(7) of the Public Sector Directive; Article 1(6) of the Utilities Direc-tive.

1105   Article 41 of the Public Sector Directive.

1106   Cf. to the criteria Article 44 of the Public Sector Directive.

III. LEGAL PROTECTION RELATING TO THE AWARD PROCESS

Legal protection for contractors who feel that a public procurement exercise was undertaken incorrectly lies in national law, which must comply with standards set out in European legislation.[1111] In England and Wales this is achieved through the Public Contracts (Amendment) Regulations 2009 and the Utilities Contracts (Amendment) Regulations 2009; notable provisions include:

(1) the enforcement of a duty of care owed by a contracting authority to an economic operator shall take place in the High Court (Reg. 47C);

(2) interim and interlocutory measures to set aside unlawful decisions and to award damages (Reg. 47I);

(3) automatic suspension of the contract-making process when legal review of a contract award decision has been applied for but not yet concluded (Reg. 47G);

(4) establishment of a 'standstill period' following the announcement of an award decision to enable aggrieved parties to pursue an effective range of pre-contractual remedies (Reg. 32A);

(5) a remedy of 'ineffectiveness' under which contracts can be cancelled after they have been awarded, for certain serious breaches of public procurement rules (Reg. 47K); and

(6) penalties of fines and contract shortening which can be used either as an alternative to ineffectiveness or as an addition to prospective ineffectiveness (Reg. 47N).

Example: Legal Protection notwithstanding Expiry of Limitation Periods

Can the Commission bring an action relating to infringement of public procurement law if the deadline for doing so under national law has expired?

In two cases of *Commission v Germany* (Case C-275/08 and Case C-17/09), the Court of Justice had to consider whether infringement proceedings for the infringement of public procurement rules can be brought against a Member State after the deadline for any such claims under national law has passed.

The German government did not dispute that infringements of public procurement rules had taken place, but pointed out that the aggrieved party had known about the

---

1107   Article 41 of the Public Sector Directive.

1108   Cf. the legal definition in Article 1(7) of the Public Sector Directive; Article 1(6) of the Utilities Directive.

1109   Article 33 of the Public Sector Directive.

1110   Articles 1(6) and 33 of the Public Sector Directive; Articles 1(5) and 15 of the Utilities Directive.

1111   Council Directive 89/665/EEC of 21 December 1989 on the coordination of the laws, regulations and administrative provisions relating to the application of review procedures to the award of public supply and public works contracts, [1989] OJ L395/33, and Council Directive 92/13/EEC of 25 February 1992 coordinating the laws, regulations and administrative provisions relating to the application of Community rules on the procurement procedures of entities operating in the water, energy, transport and telecommunications sector, [1992] OJ L76/14, both directives being amended by Directive 2007/66/EC of the European Parliament and of the Council of 11 December 2007 amending Council Directives 89/665/EEC and 92/13/EEC with regard to improving the effectiveness of review procedures concerning the award of public contracts, [2007] OJ L335/31.

breach for a number of years, yet not brought any action in the German courts until after the German statute of limitation for bringing such a claim under German law had passed.[1112]

The Court of Justice held that, notwithstanding the time limits imposed by national law, the Commission could still initiate infringement proceedings against Germany in the European courts.[1113] The Court noted that the purpose of the Commission bringing proceedings against a Member State was not to preserve the rights of one potential contractor (which is an element of national law) but rather was to ensure that certain rights granted under EU law are protected generally.[1114] As such, national limitation periods could not limit the applicability of EU primary law.[1115]

Equally, even if a potential contractor contacted the Commission to report what it perceived to be a breach of EU public procurement rules, the Commission alone in its role as "guardian of the Treaties" is responsible for deciding whether to bring infringement proceedings against a Member State.[1116]

1112   Case C-17/09, *Commission v Germany*, para. 13.

1113   Case C-17/09, *Commission v Germany*, paras. 19–29.

1114   Case C-275/08, *Commission v Germany*, [2009] ECR I-168, paras. 34–37; Case C-17/09, *Commission v Germany*, paras. 25 et seq.

1115   Case C-275/08, *Commission v Germany*, [2009] ECR I-168, para. 37; Case C-17/09, *Commission v Germany*, para. 27.

1116   Case C-275/08, *Commission v Germany*, [2009] ECR I-168, paras. 26 et seq., 38 et seq.; Case C-17/09, *Commission v Germany*, paras. 19–21, 28 et seq.

OVERVIEW:
IMPORTANT DECISIONS – EXAMPLES

The numbers at the end of each line refer to the page(s) on which the specific decision is discussed in this book.

Decisions of the European Court of Justice

Case 6/72, *Continental Can*, [1973] ECR-215	142
Joined Cases 40 to 48, 50, 54 to 56, 111, 113 and 114/73, *Suiker Unie*, [1975] ECR 1663	100
Case 27/76, *United Brands*, [1978] ECR 207	34/35
Case 77/77, *Benzine en Petroleum Handelsmaatschappij BV and others*, [1978] ECR 1513	103
Case 22/78, *Hugin*, [1979] ECR 1869	36/37
Case 155/79, *AM&S*, [1982] ECR 1575	130
Case 7/82, *GVL*, [1983] ECR 483	100, 120
Case 322/81, *N.V. Nederlandsche Banden-Industrie-Michelin*, [1983] ECR 3461	37
Joined Cases 142/84 and 156/84, *British American Tobacco*, [1987] ECR-4487	142
Case 238/87, *AB Volvo v Erik Veng*, [1988] ECR 6211	100
C-301/87, *France v Commission*, [1990] ECR I-307	178
Case C-41/90, *Höfner and Elser*, [1991] ECR I-1979,	18
Case C-62/86, *Akzo*, [1991] ECR I-3359	110
Joined Cases C-89/85, C-104/85, C-114/85, C-116/85, C-117/85 and C-125/85 to C-129/85, *Ahlström*,[1993] ECR I-1307	53/54
Case C-320/91, *Corbeau*, [1993] ECR I-2533	122
Case C-364/92, *Eurocontrol*, [1994] ECR I-43	18
Joined Cases C-241/91 P and C-242/91 P, *Magill*, [1995] ECR I-743	105, 106
Case C-244/94, *Fédération Française des Sociétés d'Assurance*, [1995] ECR I-4013	16/17
Case C-387/93, *Banchero*, [1995] ECR I-4663	18
Case C-343/95, *Diego Calí & Figli*, [1997] ECR I-1547	18
Case C-7/97, *Bronner*, [1998] ECR I-7791	41, 105
Case C-75/97, *Maribel*, [1999] ECR I-3671	177
Polypropylene cases, e.g. Case C-51/92 P, *Hercules Chemicals*, [1999] ECR I-4235; Case C-199/92 P, *Hüls*, [1999] ECR I-4287; Case C-49/92 P, *Commission v Anic Partecipazioni*, [1999] ECR I-4125	55, 57
Case C-124/97, *Läärä*, [1999] ECR I-6067	213
Joined Cases C-395/96 P and C-396/96 P, *Compagnie maritime belge transports*, [2000] ECR I-1365	92

Case C-156/98, *Germany v Commission*, [2000] ECR I-6857	178
Case C-324/98, *Telaustria*, [2000] ECR I-10745	208
Case C-237/99, *Commission v France*, [2001] ECR I-939	202
Case C-379/98, *PreussenElektra*, [2001] ECR I-2099	174
Case C-475/99, *Ambulanz Glöckner*, [2001] ECR I-8089	100/101
Case C-35/99, *Arduino*, [2002] ECR I-1529	23, 24
Case C-309/99, *Wouters*, [2002] ECR I-1577	14, 51, 68
Case C-482/99, *Stardust Marine*, [2002] ECR I-4397	174
Joined Cases C-328/99 and C-399/00, *Seleco*, [2003] ECR I-4035	193
Case C-462/99, *Connect Austria*, [2003] ECR I-5197	19/20
Case C-18/01, *Korhonen*, [2003] ECR I-5321	199/200
Case C-280/00, *Altmark Trans*, [2003] ECR I-7747	180
Case C-198/01, *CIF*, [2003] ECR I-8055	29
Case C-283/00, *Commission v Spain*, [2003] ECR I-11697	200
Joined Cases C-2/01 P and C-3/01 P, *Bayer*, [2004] ECR I-23	49/50
Joined Cases C-204/00 P, C-205/00 P, C-211/00 P, C-213/00 P, C-217/00 P and C-219/00 P, *Aalborg Portland A/S and others*, [2004] ECR I-123	130
Joined Cases C-264/01, C-306/01, C-354/01 and C-355/01, *AOK Bundesverband and others*, [2004] ECR I-2493	16/17
Case C-277/00, *SMI*, [2004] ECR I-3925	193
Case C-418/01, *IMS Health*, [2004] ECR I-5039	105, 106, 107
Case C-345/02, *Pearle*, [2004] ECR I-7139	174
Opinion of Advocate General Kokott of 28 October 2004, Case C-134/03, *Viacom Outdoor*, [2005] ECR I-1164	18
Joined Cases C-189/02 P, C-202/02 P, C-205/02 P to C-208/02 P and C-213/02 P, *Dansk Rørindustri A/S*, [2005] ECR I-5425	65
Case C-451/03, *Servizi Ausiliari Dottori Commercialisti Srl*, [2006] ECR I-2941	182
Case C-158/06, *ROM-projecten*, [2007] ECR I-5103	194/195
Case C-260/04, *Commission v Italy*, [2007] ECR I-7083	208
Case C-162/06, *International Mail Spain*, [2007] ECR I-9911	123/124
Case C-337/06, *Bayerischer Rundfunk*, [2007] ECR I-11173	201/202
Case C-49/07, *MOTOE*, [2008] ECR I-4863	14, 20
Joined Cases C-468/06 to C-478/06, *GlaxoSmithKline*, [2008] ECR I-7139	101/102
Case C-324/07, *Coditel Brabant*, [2008] ECR I-8457	210/211
Case C-384/07, *Wienstrom*, [2008] ECR I-10393	174
Case C-275/08, *Commission v Germany*, [2009] ECR I-168	219/220
Case C-113/07 P, *Selex*, [2009] ECR II-I-2207	15/16
Case C-202/07 P, *France Télécom*, [2009] ECR I-2369	42, 97/98
Case C-357/07, *TNT Post UK*, [2009] ECR I-3025	121/122

Case C-8/08, *T-Mobile Netherlands*, [2009] ECR I-4529	55, 56, 57, 63/64
Case C-300/07, *Hans & Christophorus Oymanns*, [2009] ECR I-4779	205
Case C-385/07, *Der Grüne Punkt*, [2009] ECR I-6155	96/97
Case C-440/07 P, *Commission v Schneider Electric*, [2009] ECR I-6413	135-137
Case C-42/07, *Liga Portuguesa*, [2009] ECR I-7633	213
Case C-97/08 P, *Akzo Nobel*, [2009] ECR I-8237	21/22, 193
Joined Cases C-501/06 P, C-513/06 P, C-515/06 P and C-519/06 P, *GlaxoSmithKline*, [2009] ECR I-9291	6, 50
Case C-196/08, *Acoset*, [2009] ECR I-9913	208
Case C-17/09, *Commission v Germany*	219/220
Case C-451/08, *Helmut Müller*	206/207
Case C-203/08, *Sporting Exchange*	211-213
Case C-280/08 P, *Deutsche Telekom* AG	25-28, 39, 99
Case C-537/08 P, *Kahla*	193/194

Decisions of the General Court

Case T-65/89, *BPB Industries Plc and British Gypsum*, [1993] ECR II-389	103/104
Case T-83/91, *Tetra Pak*, [1994] ECR II-755	37/38, 110
Case T-141/89, *Tréfileurope Sales*, [1995] ECR II-791	46
Case T-334/94, *Sarrió SA*, [1998] ECR II-1439	45/46
Case T-65/96, *Kish Glass*, [2000] ECR II-1885	38/39
Case T-62/98, *Volkswagen*, [2000] ECR II-2707	62
Case T-288/97, *Friuli Venezia Giulia*, [2001] ECR II-1169	178
Case T-25/99, *Roberts*, [2001] ECR II-1881	41
Case T-48/98, *Acerinox*, [2001] ECR II-3859	53
Case T-342/99, *Airtours*, [2002] ECR II-2585	153
Case T-310/01, *Schneider Electric*, [2002] ECR II-4071	135-137
Case T-213/00, *CMA CGM*, [2003] ECR II-913	61/62
Case T-114/02, *BaByliss*, [2003] ECR II-1279	158
Case T-203/01, *Michelin*, [2003] ECR II-4071	104
Case T-65/98, *Van den Bergh Foods*, [2003] ECR II-4653	89/90
Case T-219/99, *British Airways*, [2003] ECR II-5917	40
Case T-193/02, *Laurent Piau*, [2005] ECR II-209	14
Joined Cases T-49/02 to T-51/02, *Brasserie nationale SA, Brasserie Jules Simon et Cie SCS and Brasserie Battin SNC*, [2005] ECR II-3033	65, 68/69
Case T-209/01, *Honeywell Internationally*, [2005] ECR II-5527	159
Case T-279/02, *Degussa*, [2006] ECR II-897	54/55

Decisions of the Commission

Microsoft (Case COMP /C-3/37.792) Commission Decision of 24 March 2004	105, 109
Sony/BMG (COMP /M.3333) Commission Decision of 19 July 2004	153/154
Choline chloride (COMP /37.533) Commission Decision of 9 December 2004	21/22
Clearstream (COMP /38096)	35/36
AstraZeneca (Case COMP /37.507) Commission Decision of 15 July 2005	40, 107/108
T-Mobile Austria/Tele.ring (COMP /M.3916) Commission Decision of 26 April 2006	156/157
Axalto/Gemplus (COMP /M.3998) Commission Decision of 19 May 2006	159
Wienstrom (Case N317A/2006) Commission Decision of 4 July 2006, [2006] OJ C221/6	174
Privatisation of Bank Burgenland (Case State aid C 56/06 (ex NN 77/06)), Commission Decision 2008/719/EC of 30 April 2008 (notified under document number C(2008) 1625), [2008] OJ L239/32	171/172
Carglass (Case COMP /39.125) Commission Decision of 12 November 2008	50
RWE (Case COMP /39.402) Commission Decision of 18 March 2009	132
Intel (Case COMP /C-3/37.990) Commission Decision of 13 May 2009	109/110
E.ON/GDF (Case COMP /39.401) Commission Decision of 8 July 2009, [2009] OJ C248/5	50/51
E.ON (Case COMP /39.388 and COMP /39.389) Commission Decision of 8 July 2009	132
Austrian Airlines (Case State aid C 6/09 (ex N 663/08)) Commission Decision of 28 August 2009, [2010] OJ L59/1	171

REGISTER